NEW
DIRECTIONS IN
LITERARY
HISTORY

NEW
DIRECTIONS IN
LITERARY
HISTORY

Edited by

Ralph Cohen

Professor of English Literature,
University of Virginia

The Johns Hopkins University Press
Baltimore, Maryland

Published in the United States by The Johns Hopkins University
Press, Baltimore, Maryland 21218

Library of Congress Catalog Card Number 73-8115
ISBN 0-8018-1549-5

Published in England in 1974 by
Routledge & Kegan Paul Ltd.,
Broadway House, 68-74 Carter Lane,
London EC4V 5EL

Contents

Illustrations

between pages 200 and 201

Notes on Contributors

PAUL ALPERS, Professor of English at the University of California, Berkeley, is the author of *The Poetry of "The Faerie Queene"* and is working on a study of pastoral literature of the English Renaissance.

SVETLANA ALPERS, Associate Professor of the History of Art at the University of California, Berkeley, is the author of a book on Rubens and is studying the representation of the peasant in sixteenth- and seventeenth-century art.

RALPH COHEN, William R. Kenan Jr Professor of English at the University of Virginia, is the author of *The Art of Discrimination* and *The Unfolding of The Seasons* and the editor of *New Literary History*.

ALASTAIR FOWLER is Regius Professor of Rhetoric and English Literature at the University of Edinburgh. His books include *Triumphal Forms: Structural Patterns in Elizabethan Poetry* and an edition of Milton's *Paradise Lost*.

GEORGE GARRETT wrote *Death of the Fox* which was published in 1971. His latest work of fiction is *The Magic Striptease*.

FRANCIS R. HART is Professor of English at the University of Massachusetts at Boston. His books to date include *Scott's Novels* and *Lockhart as Romantic Biographer*, and his chief essays have to do with biography and autobiography, the Gothic Novel, and the fiction and life of Neil Gunn. He is at work on books about the novel in Scotland and about the novel and society from Fanny Burney through Walter Scott.

GEOFFREY H. HARTMAN, author of *The Unmediated Vision, Wordsworth's Poetry 1781–1814* and *Beyond Formalism: Literary Essays 1958–1970*, is Professor of English and Comparative Literature at Yale University.

WOLFGANG ISER, Professor of English and Comparative Literatures at the University of Konstanz, is founder and co-editor of *Poetik und Hermeneutik* and author of, among others, *Die Weltanschauung Henry*

Fieldings and *Texte und Adressaten. Literarische Kommunikation von Bunyan bis Beckett.* He is presently concerned with the theory of literary response.

HANS ROBERT JAUSS is Professor of Literary Science at the University of Konstanz and a member of the research group *Poetik und Hermeneutik.* He is the author of "Zeit und Erinnerung in Marcel Proust's *A la recherche du temps perdu,*" *Untersuchungen zur mittelalterlichen Tierdichtung, Literaturgeschichte als Provokation,* and *Kleine Apologie der ästhetischen Erfahrung.*

HENRYK MARKIEWICZ, Professor of Polish Literature, Jagellonian University, Krakow, is the author of *Main Problems of Literary Scholarship* and collections of studies on theory of literature and the Polish novel of the nineteenth and twentieth centuries. He has also published some anthologies of the methodology of literary studies in Poland and abroad.

LOUIS O. MINK, Professor of Philosophy, Chairman and Senior Tutor, College of Social Studies, Wesleyan University, is author of *Mind, History, and Dialectic: The Philosophy of R. G. Collingwood.* He has contributed essays to books and journals on philosophy of history, social science, and aesthetics. Currently he is preparing a gazetteer of James Joyce's *Finnegans Wake.*

MICHAEL RIFFATERRE, Professor of French at Columbia University and General Editor of the *Romanic Review,* has recently published articles in *Poétique* and *Diacritics.* His *Essais de stylistique structurale* has been translated into German, Spanish, Portuguese, and Japanese.

D. W. ROBERTSON JR is Murray Professor of English Literature at Princeton University and the author of *A Preface to Chaucer, Chaucer's London,* and *The Literature of Medieval England.*

BARBARA HERRNSTEIN SMITH teaches literature at Bennington College and is Visiting Lecturer at the Annenberg School of Communications, University of Pennsylvania. She is the author of *Poetic Closure* and is completing a work on "fictive discourse."

ROBERT WEIMANN is Professor of Literary Theory at the Akademie der Wissenschaften der DDR. His most recent book is *Literaturgeschichte und Mythologie.*

Introduction

Ralph Cohen

W HAT is meant by "New Directions in Literary History"? What are the old directions? The critics whose essays are collected in this volume are engaged in reconsidering the systematic study of literature, and since guides to such a study have been offered by René Wellek, Northrop Frye, György Lukács, and others, the "new directions" represent new guides, maps, routes to old destinations. These critics build upon foundations laid by their predecessors, sometimes to reinforce them, at others to alter the shape of the structure. In this respect the metaphor of stable structure is inaccurate because terms like "objects" and "monuments" are precisely what they resist. For them the literary work is an "event," an "action," a relation established between reader and what he reads, audience and performance. This relationship is inevitably historical for some; for others it is historically indeterminate—but for all these critics the arguments for interpreting or justifying literary works as "objects" are no longer adequate.

The critics—especially the continental members of the group (H. R. Jauss, Wolfgang Iser, Henryk Markiewicz, Robert Weimann) —do not accept the premise that the languages of criticism are self-reflexive and that different critical languages have no translation systems. Rather, they proceed to analyze the statements of their predecessors, indicating what might be considered the unresolved, unexamined, inconsistent, or vague statements of this criticism and asking questions about these very statements. Thus, if William Wimsatt asks, "What To Say about a Poem," these critics, in dealing with this question, might ask, "Why do we say what we do about a poem?"

Put this way, the essays in this collection are concerned with the theoretical basis for practical inquiries. Partly, this is a result of the policy of the journal, *New Literary History*, which first published these articles. But in a more general sense, theoretical inquiry becomes a way of identifying the critic's assumptions and revealing his presuppositions in dealing with his subject. The commitment to criticism as necessarily theoretical is analogous to the view that the consciousness of the reader is a necessary involvement in the interpretation of a work. All the essays share the new awareness of the role of the reader—in his responses, in the process by which he arrives at his responses, in the different responses of readers at the same and different times.

This formulation of the critic's "consciousness," the effort to assert the individuality both of reader and work, is an attack on the work as "object." Some of these critics observe, for example, that the Marxists related a literary work to its genesis in society, and they object that literary value seems to persist even after the conditions of genesis change. Acknowledging that Marx was not unaware of this problem, since he specifically refers to it in *A Contribution to the Critique of Political Economy*, they argue that it is the explanations for the phenomenon that are unsatisfactory. Thus, one Marxist critic in this collection deliberately sets himself to explain once again "Past Significance and Present Meaning in Literary History." Like the Marxist critics, the formalists are acknowledged and confronted, but many of their explanations are superseded.

In taking account of the responses of different readers, the critics inevitably find themselves writing literary history. They inherit the tripartite division of literary study—literary theory, literary criticism, literary history—in which theory is "the study of the principles of literature, its categories, criteria, and the like, while the studies of concrete works of art are either 'literary criticism' (primarily static in approach) or 'literary history.' " (R. Wellek, *Concepts of Criticism*, Yale University Press, New Haven, 1963, p. 1.) Literary criticism, according to this view, is the study of literature as a simultaneous order, whereas literary history is a study of a series of works arranged in chronological order as integral parts of the historical process.

But most critics in this volume resist the idea of literature as a "simultaneous order" because it overlooks the complex relation between a present reader and past work, especially the pastness of the past. "Simultaneity" draws attention to those aspects of a work that exist for us, not those which had existence for other, earlier readers, and to this extent the "work" is not properly distinguished from a particular historical interpretation of it. The critics also resist the vagueness of a concept such as "historical process"; they argue that the historical ordering of works involves conceptual hypotheses, and it is to the unfolding of these hypotheses that they address themselves.

The essays in this collection fall into four groups: the first deals with the continuity or succession of relations between readers and works; the second with the kind of processes involved in reading; the third with distinctions between literary and nonliterary works; and the fourth with exploratory inquiries in making statements about literature and art, about the "genre" of self-examination called autobiography and about the author's awareness of a historical past in a historical novel. The ordering of the collection is such that it moves from the most extensive generalizations about historical relations to statements that are antecedent to generalizing, from the presentations of varieties of response, to analyses of how responses are elicited, to inquiries regarding responses to literary and non-literary works, to explorations that seek to expand the range of literary inquiries. I need not add, of course, that there are other ways of ordering these essays and that readers will have little difficulty in doing so.

The first group, which includes articles by Hans Robert Jauss, Robert Weimann, D. W. Robertson, Jr, and Alastair Fowler, deals with interaction of present readers and past works and the manner in which such relations can be formulated systematically. All of these critics recognize that there is a gap between the contemporary responders to a past work and its present audience. And they also recognize that "responders" or "audience" can refer not only to a "critic" or "scholar" or learned reader but to untrained readers as well. Jauss's theory takes account of this variety of readers; the others prefer to discuss responses in terms of the learned reader.

How does a modern critic come to understand a past work since it is clearly from another time and place? One answer, in the language of R. G. Collingwood, is to understand the questions a past work asks and the answers it gives. Literary history, then, becomes a history of the sequence of questions and answers that works provide and the reader reconstructs. Not only do works ask implicit questions, but so, too, does the critic. The questions that the modern critic asks are inevitably a result of problems that are important to him; but the historical sequence of questions is what leads the critic to his own inquiries. His relation to the work, then, considers the questions asked by the earliest and subsequent readers as well as present readers so that his own consciousness of the work is shaped, in part, by his knowledge of the consciousness of other readers. Since Jauss's discussion makes reference to phenomenological terms, it is appropriate to note that both he and Wolfgang Iser are members of the group identified with *Poetik und Hermeneutik*.

In distinguishing among the four contributors, it is necessary to point out that their explanations are not identical. Weimann bases

his relation on the two-fold function of art—imitation and creation—
and with reference to Shakespeare's work he declares: "to re-create
the mimetic and the expressive dimensions is impossible without
reference to Shakespeare's world and his intentions; to reassess their
affective and moral effects is impossible without reference to our
audience and our world."

D. W. Robertson, while agreeing with the need for methodological
and pedagogical reconsideration of past works, opts for only one of
the terms that Weimann offers. His argument, based on "reconstructing" past works and periods, agrees that such reconstructions
are inevitably partial because of the readers' own conventions. But
Robertson does not resolve what the others consider a dilemma:
the conflict between the kind of value a work had for its contemporary readers and the value it may have for us. For him, the
value lies in the effort of reconstruction (which is a "modern" value)
and in the comparison of past with present as a basis for self-defini-
tion, not with any past values that persist in the present.

Alastair Fowler offers a model for changes and transformations
that generic forms undergo. Although he is aware that genres
involve networks of expectation both in author and reader, he is
primarily concerned with the diachronic development of forms.
Why genres undergo the changes they do, becomes subsidiary to the
description of those changes.

The direction of these essays is relativistic; without assuming that
changes are either good or bad, the assertions that significance
endures, that forms have vigor, that reconstruction is desirable,
introduce value problems that remain unexplored in the articles.
Their aim is to offer methods for systematizing literary study or to
offer more adequate solutions to problems of interpreting works of
the past. These papers, therefore, deal with general statements about
literature rather than specific statements about individual poems,
novels, or dramas.

In treating works as part of a comprehensive scheme, the first
group necessarily minimizes the reader's relation to the individuality
of the work, just as their essays must push to the background the criteria for reliability of interpretation. The four critics whose essays
constitute the second group—Geoffrey Hartman, Louis Mink,
Wolfgang Iser, Michael Riffaterre—draw attention to this limitation
(or, if one prefers, this advantage) which seems inherent in the
strategies of literary history. In doing so, they turn to criteria such
as the "being" of a work or the primary acts of consciousness, which,
in order to go "beyond formalism," seem to imply some intuitive or
perceptual or linguistic absolute. These are alternatives to the

"concrete universal," but they are not the only alternatives that the critics offer.

For Geoffrey Hartman, literary works have a "reserve," a style of resisting ideas, a recalcitrance to yield to the inquiries of the literary historian. The crucial problem is to discover how the reader can make the work reveal its authentic quality, while taking account of the limited, historical conditions governing it: "Can history-writing, or interpretation in touch with it, become a new medium—a supreme fiction which does not reduce being to meaning but defines a thing sharply in 'the difficulty of what is to be'?" Works or groups of works must be seen as historically individuated, as participating in and also resisting the burden of the past. Geoffrey Hartman argues that literary history must not overlook or disregard the "being" of a poem, and he suggests that it need not do so. But to what extent is the "being" of a poem recoverable so that it can become a basis for a history of "authentic" responses?

To answer such a question, and it is one that these critics recognize as important, it is necessary to probe what is meant by the "reading" or "comprehending" of a text. How, indeed, does one approach "being"? Louis Mink undertakes to define the processes of "comprehending" literature or history. For him, these processes are primary acts of consciousness, and, as such, they can apply to any narrative work. Mink defines three ways of "comprehending" a number of objects in a single mental act: the "theoretical" mode, the "categoreal," and the "configurational." Each of these modes is incompatible with the other, and it is "the configurational mode alone which is relevant to the concept of a story." In arguing for "comprehension," Mink finds grounds for considering diverse types of narratives together. He thus provides a common basis for responding to literary and other texts in what might be considered a perceptual absolute—"a characteristic kind of understanding."

Louis Mink is interested in the procedures which are prior to any specific analysis so that, for him, the important distinctions are those between "comprehension" and "knowledge," between "comprehending" and logical procedures for knowing. Wolfgang Iser may be seen as extending this inquiry into the actual processes a critical reader undergoes both in "comprehending" a text, and in arriving at a complex interpretation of it. He describes how the trained reader responds to the clues of the work, noting that these, apparently, are not always organized by the same reader in the same way. Iser has argued elsewhere ("Indeterminacy and the Reader's Response in Prose Fiction," *Aspects of the Narrative*, ed. J. Hillis Miller, Columbia University Press, New York, 1971) that different historical periods result in different uses of literary techniques demanding different kinds of readings. Although reading involves comprehension, he implies that there is no need to assume that comprehension of narrative always proceeds in the same way. And he draws attention to an important distinction between the text and the experience of reading it: "the literary work cannot be completely identical with the text, or with the realization of the text, but in fact must lie halfway between the two." Is there a way to discover the proper "reading" or "realization" of a text?

This question of a "proper" reading is, for these critics, converted into a question about relations, about processes. In so far as "proper" is a value term, it is subsumed under descriptions of how reading takes place. There are readers who neglect the kind of processes necessary to establish a "proper" relation with a work. Their judgments are necessarily limited by their own shortcomings.

Wolfgang Iser distinguishes among text, realization (actualization), and work so that he can refer to the composed words, to the reader's response to these words, and to the totality of such responses. Michael Riffaterre, developing what he calls "stylistic" criticism, proposes a theory of language that differs from that accepted by phenomenologically oriented critics like Jauss and Iser. For him, the text is unchanging and is composed of "descriptive systems." Every descriptive system provides the general language from which the poet makes his private or individual language; thus questions of genre, tradition, influence are "peripheral to the problem of the very existence of the literary work." But he does recognize that the "mechanisms" of poetry, as encoded in a poem, become elusive in time. What the critic must do, therefore, is construct a series of composite descriptive systems, to check not only the "particular case in hand against its composite model, but to sort out and discard all the components of the model that the text has not actualized." The hypothesis of "descriptive systems" serves as an alternative to a theory of genres as well as a basis for reconstruction of texts. And since descriptive systems are involved in changes of meaning, how such changes occur and how "original" meanings can be reconstructed becomes a central problem. To solve this problem Riffaterre offers a theory of literary history which is "a history of words."

Michael Riffaterre prefers the terms of the formalists in describing the relation of reader to text. The latter, in its "monumentality," has all future interpretations implicit in it; Iser, on the other hand, suggests that the text merely provides one element of a relation that requires the reader to complete the process of reading. Of course, Riffaterre does not ignore the reader; but he attributes to the work the capacities that Iser attributes to readers. Still, even when formalist premises are retained, they are accompanied by new explanations, and the theoretical sophistication of these critics can be seen with particular clarity when they provide theoretical rationales for commonly received ends.

For example, the two critics—Barbara H. Smith and Henryk Markiewicz—who address themselves to defining literature or the nature of literary discourse do indeed take for granted that literary texts differ from nonliterary ones. Their arguments, since they rest on how readers can, do, or ought to recognize such texts, follow appropriately upon the preceding essays. They serve, too, to illustrate the ties of old directions to new. For the formalists, texts were considered literature if, in them, the "aesthetic function" was dominant or if the work was characterized by "fictionality," "invention," or "imagination." Their distinction of literary from nonliterary discourse arose from the aim to systematize literature, to give "literature" an autonomous status in society. The governing hypothesis was to identify literature as a single class that remained monolithic rather than one governed by a group of diverse "family" characteristics. And the method was to posit a coherent theory rather than to relate it to what critics might empirically, at different times, identify as "literature." This procedure of providing a reductive but thoroughly consistent definition is followed by Barbara H. Smith in her distinction between natural and fictive discourse. Natural language, she states, requires a historical context, the speaker's on-going total behavior. Poems, on the other hand, "are not natural utterances, not historically unique verbal acts or events; indeed a poem is not an event at all, and cannot be said ever to have 'occurred' in the usual sense." A poem, or "mimetic discourse," is governed by special conventions, and it is the "understanding that these conventions are operating that distinguishes the poem as a verbal artwork from natural discourse."

By separating fictive discourse from natural utterance in terms of the mode of discourse, Barbara Smith avoids the dilemma of having to explain how natural utterances can also be considered fictive discourse. But she does rest her argument on conventions, and to this extent her argument is historical, even if she finds mimetic discourse "historically indeterminate."

Henryk Markiewicz, in treating the same problem as Barbara H. Smith, seeks to base his definition of literary discourse on those given by contemporary critics. Since they do not agree, he provides an eclectic definition composed of three criteria: "fictionality," "superimposed ordering," and "figurativeness." By confining the inquiry to what "literature" means today, he necessarily limits his definition to a specific historical moment. This procedure extends the range of "literature" to apply to what is actually called such, but it makes apparent the need to include a wider historical overview that will provide an even more extensive series of features. The definitions of "literature" or "belles lettres" include, historically, a far wider range than modern critics accept. To mention only one example, Samuel Johnson's definition of "literature" as "learning; skill in letters" and his definition of "literary history" as an "account of the state of learning, and the lives of learned men" imply that for eighteenth-century critics the distinction between literary and nonliterary discourse was that between learning and ignorance, between "belles lettres" or polite literature and inelegant or crude writings, between true wit and false wit.

Some of the possibilities of new directions available to postformalist critics are examined in the essays by Svetlana and Paul Alpers, Francis R. Hart, and George Garrett. The Alpers reconsider the traditional arguments for treating literature and art in the same way, and they urge that the "great questions" are: "In what sense and in what ways are intention, comprehension, historical reality, social situation and purpose, human use implicit or implicated—literally, enfolded—in works of art?" These are historical questions the answers to which will provide information about the possibilities of a "cooperative pursuit of historical generalizations."

The conclusions to which the Alpers come are not particularly novel, but their arguments are based on assumptions opposing those of the "New Critics" as well as those of traditional historians of art styles. They do not open new roads; but they find more direct or accessible routes to the old ones.

Francis R. Hart's essay on autobiography discusses "the wide plurality of mimetic and formal value of which autobiography has proved capable." His essay, too, is part of the new historical enterprise, analyzing autobiography and its associated kinds as a task prior to making a generalization about them; only after the accumulation of individual autobiographies has "undergone testing and sorting, then and only then will it be possible to make real and meaningful descriptive generalizations about the historical development of modern autobiography."

His gathering and testing of evidence before engaging in generalizations is, of course, governed by conceptual hypotheses, and these are apparent in the manner in which he identifies his "preoccupations" in the study. The method of inquiry—the setting up of questions, the recognition of the usefulness of the pursuit of "solution," the latitude of development of form—places the essay within the aim of literary history. The essay by the novelist George Garrett offers an inquiry into the consciousness of a novelist engaged in writing a historical novel. Unlike the critics who need to explain an Elizabethan work, Garrett set out to create one. To the extent that critic and author find themselves decoding or encoding the past, they must both determine the language code and the manner in which Elizabethan experience is implicit in it. Garrett explains how he sought to unlearn modern prejudices about technology and how he sought to achieve the appropriate language style. The "unlearning" which he describes in his effort to enact a historical consciousness for readers has its parallel in the critic's effort to relearn a past work. In doing so, he finds that the subject of his novel "is the larger imagination, the possibility of imagining lives and spirits of other human beings, living or dead, without assaulting their essential and, anyway, ineffable mystery." Just as the reader defines himself in his reading, the author defines himself in his writing.

Garrett argues that it is for the writer to present people in their "ineffable mystery," not to "understand" them, but the critic has no way of communicating this being without understanding unless as critic he wishes to imitate, not explain, words and people. And even such a task, however dubious it may be as communication, rests on historical reconstruction.

What, then, is the "literary history" that engages these critics? It is, to begin with, a history of the relation of readers to works. These relations, governed as they are by the method of question and answer, permit a systematized succession. And this system of relations is literary, because it deals with the changing functions of literary features, with changes of conventions, with changes in the meaning of language codes. But the concept of "change" is itself a historical category, so that theoretical premises, no less than relations, require historical explanations for their genesis and revision. Thus "literary history," even if critics consider it peripheral to interpretation, becomes a presupposition of all critical activity. The tripartite distinction of literary theory, literary criticism, literary history breaks down into different functions of the critic-text relationship. Theory, criticism, history all presuppose organizing concepts that are necessarily historical. And the purpose of this activity is not only to systematize the study of literature, but to make it possible for the critic to define himself in his responses by attending to those of others.

The journal, *New Literary History*, from which these essays have been collected, continues with its inquiries. It is appropriate, therefore, to hope that the questions these essays raise will provoke readers to further inquiry—into the nature of literary change, into categories prior to interpretation, into the "being" of a literary work, into alternatives to generic explanations, into the relation between interpretation, explanation, and value—indeed, into the very nature of the new directions in literary history.

A Note on the Texts

All translations included in this collection have been authorized and approved by the authors. The articles originally appeared in *New Literary History*.

I

Literary History as a Challenge to Literary Theory *

Hans Robert Jauss

LITERARY history may be seen as challenging literary theory to take up once again the unresolved dispute between the Marxist and formalist schools. My attempt to bridge the gap between literature and history, between historical and aesthetic approaches, begins at the point at which both schools stop. Their methods understand the literary fact in terms of the circular aesthetic system of production and of representation. In doing so, they deprive literature of a dimension which unalterably belongs to its aesthetic character as well as to its social function: its reception and impact. Reader, listener and spectator—in short, the audience—play an extremely limited role in both literary theories. Orthodox Marxist aesthetics treats the reader— if at all—the same way as it does the author; it inquires about his social position or describes his place within the structure of the society. The formalist school needs the reader only as a perceiving subject who follows the directions in the text in order to perceive its form or discover its techniques of procedure. It assumes that the reader has the theoretical knowledge of a philologist sufficiently versed in the tools of literature to be able to reflect on them. The Marxist school, on the other hand, actually equates the spontaneous experience of the reader with the scholarly interest of historical materialism, which seeks to discover relationships between the economic basis of production and the literary work as part of the intellectual superstructure. However, as Walther Bulst has stated, "no text was ever written to be read and interpreted philologically by philologists," [1] nor, may I add, historically by his-

---

* This essay is a translation of chapters V — XII of *Literaturgeschichte als Provokation der Literaturwissenschaft*, Konstanz, 1967; it forms part of a later published collection of essays, *Literaturgeschichte als Provokation*, Frankfurt, 1970 (edition suhrkamp, 418).

1 "Bedenken eines Philologen," *Studium générale*, VII (1954), 321-23. The new approach to literary tradition which R. Guiette has sought in a series of pioneering essays (partly in *Questions de littérature* [Gent, 1960]), using his own original methods of combining aesthetic criticism with understanding of history, follows his (unpublished) axiom, "The greatest error of philologists is to believe that literature has been written for philologists." See also his "Eloge de la lecture," *Revue générale belge* (January, 1966), pp. 3-14.

torians. Neither approach recognizes the true role of the reader to whom the literary work is primarily addressed, a role as unalterable for aesthetic as for historical appreciation.

For the critic who judges a new work, the writer who conceives of his work in light of positive or negative norms of an earlier work and the literary historian who classifies a work in his tradition and explains it historically are also readers before their reflexive relationship to literature can become productive again. In the triangle of author, work and reading public the latter is no passive part, no chain of mere reactions, but even history-making energy. The historical life of a literary work is unthinkable without the active participation of its audience. For it is only through the process of its communication that the work reaches the changing horizon of experience in a continuity in which the continual change occurs from simple reception to critical understanding, from passive to active reception, from recognized aesthetic norms to a new production which surpasses them. The historicity of literature as well as its communicative character presupposes a relation of work, audience and new work which takes the form of a dialogue as well as a process, and which can be understood in the relationship of message and receiver as well as in the relationship of question and answer, problem and solution. The circular system of production and of representation within which the methodology of literary criticism has mainly moved in the past must therefore be widened to include an aesthetics of reception and impact if the problem of understanding the historical sequence of literary works as a continuity of literary history is to find a new solution.

The perspective of the aesthetics of reception mediates between passive reception and active understanding, norm-setting experience and new production. If the history of literature is viewed in this way as a dialogue between work and public, the contrast between its aesthetic and its historical aspects is also continually mediated. Thus the thread from the past appearance to the present experience of a work, which historicism had cut, is tied together.

The relationship of literature and reader has aesthetic as well as historical implications. The aesthetic implication is seen in the fact that the first reception of a work by the reader includes a test of its aesthetic value in comparison with works which he has already read. [2] The obvious historical implication of this is that the appreciation of the first reader will be continued and enriched through further "receptions" from generation to generation; in this way the historical significance

---

2   This thesis is one of the main points of the *Introduction à une esthétique de la littérature* by G. Picon (Paris, 1953), see esp. pp. 90 ff.

of a work will be determined and its aesthetic value revealed. In this process of the history of reception, which the literary historian can only escape at the price of ignoring his own principles of comprehension and judgment, the repossession of past works occurs simultaneously with the continual mediation of past and present art and of traditional evaluation and current literary attempts. The merit of a literary history based on an aesthetics of reception will depend upon the degree to which it can take an active part in the continual integration of past art by aesthetic experience. This demands on the one hand—in opposition to the objectivism of positivist literary history—a conscious attempt to establish canons, which, on the other hand—in opposition to the classicism of the study of traditions—presupposes a critical review if not destruction of the traditional literary canon. The criterion for establishing such a canon and the ever necessary retelling of literary history is clearly set out by the aesthetics of reception. The step from the history of the reception of the individual work to the history of literature has to lead us to see and in turn to present the historical sequence of works in the way in which they determine and clarify our present literary experience. [3]

Literary history can be rewritten on this premise, and the following remarks suggest seven theses that provide a systematic approach to such rewriting.

I

If literary history is to be rejuvenated, the prejudices of historical objectivism must be removed and the traditional approach to literature must be replaced by an aesthetics of reception and impact. The historical relevance of literature is not based on an organization of literary works which is established *post factum* but on the reader's past experience of the "literary data." This relationship creates a dialogue that is the first condition for a literary history. For the literary historian must first become a reader again himself before he can understand and classify a work; in other words, before he can justify his own evaluation in light of his present position in the historical progression of readers.

R. G. Collingwood's criticism of the prevailing ideology of objectivity in history—"History is nothing but the re-enactment of past thought in the historian's mind" [4]—is even more valid for literary history. For the

---

3   W. Benjamin (1931) formulated a corresponding idea: "For it is not a question of showing the written works in relation to their time but of presenting the time which knows them—that is our time—in the time when they originated. Thus literature becomes an organon of history and the task of literary history is to make it this—and not to make it the material of history" (*Angelus Novus,* Frankfurt, 1966, p. 456).

4   *The Idea of History* (New York and Oxford, 1956), p. 228.

positivistic view of history as the "objective" description of a series of events in an isolated past neglects the artistic quality as well as the specific historical relevance of literature. A literary work is not an object which stands by itself and which offers the same face to each reader in each period.[5] It is not a monument which reveals its timeless essence in a monologue. It is much more like an orchestration which strikes ever new chords among its readers and which frees the text from the substance of the words and makes it meaningful for the time: "words which must, at the same time that they speak to him, create an interlocutor capable of listening."[6] A literary work must be understood as creating a dialogue, and philological scholarship has to be founded on a continuous re-reading of texts, not on mere facts.[7] Philological scholarship is continuously dependent upon interpretation, which must have as its goal, along with learning about the object, the reflection upon and description of the perfection of this knowledge as an impulse to new understanding.

History of literature is a process of aesthetic reception and production which takes place in realization of literary texts on the part of the receptive reader, the reflective critic and the author in his continued creativity. The continuously growing "literary data" which appear in the conventional literary histories are merely left over from this process; they are only the collected and classified past and therefore not history at all, but pseudohistory. Anyone who considers such literary data as history confuses the eventful character of a work of art with that of historical matter-of-factness. *Perceval* by Chrétien de Troyes, a literary event, is not historical in the same sense as the Third Crusade,

5   Here I am following A. Nisin in his criticism of the latent Platonism of philological methods, that is, of their belief in the timeless nature of a literary work and in a timeless point of view of the reader: "For the work of art, if it cannot incarnate the essence of art, is no longer an object which we can regard according to the Cartesian rule 'without putting anything of ourselves into it but what can apply indiscriminately to all objects,' " *La Littérature et le lecteur* (Paris, 1959), p. 57 (see also my critique in *Archiv für das Studium der neueren Sprachen*, CXCVII [1960], 223-25).

6   Picon, *Introduction*, p. 34. This view of the dialogue-like nature of a literary work of art is found in Malraux (*Les vois du silence*) as well as in Picon, Nisin, and Guiette—a tradition of literary aesthetics which is still alive in France and to which I am especially indebted; it finally goes back to a famous sentence in Valéry's poetics, "C'est l'exécution du poème qui est le poème."

7   P. Szondi, "Uber philologische Erkenntnis," *Hölderlin-Studien* (Frankfurt, 1967), rightly sees in this the decisive difference between literary and historical scholarship, p. 11: "No commentary, no criticism of the style of a poem should aim to give a description of the poem which one could gain by oneself. Even the least critical reader will want to confront it with the poem and will not understand it until he has traced the course of the argument back to the original idea upon which it was based." Guiette says something very similar in "Éloge de la lecture" (see note 1).

which was occurring at the same time.[8] It is not a "fact" which could be explained as caused by a series of situational preconditions and motives, by the intent of an historical action as it can be reconstructed, and by the necessary and secondary results of this deed as an eventful turning point. The historical context in which a literary work appears is not a factual, independent series of events which exists apart from the reader. *Perceval* becomes a literary event only for the reader who reads this last work of Chrétien in light of his earlier works and who recognizes its individuality in comparison with these and other works which he has already read, so that he gains a new criterion for evaluating works. In contrast to a political event, a literary event has no lasting results which succeeding generations cannot avoid. It can continue to have an effect only if future generations still respond to it or rediscover it—if there are readers who take up the work of the past again or authors who want to imitate, outdo, or refute it. The organization of literature according to events is primarily integrated in the artistic standards of contemporary and succeeding readers, critics, and authors. Whether it is possible to comprehend and present the history of literature in its specific historicity depends on whether these standards can be objectified.

II

The analysis of the literary experience of the reader avoids the threatening pitfalls of psychology if it describes the response and the impact of a work within the definable frame of reference of the reader's expectations: this frame of reference for each work develops in the historical moment of its appearance from a previous understanding of the genre, from the form and themes of already familiar works, and from the contrast between poetic and practical language.

My thesis is opposed to a widespread skepticism that doubts that an analysis of the aesthetic impact can approach the meaning of a work of art or can produce at best more than a plain sociology of artistic taste. René Wellek directs such doubts against the literary theory of I. A. Richards. Wellek argues that neither the individual consciousness, since it is immediate and personal, nor a collective consciousness, as J. Mukarovsky assumes the effect of an art work to be, can be determined by empirical means.[9] Roman Jakobson wanted to replace the "collective consciousness" by a "collective ideology." This he thought of

8 Note also J. Storost, "Das Problem der Literaturgeschichte," *Dante-Jahrbuch,* XXXVIII (1960), 1-17, who simply equates the historical event with the literary event ("A work of art is first of all an artistic achievement and hence historical like the Battle of Isos").

9 R. Wellek, "The Theory of Literary History," *Études dédiées au quatrième Congrès de linguistes,* Travaux du Cercle Linguistique de Prague (Prague, 1936), p. 179.

as a system of values which exists for each literary work as *langue* and which becomes *parole* for the respondent—although incompletely and never as a whole.[10] This theory, it is true, limits the subjectivity of the impact, but it leaves open the question of which data can be used to interpret the impact of a unique work on a certain public and to incorporate it into a system of values. In the meantime there are empirical means which had never been thought of before—literary data which give for each work a specific attitude of the audience (an attitude that precedes the psychological reaction as well as the subjective understanding of the individual reader). As in the case of every experience, the first literary experience of a previously unknown work demands a "previous knowledge which is an element of experience itself and which makes it possible that anything new we come across may also be read, as it were, in some context of experience."[11]

A literary work, even if it seems new, does not appear as something absolutely new in an informational vacuum, but predisposes its readers to a very definite type of reception by textual strategies, overt and covert signals, familiar characteristics or implicit allusions. It awakens memories of the familiar, stirs particular emotions in the reader and with its "beginning" arouses expectations for the "middle and end," which can then be continued intact, changed, re-oriented or even ironically fulfilled in the course of reading according to certain rules of the genre or type of text. The psychical process in the assimilation of a text on the primary horizon of aesthetic experience is by no means only a random succession of merely subjective impressions, but the carrying out of certain directions in a process of directed perception which can be comprehended from the motivations which constitute it and the signals which set it off and which can be described linguistically. If, along with W. D. Stempel, one considers the previous horizon of expectations of a text as paradigmatic isotopy, which is transferred to an immanent syntactical horizon of expectations to the degree to which the message grows, the process of reception becomes describable in the expansion of a semiological procedure which arises between the development and the correction of the system.[12] A corresponding

10 In *Slovo a slovenost*, I, 192, cited by Wellek, "The Theory of Literary History," pp. 179 ff.

11 G. Buck, *Lernen und Erfahrung* (Stuttgart, 1967), p. 56, who refers here to Husserl (*Erfahrung und Urteil*, esp. § 8) but goes farther than Husserl in a lucid description of negativity in the process of experience, which is of importance for the horizon structure of aesthetic experience (cf. note 74 below).

12 W. D. Stempel, "Pour une description des genres littéraires," in *Actes du XIIe congrès internat. de linguistique Romane* (Bucharest, 1968), also in *Beiträge zur Textlinguistik*, ed. by W. D. Stempel (Munich, 1970).

process of continuous horizon setting and horizon changing also determines the relation of the individual text to the succession of texts which form the genre. The new text evokes for the reader (listener) the horizon of expectations and rules familiar from earlier texts, which are then varied, corrected, changed or just reproduced. Variation and correction determine the scope, alteration and reproduction of the borders and structure of the genre.[13] The interpretative reception of a text always presupposes the context of experience of aesthetic perception. The question of the subjectivity of the interpretation and the taste of different readers or levels of readers can be asked significantly only after it has been decided which transsubjective horizon of understanding determines the impact of the text.

The ideal cases of the objective capability of such literary frames of reference are works which, using the artistic standards of the reader, have been formed by conventions of genre, style, or form. These purposely evoke responses so that they can frustrate them. This can serve not only a critical purpose but can even have a poetic effect. Thus Cervantes in *Don Quixote* fosters the expectations of the old tales of knighthood, which the adventures of his last knight then parody seriously.[14] Thus Diderot in the beginning of *Jacques le Fataliste* evokes the expectations of the popular journey novel along with the (Aristotelian) convention of the romanesque fable and the providence peculiar to it, so that he can then confront the promised journey and love novel with a completely unromanesque "verité de l'histoire": the bizarre reality and moral casuistry of the inserted stories in which the truth of life continually denies the lies of poetic fiction.[15] Thus Nerval in *Chimères* cites, combines, and mixes a quintessence of well-known romantic and occult motives to produce the expectation of a mythical metamorphosis of the world only in order to show his renunciation of romantic poetry. The mythical identification and relationships which are familiar to the reader dissolve in the unknown to the same degree as the attempted private myth of the lyrical "I" fails; the law of sufficient

13 See also my treatment of this in "Littérature médiévale et théorie des genres," *Poétique*, I (1970), 79-101, later published in expanded form in *Grundriss der romanischen Literaturen des Mittelalters* (Heidelberg, 1970).

14 According to the interpretation of H. J. Neuschäfer, *Der Sinn der Parodie im Don Quijote*, Studia Romanica V (Heidelberg, 1963).

15 According to the interpretation of R. Warning, *Allusion und Wirklichkeit in Tristram Shandy und Jacques le Fataliste*, Theorie und Geschichte der Literatur und der schönen Kunste, IV (Munich, 1965), esp. pp. 80 ff.

information is broken and the darkness which has become expressive
gains a poetic function. [16]

There is also the possibility of objectifying the expectations in works
which are historically less sharply delineated. For the specific reception which the author anticipates from the reader for a particular work
can be achieved, even if the explicit signals are missing, by three generally acceptable means: first, by the familiar standards or the inherent poetry of the genre; second, by the implicit relationships to familiar
works of the literary-historical context; and third, by the contrast between fiction and reality, between the poetic and the practical function
of language, which the reflective reader can always realize while he
is reading. The third factor includes the possibility that the reader of
a new work has to perceive it not only within the narrow horizon of his
literary expectations but also within the wider horizon of his experience
of life. I shall return to this horizon structure and its ability to be ob-
jectivized by means of the hermeneutics of question and answer in the
discussion of the relationship between literature and practical life
(see VII).

III

If the horizon of expectations of a work is reconstructed in this way,
it is possible to determine its artistic nature by the nature and degree of
its effect on a given audience. If the "aesthetic distance" is considered
as the distance between the given horizon of expectations and the appearance of a new work, whose reception results in a "horizon change"
because it negates familiar experience or articulates an experience for
the first time, this aesthetic distance can be measured historically in the
spectrum of the reaction of the audience and the judgment of criticism (spontaneous success, rejection or shock, scattered approval, gradual or later understanding).

The way in which a literary work satisfies, surpasses, disappoints,
or disproves the expectations of its first readers in the historical moment
of its appearance obviously gives a criterion for the determination of its
aesthetic value. The distance between the horizon of expectations and
the work, between the familiarity of previous aesthetic experiences and
the "horizon change" [17] demanded by the response to new works, determines the artistic nature of a literary work along the lines of the
aesthetics of reception: the smaller this distance, which means that no

16   According to the interpretation of K. H. Stierle, "Dunkelheit und Form in Gérard
de Nervals 'Chimères,'" *Theorie und Geschichte der Literatur und der schönen Künste*, V
(Munich, 1967), esp. pp. 55 and 91.

17   See Buck, pp. 64 ff., about this idea of Husserl in *Lernen und Erfahrung*.

demands are made upon the receiving consciousness to make a change on the horizon of unknown experience, the closer the work comes to the realm of "culinary" or light reading. This last phrase can be characterized from the point of view of the aesthetics of reception in this way: it demands no horizon change but actually fulfills expectations, which are prescribed by a predominant taste, by satisfying the demand for the reproduction of familiar beauty, confirming familiar sentiments, encouraging dreams, making unusual experiences palatable as "sensations" or even raising moral problems, but only to be able to "solve" them in an edifying manner when the solution is already obvious. [18] On the other hand, if the artistic character of a work is to be measured by the aesthetic distance with which it confronts the expectations of its first readers, it follows that this distance, which at first is experienced as a happy or distasteful new perspective, can disappear for later readers to the same degree to which the original negativity of the work has become self-evident and, as henceforth familiar expectation, has even become part of the horizon of future aesthetic experience. Especially the classic nature of so-called masterworks belongs to this second horizon change; their self-evident beauty and their seemingly unquestionable "eternal significance" bring them, from the point of view of the aesthetics of reception, into dangerous proximity with irresistible convincing and enjoyable "culinary" art, and special effort is needed to read them "against the grain" of accustomed experience so that their artistic nature becomes evident again (compare with IV).[19]

The relationship between literature and the public encompasses more than the fact that every work has its specific, historically and sociologically determined audience, that every writer is dependent upon the milieu, views and ideology of his readers and that literary success re-

18   Here I am incorporating the results of the discussion of "Kitsch," as a fringe manifestation of aesthetics, which took place during the third colloquium of the "Forschungsgruppe Poetik und Hermeneutik" in the volume, *Die nicht mehr schönen Künste—Grenzphänomene des Asthetischen*, ed. H. R. Jauss (Munich, 1968). For the "culinary" approach, which presupposes mere light reading, the same thing holds true as for "Kitsch," namely, that the "demands of the consumers are *a priori* satisfied" (P. Beylin), that "the fulfilled expectation becomes the standard for the product" (W. Iser), or that "a work appears to be solving a problem when in reality it neither has nor solves a problem" (M. Imdahl), pp. 651-67.

19   As also "Epigonentum" (Decadence), for this see B. Tomasevskij (in: *Théorie de la littérature. Texts des formalistes russes,* ed. by T. Todorov [Paris 1965], p. 306): "L'apparition d'un génie équivaut toujours à une révolution littéraire qui détrône le canon dominant et donne le pouvoir aux procédés jusqu'alors subordonnés. [. . .] Les épigones répètent une combinaison usée des procédés, et d'originale et révolutionnaire qu'elle était, cette combinaison devient stéréotypée et traditionnelle. Ainsi les épigones tuent parfois pour longtemps l'aptitude des contemporains à sentir la force esthétique des exemples qu'ils imitent: ils discréditent leurs maîtres."

quires a book "which expresses what the group expects, a book which presents the group with its own portrait . . . ."[20] The objectivist determination of literary success based on the congruence of the intent of a work and the expectation of a social group always puts literary sociology in an embarrassing position whenever it must explain later or continuing effects. This is why R. Escarpit wants to presuppose a "collective basis in space or time" for the "illusion of continuity" of a writer, which leads to an astonishing prognosis in the case of Molière: he "is still young for the Frenchman of the 20th century because his world is still alive and ties of culture, point of view and language still bind us to him . . . but the ties are becoming ever weaker and Molière will age and die when the things which our culture has in common with the France of Molière die" (p. 117). As if Molière had only reflected the manners of his time and had only remained successful because of this apparent intention! Where the congruence between work and social group does not exist or no longer exists, as for example in the reception of a work by a group which speaks a foreign language, Escarpit is able to help himself by resorting to a "myth": "myths which are invented by a later period which has become estranged from the reality which they represent" (p. 111). As if all reception of a work beyond the first socially determined readers were only "distorted echoes," only a consequence of "subjective myths" (p. 111) and did not have its objective a priori in the received work which sets boundaries and opens possibilities for later understanding! The sociology of literature does not view its object dialectically enough when it determines the circle of writers, work and readers so one-sidedly.[21] The determination is reversible: there are works which at the moment of their publication are not directed at any specific audience, but which break through the familiar horizon of literary expectations so completely that an audience can only gradually develop for them.[22] Then when the

20 R. Escarpit, *Das Buch und der Leser: Entwurf einer Literatursoziologie* (Cologne and Opladen, 1961; first German expanded edition of *Sociologie de la littérature* [Paris, 1958]), p. 116.

21 K. H. Bender, *König und Vasall: Untersuchungen zur Chanson de Geste des XII. Jahrhunderts,* Studia Romanica, XIII (Heidelberg, 1967), shows which step is necessary in order to escape from this one-sided determination. In this history of the early French epic the apparent congruence of feudal society and epic ideality is represented as a process which is maintained through a continually changing discrepancy between "reality" and "ideology," that is between the historical constellations of feudal conflict and the poetic answers of the epic.

22 The much more sophisticated sociology of literature by Erich Auerbach brought to light this aspect in the variety of epoch-making disruptions of the relationship between author and reader. See also the evaluation of F. Schalk in his edition of E. Auerbach's *Gesämmelte Aufsätze zur romanischen Philologie* (Bern and Munich, 1967), pp. 11 ff.

new horizon of expectations has achieved more general acceptance, the authority of the changed aesthetic norm can become apparent from the fact that readers will consider previously successful works as obsolete and reject them. It is only in view of such a horizon change that the analysis of literary effect achieves the dimension of a literary history of readers[23] and provides the statistical curves of the historical recognition of the bestseller.

A literary sensation from the year 1857 may serve as an example of this. In this year two novels were published: Flaubert's *Madame Bovary*, which has since achieved world-wide fame, and *Fanny* by his friend Feydeau, which is forgotten today. Although Flaubert's novel brought with it a trial for obscenity, *Madame Bovary* was at first overshadowed by Feydeau's novel: *Fanny* had thirteen editions in one year and success the likes of which Paris had not seen since Chateaubriand's *Atala*. As far as theme is concerned, both novels fulfilled the expectations of the new audience, which—according to Baudelaire's analysis—had rejected anything romantic and scorned grand as well as naive passion.[24] They treated a trivial subject—adultery—the one in a bourgeois and the other in a provincial milieu. Both authors understood how to give a sensational twist to the conventional, rigid triangle which in the erotic scenes surpassed the customary details. They presented the worn-out theme of jealousy in a new light by reversing the expected relationship of the three classic roles. Feydeau has the youthful lover of the "femme de trente ans" becoming jealous of his lover's husband, although he has already reached the goal of his desires, and perishing over this tormenting situation; Flaubert provides the adulteries of the doctor's wife in the provinces, which Baudelaire presents as a sublime form of "dandysme," with a surprising ending, so that the ridiculous figure of the deceived Charles Bovary takes on noble traits at the end. In official criticism of the time there are voices which reject *Fanny* as well as *Madame Bovary* as a product of the new school of "réalisme," which they accuse of denying all ideals and attacking the ideas on which

23 See H. Weinrich, "Für eine Literaturgeschichte des Lesers," *Merkur*, XXI (November, 1967). Just as the linguistics of the speaker, which was earlier customary, has been replaced by the linguistics of the listener, Weinrich pleads for a methodical consideration for the perspective of the reader in literary history and thereby supports my aims. Weinrich shows especially how the empirical methods of literary sociology can be supplemented by the linguistic and literary interpretation of the role of the reader, which is implicit in the work.

24 In "*Madame Bovary* par Gustave Flaubert," Baudelaire, *Oeuvres complètes*, Pléiade ed. (Paris, 1951), p. 998: "The last years of Louis-Philippe witnessed the last explosions of a spirit still excitable by the play of the imagination; but the new novelist found himself faced with a completely worn-out society—worse than worn-out—stupified and gluttonous, with a horror only of fiction and love only for possession."

the order of the society in the Second Empire was based.[25] The horizon of expectations of the public of 1857, here only sketched in, which did not expect anything great in the way of novels after the death of Balzac,[26] explains the differing success of the two novels only when the question of the effect of their narrative form is posed. Flaubert's innovation in form, his principle of "impersonal telling" (*impassibilité*, which Barbey d'Aurevilly attacked with this comparison: if a story-telling machine could be made of English steel, it would function the same as Monsieur Flaubert[27]), must have shocked the same audience which was offered the exciting contents of *Fanny* in the personable tone of a confessional novel. It could also have found in Feydeau's descriptions[28] popular ideals and frustrations of the level of society which sets the style, and it could delight unrestrainedly in the lascivious main scene in which Fanny (without knowing that her lover is watching from the balcony) seduces her husband—for their moral indignation was forestalled by the reaction of the unfortunate witness. However, as *Madame Bovary,* which was understood at first only by a small circle of knowledgeable readers and called a turning point in the history of the novel, became a world-wide success, the group of readers who were formed by this book sanctioned the new canon of expectations, which made the weaknesses of Feydeau—his flowery style, his modish effects, his lyrical confessional clichés—unbearable and relegated *Fanny* to the class of bestsellers of yesterday.

IV

The reconstruction of the horizon of expectations, on the basis of which a work in the past was created and received, enables us to find

25 Cf. *ibid.*, p. 999, as well as the accusation, speech for the defense, and verdict of the *Bovary* trial in Flaubert, *Oeuvres*, Pléiade ed. (Paris, 1951), I, 649-717, esp. 717; also about *Fanny*, E. Montegut, "Le roman intime de la littérature réaliste," *Revue des deux mondes*, XVIII (1858), 196-213, esp. 201 and 209 ff.

26 As Baudelaire testifies (*"Madame Bovary* par Gustave Flaubert," p. 996): "for since the disappearance of Balzac . . . all curiosity relative to the novel has been stilled and slumbers."

27 For these and other contemporary verdicts see H. R. Jauss "Die beiden Fassungen von Flauberts 'Education Sentimentale,' " *Heidelberger Jahrbücher,* II (1958), 96-116, esp. 97.

28 See the excellent analysis by the contemporary critic E. Montegut (see note 25), who explains in detail why the dreams and the figures in Feydeau's novel are typical for the readers in the section between the *Bourse* and the boulevard Montmartre (p. 209) : they need an "alcool poétique," enjoy seeing "their vulgar adventures of yesterday and their vulgar projects of tomorrow poeticized" (p. 210) and have an "idolatry of the material" by which term Montegut understands the ingredients of the "dream factory" of 1959—"a sort of sanctimonious admiration, almost devout, for furniture, wallpaper, dress, escapes, like a perfume of patchouli, from each of its pages" (p. 201).

the questions to which the text originally answered and thereby to discover how the reader of that day viewed and understood the work.
This approach corrects the usually unrecognized values of a classical
concept of art or of an interpretation that seeks to modernize, and it
avoids the recourse to a general spirit of the age, which involves circular
reasoning. It brings out the hermeneutic difference between past and
present ways of understanding a work, points up the history of its reception—providing both approaches—and thereby challenges as plato-
nizing dogma the apparently self-evident dictum of philological
metaphysics that literature is timelessly present and that it has
objective meaning, determined once and for all and directly open to
the interpreter at any time.

The method of the history of reception[29] is essential for the understanding of literary works which lie in the distant past. Whenever the
writer of a work is unknown, his intent not recorded, or his relationship
to sources and models only indirectly accessible, the philological question
of how the text is "properly" to be understood, that is according to its
intention and its time, can best be answered if the text is considered in
contrast to the background of the works which the author could expect
his contemporary public to know either explicitly or implicitly. For example, the creator of the oldest branches of the *Roman de Renart* assumed— ˆs his prologue testifies—that his listeners knew romances like
the story of Troy, *Tristan,* heroic epics (*chansons de geste*) and verse
fables (*fabliaux*) and that they were, therefore, curious about the "un-
precedented war of the two barons, Renart and Ysengrin," which was
to overshadow everything familiar. The works and genres which are
called to mind are all ironically alluded to in the course of the poem.
The success of this work, which rapidly became famous even outside of
France, and which for the first time took a position opposed to all heroic
and courtly poetry up to that time,[30] can probably be explained by this
change of horizon.

Philological investigation long misunderstood the original satirical

---

29 Examples of this method, which not only follows the fame, image, and influence of a writer through history but also examines the historical conditions and
changes in his understanding, are rare. The following should be mentioned: G. F.
Ford, *Dickens and His Readers* (Princeton, 1955); A. Nisin, *Les Oeuvres et les
siècles* (Paris, 1960), discusses Virgil, Dante et nous, Ronsard, Corneille, Racine;
E. Lämmert, "Zur Wirkungsgeschichte Eichendorffs in Deutschland," *Festschrift
für Richard Alewyn,* ed. H. Singer and B. von Wiese (Cologne and Graz, 1967).
The methodological problem of the step from the impact to the reception of a work
is shown most sharply by F. Vodicka in *Die Problematik der Rezeption von Nerudas
Werk* (1941, now in *Struktur vyvoje* [Prague, 1969]), where he discusses the changes
of the work which are realized in its successive aesthetic perceptions.

30 See H. R. Jauss, *Untersuchungen zur mittelalterlichen Tierdichtung* (Tübingen, 1959),
esp. Chap. IV, A and D.

intention of the medieval *Reineke Fuchs* and along with it the ironic-didactic sense of the analogy between animals and human nature, because ever since Jacob Grimm it had been wedded to the romantic notion of pure nature poetry and naive animal fairy tales. To give a second example for modernizing values, one could reproach French epic research since Bédier for continuing the criteria of Boileau's poetics —without realizing it—and judging literature which is not classical by the standards of simplicity, harmony of the parts and the whole, probability, and others.[31] The philological method of criticism is obviously not protected by its historical objectivity from the interpreter who, though supposedly eliminating his subjective evaluation, unconsciously raises his preconceived aesthetic sense to an unacknowledged standard and unwittingly modernizes the meaning of a text from the past. Whoever believes that the "timeless truth" of a work must reveal itself to the interpreter directly and through simple absorption in the text as if he had a point of view outside of history, disregarding all "errors" of his predecessors and of the historical reception, "conceals the fabric of impact and history in which historical consciousness itself stands"; he disavows the "preconditions, which are neither intentional nor random but all-inclusive, which govern his own understanding," and can only feign objectivity "which actually depends on the legitimacy of the questions."[32]

Hans Georg Gadamer, whose criticism of historical objectivism I am incorporating here, described in *Wahrheit und Methode* the principle of the history of impact, which seeks to show the reality of history in understanding itself,[33] as an application of the logic of question and answer to historical tradition. Continuing Collingwood's thesis that "one can only understand a text when one understands the question which it answers,"[34] Gadamer suggests that the reconstructed question can no longer stand in its original context because this historical context is always surrounded by the context of our present: "Understanding is always the process of fusion of such horizons which seem to exist independently."[35] The historical question cannot exist independently; it has to be fused with another question which will result from our attempt to integrate the past.[36] This logic of question and answer is the solution

---

31 A. Vinaver, "A la recherche d'une poétique médiévale," *Cahiers de civilisation médiévale*, II (1959), 1-16.

32 H. G. Gadamer, *Wahrheit und Methode* (Tübingen, 1960), pp. 284-85.

33 *Ibid.*, p. 283.

34 *Ibid.*, p. 352.

35 *Ibid.*, p. 289.

36 *Ibid.*, p. 356.

to what René Wellek described as the problem of literary judgment: should the philologist evaluate a literary work according to the perspective of the past, according to the viewpoint of the present or according to the "verdict of the ages?"[37]   The actual criteria of the past could be so narrow that their use would only make a work, whose historical impact had a great potential, poorer. The aesthetic judgment of the present would favor a group of works which appeal to the modern taste and would evaluate all other works unjustly because their function in their own day is no longer evident. And the history of the impact itself, as instructive as it may be, is "as authority open to the same objections as the authority of the author's contemporaries."[38] Wellek argues that it is impossible to avoid one's own opinion; one must only make it as objective as possible by doing what every scholar does— "isolating his object."[39] This view, however, is not a solution for the dilemma, but a relapse into objectivism. The "verdict of the ages" of a literary work is more than just "the accumulated judgment of other readers, critics, viewers, and even professors";[40] it is the successive development of the potential meaning which is present in a work and which is gradually realized in its historical reception by knowledgeable criticism. This judgment must, however, take place in contact with tradition and thus cause a controlled fusion of the horizons.

The agreement between my attempts at basing a possible literary history on an aesthetics of reception and H. G. Gadamer's principle of a history of impact ends, however, at the point where Gadamer wants to elevate the concept of the classical to the prototype of all historical contact between past and present. His pronouncement, "whatever is called 'classical' does not first require the surmounting of historical distance—for it continuously accomplishes this surmounting itself,"[41] denies the constitutive relationship of question and answer in historical tradition. If classical is "what is said for the present in such a way as if it were said especially for it,"[42] then it would not be a matter of looking for the question that the classical text answers. Doesn't one find described in the classical, which "means itself and interprets itself,"[43] simply the

---

37   Wellek, "Theory of Literary History," p. 184; *ibid.*, "Der Begriff der Evolution in der Literaturgeschichte," *Grundbegriffe der Literaturkritik* (Stuttgart, 1965), pp. 20-22.

38   Wellek, "Der Begriff der Evolution," p. 20.

39   *Ibid.*

40   *Ibid.*

41   *Wahrheit und Methode*, p. 274.

42   *Ibid.*

43   *Ibid.*

result of what I called the second horizon change: the unquestioning acceptance as self-evident of a so-called masterwork, which conceals its negativity in the retrospective horizon of an exemplary tradition and necessitates our regaining the "right horizon of questioning" in the face of guaranteed classicism? The classical work, too, calls for its conscious reception and thus for a realization of the "tension between text and present."[44] The concept of the classical which interprets itself, taken from Hegel, must lead to a reversal of the historical relationship between question and answer[45] and contradicts the principle of the history of impact that understanding is "not only reproductive but also productive."[46]

This contradiction is evidently determined by Gadamer's holding fast to his concept of classical art, which has not been able to support a general basis of an aesthetics of reception beyond the period of humanism. It is the concept of *mimesis*, understood as "recognition," as Gadamer presents it in his ontological explanation of experience in art: "What one actually experiences in a work of art and what one looks for is, how true it is, that is, how much it makes one know and recognize the world and one's own self."[47] This concept of art may hold true for the humanistic period, but not for the preceding medieval period and definitely not for the succeeding period of modernity, in which the aesthetics of mimesis has lost its authority like the metaphysics of substance (*Erkenntnis des Wesens*) which founded it. But the cognitive function of art does not end with this epochal development,[48] which demonstrates that art was in no way bound to the classical function of recognition. The work of art can also communicate knowledge which does not fit the Platonic scheme since it can anticipate ways to future experience, imagine as yet untested models of perception and conduct, or contain an answer to new questions.[49] In Gadamer's conception of

---

44   *Ibid.*, p. 290.

45   This reversal becomes obvious in the chapter "Die Logik von Frage und Antwort" (*ibid.*, pp. 351-360), where Gadamer at first demands of the traditional text (also the unclassical text or the simply historical text!) *per se* "that it ask a question of the interpreter. Thus exposition always includes reference to this question which has been asked. Understanding a text means understanding this question." The further argument show, however, that a past text cannot ask a question of *us* but that it must be revealed first by the answer, which the text contains.

46   *Ibid.*, p. 280.

47   *Ibid.*, p. 109.

48   See *ibid.*, p. 110.

49   That also follows from formalistic aesthetics and especially from V. Sklovskij's theory of *"Entautomatisierung"*; see also V. Erlich's reply, *Russischer Formalismus* (Munich, 1964), p. 84: "Since the 'tortuous, consciously restrained form' places artificial barriers between the perceiving subject and the perceived object, the chain of familiar connections and automatic reactions is broken; in this manner we become able to really see the things instead of merely recognizing them."

the "classical," the history of the impact of literature lacks just this virtual meaning and productive function in the process of experience. For to think of the "classical" as overcoming by itself the historical distance between the past and the present is to hypostatize tradition. Gadamer does not take into account the fact that classical art at the time of its creation did not yet appear classical, but may rather have once opened new ways of seeing things and may have formed new experiences, which only in historical perspective—in recognition of what is now familiar—give the appearance that the work contains a timeless truth.

The impact of even the greatest literary work of the past cannot be compared either with an event which communicates itself automatically or with an emanation: the tradition of art presupposes a dialogue between the present and the past, according to which a past work cannot answer and speak to us until a present observer has posed the question which retrieves it from its retirement. In *Wahrheit und Methode*, when understanding—analogous to Heidegger's *Seinsgeschehen*—is thought of as "becoming part of a self-sufficient tradition in which the past and the present are continuously in mutual mediation," [50] the "productive moment which lies in understanding" [51] must be short-changed. This productive function of progressive understanding, which necessarily also includes the criticizing and even forgetting of tradition, forms the basis of the aesthetics of reception of literary history outlined in the following chapter. This outline must consider the historical relevance of literature in three ways: diachronically in the relationship of literary works based upon reception (see V), synchronically within the frame of reference of literature of the same period as well as in the sequence of such frames of reference (see VI) and finally in the relationship of the immanent literary development to the general process of history (see VII).

V

The theory of the aesthetics of reception not only allows the understanding of the meaning and form of a literary work within the historical development of its reception. It also demands the ordering of the individual work in its "literary series" so that its historical position and significance in the context of literary experience can be recognized. Literary history based on the history of reception and impact will reveal itself as a process in which the passive reception of the reader and critic

50 *Wahrheit und Methode*, p. 275.

51 *Ibid.*, p. 280.

changes into the active reception and new production of the author, or in which—stated differently—a subsequent work solves formal and moral problems that the last work raised and may then itself present new problems.

How can the individual work, which determines chronological order in positivistic literary history and thereby superficially turns it into a "fact," be brought back into its historical order and thus be understood as an "event" again? The theory of the formalist school seeks to solve this problem with its principle of "literary evolution." In this theory the new work appears against a background of previous or competing works, reaches the "high ridge" of a literary epoch as a successful form, is reproduced and thereby continuously automated so that finally, when the next form has won out, it vegetates on as a worn-out genre and thus as a part of commonplace literature. If one analyzed and described a literary period according to this program, which so far has hardly been begun,[52] one might expect a result far superior to the conventional literary history. It would relate the separate categories, which stand side by side unconnected or at least connected only by a sketchy general history (for example, works of one author, one direction or one style, as well as different genres), to each other and disclose the evolutionary give and take of function and form.[53] Works either striking, related, or interdependent would appear as factors in a process which would no longer have to aimed at one central point because, as a dialectic producing new forms, the process requires no teleology. Seen in this way, the dynamics of literary evolution would eliminate the dilemma of selective criteria. The unique criterion is the work entering the literary series as a new form, not the reproduction of worn-out forms, styles and genres which now move to the background until a new turn in the evolutionary development makes them perceptible again. Finally, in the formalist plan of literary history, which is understood as "evolution" and, contrary to the normal meaning of this term, rejects every directed course, the historical character of a work would remain the same as its artistic character. The evolutionary meaning and characteristics of a literary work presuppose innovation as the decisive feature just as does

52   In the 1927 article, "Über literarische Evolution," by Jurii Tynjanov (*Die literarischen Kunstmittel und die Evolution in der Literatur* [Frankfort, 1967], pp. 37-60), this program is presented most exactly. It was only partially fulfilled—as J. Striedter informed me—in the treatment of problems of structural change in the history of literary genres, as in the volume *Russkaja proza*, Voprosy poetiki, VIII (Leningrad, 1926). See also J. Tynjanov, "Die Ode als rhetorische Gattung" (1922), *Texte der russischen Formalisten*, II, ed. J. Striedter (Munich, 1970).

53   J. Tynjanov, "Über literarische Evolution," p. 59.

the tenet that the work of art is to be perceived against the background of other artistic works.[54]

The formalist theory of "literary evolution" is certainly one of the most significant beginnings in the renovation of literary history. The recognition that historical changes are also occurring within a system in the field of literature, the attempt to functionalize literary development, and last but not least the theory of automation are achievements which must be retained, even if the one-sided canonization of the changes requires correction. Criticism has sufficiently pointed out the weaknesses of the formalist theory of evolution: mere opposition or aesthetic variation is not enough to explain the growth of literature; the question of the direction of the change of literary forms remains unanswered; innovation alone cannot assure artistic value; and the relationship between literary evolution and social change cannot be dispensed with by simple negation.[55] My thesis VII answers the last question; the other questions demand that the descriptive literary theory of the formalists be opened up to the dimension of historical experience by means of the aesthetics of reception. The historical position of the present observer as literary historian would have to be included in this experience.

The description of literary evolution as a never-ending fight of the new with the old or as the alternation of canonizing and automation of forms reduces the historical character of literature to the one-dimensional reality of its changes and limits historical understanding to recognition of these changes. The changes of the literary order do not become a historical process until along with the opposition of old and new forms is recognized its specific mutual mediation. This mutual mediation, including the step from the old to the new form in the interaction of work and recipient (public, critic, new producer), past events and successive receptions, can be conceived of formally and substantially as the problem "which every work of art as a horizon of possible solutions creates and leaves behind."[56] But the mere description of the structural changes and new artistic means of a work does not necessarily lead to this problem, nor back to the work's function within the histori-

54 "A work of art is viewed as a positive value if it changes the structure of the preceding period; it is seen as a negative value if it adopts the structure without changing it." (J. Mukarovsky, cited by R. Wellek, "Der Begriff der Evolution," pp. 42 f.)

55 See V. Erlich, *Russischer Formalismus*, pp. 284-287, and R. Wellek, "Der Begriff der Evolution," pp. 42 ff. See also J. Striedter, *Texte der russischen Formalisten*, I (Munich, 1969), Introduction, Section X.

56 H. Blumenberg in *Poetik und Hermeneutik*, III (see note 18), p. 692.

cal order. In order to determine this function, that is, in order to recognize the remaining problem which the new work answers in the historical succession, the interpreter must call upon his own experience, because the past horizon of old and new forms, problems and solutions, can only be recognized after it has been further mediated by the present horizon of the work. Literary history as "literary evolution" presupposes the historical process of aesthetic reception and production up to the observer's time as a condition for the communicating of all formal contrasts or "qualities of difference." [57]

Founding "literary evolution" on an aesthetics of reception not only restores its lost direction by making the position of the literary historian the temporary term of this process. This procedure also emphasizes the fundamentally historical dimension of literary experience by stressing the variable distance between the immediate and the potential meaning of a literary work. This means that the artistic character of a work, whose potential importance as criterion is reduced to that of innovation by formalism, does not by any means have to be immediately perceivable in the horizon of its first appearance, nor does it have to be exhausted by the opposition between old and new forms. The distance between the immediate first perception of a work and its potential meanings, or, to put it differently, the opposition between the new work and the expectations of its first readers, can be so great that a long process of reception is necessary in order to catch up with what first was unexpected and unusable. It can happen that the potential significance of a work may remain unrecognized until the evolution of a newer form widens the horizon and only then opens up the understanding of the misunderstood earlier form. Thus the dark lyrics of Mallarmé and his school prepared the way for a re-evaluation of a baroque poetry, which had long been neglected and forgotten, and especially for the new philosophical interpretation and "rebirth" of Góngora. There are many examples of how a new literary form can open an approach to forgotten literature; they include the so-called "renaissances"—so-called because the term implies the appearance of an automatic rebirth and often obscures the fact that literary tradition does not transmit itself. That is, the literary past can only return when a new reception has brought it into the present again—whether it be that a differ-

---

57 According to V. Erlich, *Russischer Formalismus,* p. 281, this concept means three things to the formalists: "on the level of the representation of reality 'quality of difference' stands for the 'avoidance' of the real, thus for creative deformation. On the level of language the expression means the avoidance of usual speech usage. On the level of literary dynamics finally . . . a change in the prevailing artistic standard."

ent aesthetic attitude has intentionally taken up the past, or that a new phase of literary evaluation has unexpectedly illuminated past works.[58] The new is not only an *aesthetic* category. It cannot be explained completely by the factors of innovation, surprise, surpassing, rearrangement and alienation, to which the formalist theory assigned utmost importance. The new becomes an historical category when the diachronic analysis of literature is forced to face the questions of which historical forces really make the literary work new, to what degree this newness is recognizable in the historical moment of its appearance, what distance, route, or circumlocution of understanding were required for its full realization, and whether the moment of this realization was so effective that it could change the perspective of the old and thereby the canonization of the literary past.[59] How the relationship of poetic theory and aesthetically productive practice appears in this light has already been discussed in another context.[60] Certainly the possibilities of the interaction between production and reception in the historical change of aesthetic attitude are not exhausted by these remarks. I only want to indicate the dimension into which a diachronic study of literature would move, since it can no longer remain satisfied with considering a chronological series of literary "facts" as the historical appearance of literature.

VI

The results which the separation and methodological complementariness of diachronic and synchronic analysis have achieved in the study of language provide grounds for improving upon the diachronic observation which until now has been the customary method in the study of literary history. Since it reveals changes in aesthetic attitudes the perspective of the history of reception always discovers functional connections between the understanding of new works and the meaning of old works. This perspective can also make it possible to take a synchronic cross-section of a moment in the process, to arrange heterogeneous, contemporaneous works into equivalent, opposing, and hierarchical groups, and thereby to discover a general system of relationships in the litera-

58 For the first possibility the (anti-romantic) re-evaluation of Boileau and the classic *contrainte* poetics through Gide and Valéry can be introduced; for the second the tardy discovery of Hölderlin's Hymns or Novalis's concept of future poetry (for the last see H. R. Jauss in *Romanische Forschungen*, LXXVII [1965], 174-83).

59 Thus, since the reception of the "minor romantic" Nerval, whose *Chimères* only attracted attention under the influence of Mallarmé, the canonized "major romantics," Lamartine, Vigny, Musset and a large part of the "rhetorical" lyrics of Victor Hugo have been forced more and more into the background.

60 *Poetik und Hermeneutik*, II (*Immanente Aesthetik—Aesthetische Reflexion*), ed. W. Iser (Munich, 1966), esp. pp. 395-418.

ture of one historical moment. A new literary history could be developed from this if other cross-sections were made earlier and later to illustrate the literary changes of structure in epoch-making moments.

Siegfried Kracauer has questioned most decisively the primacy of diachronic observation in history. His study on "Time and History" [61] challenges the claim of general history that, within the homogeneous medium of chronological time, it can make events of all areas of life comprehensible as a unified process consistent in every historical moment. This understanding of history, still under the influence of Hegel's idea of the "objective spirit" (*objektiver Geist*), presupposes that everything which happens at one time is determined to the same degree by the meaning of this moment and thus conceals the fact that things which occur at the same time are not really simultaneous. [62] For the variety of events of one historical moment, which the universal historian, as an exponent of a unified system, believes that he grasps, are *de facto* moments of completely different time curves, determined by the laws of their special history, [63] as becomes obvious in the discrepancies of the different "histories"—of art, of law, of economics, political history, etc.: "The shaped times of the diverse areas overshadow the uniform flow of time. Any historical period must therefore be imagined as a mixture of events which emerge at different moments of their own time." [64]

It is not the question here whether this assertion presupposes a primary inconsistency in history—which would mean that the consistency of general history only appears retrospectively from the viewpoint and presentation of the historian who imparts unity to it—or whether the radical skepticism of "historical reason" which leads Kracauer from the pluralism of a chronological and morphological passage of time to the basic antinomy of the general and the special in history,

---

61   In *Zeugnisse—Theodor W. Adorno zum 60. Geburtstag* (Frankfort, 1963), pp. 50-64, and also in "General History and the Aesthetic Approach," *Poetik und Hermeneutik*, III. See also *History: The Last Things Before the Last* (New York, 1969), esp. Chap. VI: "Ahasverus, or The Riddle of Time," pp. 139-63.

62   "First, in identifying history as a process in chronological time, we tacitly assume that our knowledge of the moment at which an event emerges from the flow of time will help us to account for its appearance. The date of the event is a value-laden fact. Accordingly, all events in the history of a people, a nation, or a civilization which take place at a given moment are supposed to occur then and there for reasons bound up, somehow, with that moment." (Kracauer, *History*, p. 141.)

63   This concept is discussed by H. Foccillon, *The Life of Forms in Art* (New York, 1948), and G. Kubler, *The Shape of Time: Remarks on the History of Things* (New Haven and London, 1962).

64   S. Kracauer, *History*, p. 53.

really proves that universal history is philosophically untenable today. However, it can be said for the field of literature that Kracauer's insights into the "co-existence of the simultaneous and the unsimultaneous,"[65] far from leading historical knowledge into a dillemma, emphasize the possibility and necessity of uncovering the historical dimension of literary appearances in synchronic cross-sections. For it follows from these insights that the chronological fiction of the moment, which determines all simultaneous occurrences, corresponds as little to the concept of the historicity of literature as does the morphological fiction of a homogeneous literary order in which all occurrences follow immanent laws one after the other. Purely diachronic observation, no matter how carefully it can explain changes in the history of a genre according to the immanent logic of innovation and automation, problem and solution, only reaches a truly historical dimension when it transcends the morphological canon, confronts the work important in the history of reception with the forgotten conventional works of the genre yet does not ignore its relationship to the literary surroundings in which it had to assert itself among works in other genres.

The historical character of literature appears exactly at the intersection of the diachronic and synchronic approaches. It must be possible to analyze the literary horizon of a certain historical moment as that synchronic system in which simultaneously appearing works can be received diachronically in relation, and in which the work can appear as of current interest or not, as fashionable, out-dated or of lasting value, or before its time or after it.[66] If simultaneously appearing literature— seen from the point of view of the aesthetics of production—breaks down into a heterogeneous variety of the unsimultaneous, that is, of works formed by the different moments of the "shaped time" of their genre (as the apparently present starry sky moves apart astronomically at very different rates), then this variety of literary works moves together

65 *Poetik und Hermeneutik,* III (see note 18), p. 569. The term "simultaneity of different things," with which F. Sengle, "Aufgaben der heutigen Literaturgeschtsschreibung," *Archiv für das Studium der neueren Sprachen,* CC (1964), pp. 247 ff., refers to the same phenomenon, fails to consider one dimension of the problem which becomes evident from his belief that this difficulty of literary history can be solved by simply combining comparative methods and modern interpretation ("that is, carrying out comparative interpretations on a wider base," p. 249).

66 In 1960 R. Jakobson developed similar assertions in a lecture which is now Chap. XI, "Linguistique et poétique," of his book, *Essais de linguistique générale* (Paris, 1963). See especially p. 212: "La description synchronique envisage non seulement la production littéraire d'une époque donnée, mais aussi cette partie de la tradition littéraire qui est restée vivante ou a été ressuscitée à l'époque en question. . . . La poétique historique, tout comme l'histoire du language, si elle se veut vraiment compréhensive, doit être conçue comme une superstructure, bâtie sur une série de descriptions synchroniques successives."

again for readers who perceive them as works of *their* present and relate them to each other in a meaningful unity of a common horizon of literary expectations, memories, and anticipations.

Since every synchronic system must keep its past and its future as indivisible structural elements,[67] the synchronic cross-section analysis of the literary production at one historical point implies further cross-sections earlier and later. Analogous to the history of the language, constant and variable factors can then be localized as functions of the system. For literature is also a sort of grammar or syntax with relatively firm relationships of its own: the structure of the traditional and uncanonized genres, styles of expression, and rhetorical figures. Opposed to this is the more variable field of semantics: the literary themes, archetypes, symbols, and metaphors. This is why one can attempt to draw an analogy for literary history to what Hans Blumenberg has postulated, explained through examples of the changes in epochs and especially the resulting relations of Christian theology and philosophy, and established with his historical logic of question and answer for the history of philosophy: a "formal system of the interpretation of reality . . . within the structure of which the changes can be localized which constitute the process of history up to the radicalness of the change of epochs."[68] Once the substantial conception of a self-continuing literary tradition has been replaced by a functional explanation of the process relationship of production and reception, it must be possible to see behind the transformation of literary forms and content that change of positions in a literary system of the interpretation of reality which makes the change of horizons in the process of aesthetic experience intelligible.

On these premises a principle of presentation of a literary history could be developed which would neither have to follow the all too familiar high route of the traditional classics nor wander in the valleys of the complete descriptions of all texts which can no longer be historically articulated. The problem of the selection of the works significant for a new history of literature can be solved with the help of the synchronic view in a way which has not yet been tried: a change of horizon in the historical process of the "literary evolution" need not be seen throughout the whole complex of diachronic fact and relations, but can also be determined by the altered make-up of the synchronic literary sys-

---

67 J. Tynjanov and R. Jacobson, "Probleme der Literatur und Sprachforschung" (1928), *Kursbuch,* V (Frankfurt, 1966), 75: "The history of the system itself presents another system. Pure synchrony proves to be illusory: each synchronic system has its past and its future as an inseparable structural element of this system."

68 First in "Epochenschwelle und Rezeption," *Philosophische Rundschau*, VI (1958), 101 ff., most recently in *Die Legitimität der Neuzeit* (Frankfurt, 1966), see esp. pp. 41 ff.

tem and by further cross-section analyses. In principle a presentation of literature in the historical succession of such systems, analyzed at arbitrary points of time, would be possible. The historical dimension of literature, its eventful continuity which is lost in traditionalism as in positivism, can only be rediscovered if the literary historian finds cross-sections and points out works which articulate the process character of "literary evolution" in its history-making moments and epochal caesuras. But it is neither statistics nor subjective caprice on the part of the literary historian which determines this historical articulation. Rather it is the history of impact, that is, what results from the event and what from the present perspective constitutes the continuity of literature as the historical explanation of its present status.

VII

The task of literary history is not completed until the literary work is not only synchronically and diachronically presented in the sequence of its systems but also seen as *special history* in its own unique relationship to *general history*. The fact that the historian can find in the literature of all times a typified, idealized, satirized, or utopian picture of social existence does not completely explain this relationship. The social function becomes manifest only where the literary experience of the reader enters the horizon of expectations of his life, forms his interpretation of the world, and thereby has an effect on his social actions.

The functional relationship of literature and society is usually demonstrated by traditional literary sociology within the narrow confines of a method that has only outwardly replaced the classical principle of *imitatio naturae* with the definition that literature is the representation of a given reality and that was forced to sanction a period-determined concept of style—"Realism" of the nineteenth century the literary category *par excellence*. Even the presently fashionable literary "structuralism," which is, often with doubtful justification, founded on the archetypal criticism of Northrop Frye or on the structural anthropology of Claude Lévi-Strauss, retains the basically classical aesthetics of representation and its schematization of "reflection" (*Widerspiegelung*) and "typification."[69] By interpreting the findings of structural linguistics and literary scholarship as archaic, anthropological constants clothed in literary myths (an interpretation often made possible only by the allegorization of the text) it reduces historical existence to structures

---

69 C. Lévi-Strauss himself testifies to this involuntarily but extremely impressively in his attempt to "interpret" one of R. Jakobson's linguistic descriptions of Baudelaire's poem *Les chats* with the help of his structural method; see *L'Homme*, II (1962), 21.

of an age-old social nature and literature to its mythic or symbolic expression. Thus exactly the predominantly social, or society-*forming*,
function of literature is missed. Literary structuralism does not ask—
just as Marxist and formalist literary scholarship before it did not ask—
how literature "itself helps to determine the idea of society which is its
prerequisite" and which it has already helped to determine through
the process of history. With these words Gerhard Hess in his lecture,
"Das Bild der Gesellschaft in der französischen Literatur" (1954), formulated the unsolved problem of the connection between literary
history and sociology and thereby explained to what degree literature can claim to have first discovered certain laws of social existence. [70] Answering the question of the society-forming function
of literature from the point of view of the aesthetics of reception exceeds the competence of the traditional aesthetics of representation. The attempt to close the gap between literary-historical and sociological research by using the methods of the aesthetics of reception is
simplified by the fact that the concept of the *horizon of expectations*, [71]
has also played a role in the axioms of sociology since Karl Mannheim. [72] It is also the main point of a methodological essay, "Natur-
gesetze und theoretische Systeme", by Karl R. Popper, who anchors
the scholarly forming of theories in the pre-scholarly experience of life.
Popper develops the problem of observation from the presupposition of
a "horizon of expectations" and thus provides a basis of comparison
for any attempt to determine the specific achievement of literature within the general process of experience and to define its relationships with
other forms of social behavior. [73]

According to Popper, the procedure of scholarship shares with pre-
scholarly experience the fact that every hypothesis, like every observation, always presupposes expectations: "namely those that constitute the
horizon of expectations, a horizon that for the first time makes the observations significant and consequently gives them their place within
the order of observations." [74] For in the procedure of scholarship as in
the experience of life, the most significant moment is the "disappoint-

70 Now in *Gesellschaft—Literatur—Wissenchaft: Gesammelte Schriften 1938-
1966,* ed. by H. R. Jauss and C. Mueller-Daehn (Munich, 1967), pp. 1-13, esp. pp.
2 and 4.

71 I have introduced this concept first in *Untersuchungen zur mittelalterlichen
Tierdichtung* (Tübingen, 1959), see esp. pp. 153, 180, 225, 271; further *Archiv für
das Studium der neueren Sprachen,* CXCVII (1961), 223-25.

72 K. Mannheim, *Mensch und Gesellschaft in Zeitalter des Umbaus* (Darm-
stadt, 1958), pp. 212 ff.

73 In *Theorie und Realität,* ed. by H. Albert (Tübingen, 1964), pp. 87-102.

74 *Ibid.,* p. 91.

ment of expectations": "it resembles the experience of a blind man running into an obstacle and thereby learning of its existence. We gain contact with 'reality' by disproving our assumptions. The refutation of our errors is the positive experience that we gain from reality."[75] This model of course does not exhaustively explain the process of the scholarly formation of theories[76] though it certainly illustrates the "productive meaning of negative experience" of life.[77] It can, however, shed more light on the specific function of literature within social life. For the reader has one advantage over the (hypothetical) non-reader, that he—to adhere to Popper's metaphor— does not have to run into a new obstacle to gain new experience of reality. The experience of reading can free him from adaptations, prejudice, and predicaments in his life by forcing him to a new perception of things. The horizon of expectations of literature is differentiated from the horizon of expectations of historical life by the fact that it not only preserves real experiences but also anticipates unrealized possibilities, widens the limited range of social behavior by new wishes, demands, and goals, and thereby opens avenues for future experience.

The orientation of our experience by the creative capability of literature rests not only on its artistic character, which by virtue of a new form helps us surmount the mechanical process of everyday perception. The new form of art is not only "perceived against the background of other works of art and through association with them." Viktor Sklovskij is right in this famous sentence, the heart of the formalist credo, insofar as he turns away from the prejudice of classical aesthetics that defines beauty as harmony of form and content and accordingly reduces the

---

75 *Ibid.,* p. 102.

76 Popper's example of the blind man does not distinguish between the two possibilities of a simple reaction and experimental action assuming certain hypotheses. If the second possibility is characteristic of the reflective scholarly attitude in distinction to the unreflective attitude in life, the scholar would be "creative" on his part, that is he could be placed higher than the "blind man" and could better be compared with the poet as a creator of new expectations.

77 Buck, *Lernen und Erfahrung,* pp. 70 ff. "[Negative experience] teaches not solely by leading us to revise the context of our subsequent experience so that the new fits into the corrected unity of an objective interpretation . . . . Not only is the object of the experience represented differently, but the experiencing consciousness changes. The action of a negative experience is one of becoming conscious of oneself. Whatever one becomes conscious of are the motifs which have been guiding experience and which have remained unquestioned in this guiding function. Negative experience has primarily the character of self-experience, which frees one for a qualitatively new kind of experience." From these premises G. Buck developed the concept of hermeneutics, which as a "principle of practical life that is guided by the highest interest in practical living; the actors' understanding of each other" legitimizes the specific experience of the so-called humanities in contrast to the scientific empire. See "Bildung durch Wissenschaft," in *Wissenschaft, Bildung und pädagogische Wirklichkeit* (Heidenheim, 1969), p. 24.

new form to the secondary function shaping a given content. But the new form appears not only "in order to replace the old form, which is no longer artistic," it can also make possible a new perception of things by forming the content of an experience which first appears in the form of literature. The relationship of literature and reader can be realized in the sensuous realm as stimulus to aesthetic perception as well as in the ethical realm as a stimulation to moral reflection.[78] The new literary work is received and judged against the background of other art forms as well as the background of everyday experience of life. From the point of view of the aesthetics of reception its social function in the ethical realm is equally to be understood in the modality of question and answer, problem and solution, through which it enters the horizon of its historical effect.

How a new aesthetic form can simultaneously have moral consequences, how it can give a moral question the greatest conceivable social impact, is impressively demonstrated by the trial of Flaubert after the pre-publication of *Madame Bovary* in the *Revue de Paris* in 1857. The new literary form which forced Flaubert's readers to an unfamiliar perception of the "worn-out fable" was the principle of the impersonal (or uninvolved) narration in conjunction with the so-called "erlebte Rede," a stylistic device which Flaubert handled like a virtuoso and with a consistent perspective. What is meant by this can be seen in a description which the prosecuting attorney Pinard claimed in his indictment was immoral in the highest degree. In the novel it follows Emma's first "misstep" and tells how she looked at herself in a mirror:

En s'apercevant dans la glace, elle s'étonna de son visage. Jamais elle n'avait eu les yeux si grands, si noirs, ni d'une telle profondeur. Quelque chose de subtil épandu sur sa personne la transfigurait.

Elle se répétait: J'ai un amant! un amant! se délectant à cette idée comme à celle d'une autre puberté qui lui serait survenue. *Elle allait donc enfin posséder ces plaisirs de l'amour, cette fièvre de bonheur dont elle avait désespéré. Elle entrait dans quelque chose de merveilleux, où tout serait passion, extase, délire ...*

The prosecuting attorney regarded the last sentences as an objective description which included the judgment of the narrator and was upset over this "glorification of adultery" which he considered to be even

---

78 J. Striedter has pointed out that in the diaries and examples from the prose of Leo Tolstoy, to which Sklovskij referred in his first explanation of the process of "Verfremdung," the purely aesthetic aspect was still connected with a theory of knowledge and an ethical aspect: "however, Sklovskij was interested—in contrast to Tolstoy—primarily in the artistic 'process' and not in the question of its ethical prerequisites and effects." (*Poetik und Hermeneutik,* II [see note 60], pp. 288 ff.)

more dangerous and immoral than the misstep itself.[79] In this Flaubert's accuser fell victim to an error as the defense immediately pointed out. The incriminating sentences are not an objective determination of the narrator, which the reader can believe, but a subjective opinion of a person characterized by her feelings that are formed from novels. The scientific device consists in revealing the inner thoughts of this person without the signals of direct statement (*Je vais donc enfin posséder* ...) or indirect statement (*Elle se disait qu'elle allait donc enfin posséder* ...). The effect is that the reader must decide for himself whether he should accept this sentence as a true statement or as an opinion characteristic of this person. Indeed, Emma Bovary is actually "condemned merely by the explicit description of her existence and by her own feelings."[80] This modern analysis of style agrees exactly with the refutation of the defense attorney Senard, who stressed that disillusion begins for Emma as early as the second day: "The denouement for morality is to be found in every line of the book."[81] (Senard himself could not, however, name this artistic device which had not yet been recorded at this time.) The consternating effect of the formal innovation in Flaubert's narrative style was obvious in the trial: the impersonal narrative form forces his readers not only to perceive things differently—"photographically exact" according to the judgment of the time—but it also forced them into an alienating insecurity about their judgment. Since the new stylistic device broke with an old novelistic convention—unequivocal description and well-founded moral judgment about the characters—*Madame Bovary* could radicalize or raise questions of life, which during the trial caused the original motive for the accusation, alleged lasciviousness, to recede into the background. The defense attorney began his counter-attack by turning the charge that the novel does not present anything but the *Histoire des adultères d'une femme de province* into the question of whether the subtitle of *Madame Bovary* should not properly read *Histoire de l'education trop souvent donnée en province*.[82] But the question with which the *Réquisitoire* of the prosecuting attorney reaches its high point has not yet been answered:

Qui peut condamner cette femme dans le livre? Personne. Telle est la conclusion. Il n'y a pas dans le livre un personnage qui puisse la condam-

---

79 Flaubert, *Oeuvres*, I, 657: "thus, as early as this first mistake, as early as this first fall, she glorified adultery, its poetry, its voluptuousness. Voilà gentlemen, what for me is much more dangerous, much more immoral than the fall itself!"

80 E. Auerbach, *Mimesis: Dargestellte Wirklichkeit in der abendländischen Literatur* (Bern, 1946), p. 430.

81 Flaubert, *Oeuvres*, I, 673.

82 *Ibid.*, p. 670.

ner. Si vous y trouvez un personnage sage, si vous y trouvez un seul principe en vertu duquel l'adultère soit stigmatisé, j'ai tort. [83]

If no character presented in the novel could condemn Emma Bovary and if no moral principle is asserted in whose name she could be condemned, is not general "public opinion" and its basis in "religious feeling" questioned along with the principle of "marital fidelity"? To what authority should the case of *Madame Bovary* be presented if the previously valid standards of society, "opinion publique, sentiment religieux, morale publique, bonnes moeurs," are no longer sufficient for judging this case? [84] These open and implicit questions do not by any means indicate an aesthetic lack of understanding or moral philistinism on the part of the prosecuting attorney. Rather, there is expressed in them the unsuspected influence of a new art form which can by means of a new *manière de voir les choses* jolt the reader of *Madame Bovary* out of the belief that his moral judgment is self-evident and reopen the long-closed question of public morals. Inasmuch as Flaubert, thanks to his impersonal style, did not provide an opportunity for the banning of his novel on grounds of immorality, the court acted consistently when it acquitted Flaubert as author but damned the literary school which they supposed him to represent, but which in reality was his stylistic device, as yet not recognized:

Attendu qu'il n'est pas permis, sous prétexte de peinture de caractère ou de couleur locale, de reproduire dans leurs écarts les faits, dits et gestes des personnages qu'un écrivain s'est donnée mission de peindre; qu'un pareil système, appliqué aux oeuvres de l'esprit aussi bien qu'aux productions des beaux-arts, *conduit à un réalisme qui serait la négation du beau et du bon* et qui, enfantant des oeuvres également offensantes pour les regards et pour l'esprit, commettrait de continuels outrages à la morale publique et aux bonnes moeurs. [85]

Thus a literary work with an unusual aesthetic form can shatter the expectations of its reader and at the same time confront him with a question which cannot be answered by religiously or publicly sanctioned morals. Instead of further examples, a word of reminder is in order here: it was not Bertolt Brecht but the Enlightenment which first proclaimed the competitive relationship between literature and canonized morals. Friedrich Schiller bears witness to this when he makes this express claim in regard to bourgeois drama: "the rules of the stage begin

83 *Ibid.*, p. 666.
84 Cf. *ibid.*, pp. 666-67.
85 *Ibid.*, p. 717.

where the realm of worldly laws ends."[86] The literary work can also—
and in the history of literature this possibility characterizes the most recent period of modernity—reverse the relationship of question and
answer and in an artistic medium confront the reader with a new
"opaque" reality which can no longer be understood from the previous
horizon of expectations. Thus the newest form of the novel, the much
discussed *nouveau roman,* is a form of modern art which—according
to Edgar Wind's formulation—presents the paradoxical case "that the
solution is provided, the problem, however, is given up in order that
the solution can be understood as the solution."[87] Here the reader is
excluded from the position of the immediate audience and placed in the
position of an uninitiated third person, who in the face of a still meaningless reality must himself find the question which will enable him to
discover the perception of the world and the interpersonal problem to
which the work's answer is directed.

It follows from all of this that the specific achievement of literature
in society can be found only when the function of literature is not understood as one of imitation. If one looks at the moments in history
when literary works toppled the taboos of the prevailing morality or offered the reader new solutions for the moral casuistry of his life which
later would be sanctioned by the consensus of all readers in a society, a
little-studied area of research opens for the literary historian. The chasm
between literature and history, between aesthetic and historical knowledge, can be bridged if literary history does not simply once again describe literary works as a reflection of the process of general history,
but rather discovers in the course of "literary evolution" that truly
socially formative function which belongs to literature as it competes
with other arts and social forces in the emancipation of man from his
natural, religious, and social ties.

If the literary critic is willing to overcome his lack of historical sense
for the sake of this task, then it can provide an answer to the questions,
why and to what ends one can still—or again—study literary history.[88]

(Translated by Elizabeth Benzinger)

86 *Die Schaubühne als eine moralische Anstalt betrachtet,* Säkular-Ausgabe,
XI, 99. See also R. Koselleck, *Kritik und Krise* (Freiburg and Munich, 1959), pp.
82 ff.

87 "Zur Systematik der künstlerischen Probleme," *Jahrbuch für Asthetik*
(1925), 440; for the application of this principle to works of the art of the present
see M. Imdahl, *Poetik und Hermeneutik,* III (see note 18), pp. 493-505, 663-64.

88 For further developments of this theory of literary history, see "Geschichte der
Kunst und Historie," *Literaturgeschichte als Provokation,* pp. 208-51; *Kleine Apologie der
ästhetischen Erfahrung* (Konstanz, 1972); and "Die Partialität der rezeptionsästhetischen
Methode," *Neue Hefte für Philosophie,* 4 (1973), 30-46 which will shortly appear in
Yale French Studies).

2

Past Significance and Present Meaning in
Literary History*

Robert Weimann

OVER the last 30 years the critique of the historical method has, in the West, achieved considerable dimensions, but perhaps the time has now come to re-assess the nature and the object of this critique, and from there to proceed to some re-appraisal of the possibilities and limitations of literary history. If, in the United States, the historical study of literature is to achieve a new sense of direction and purpose, it must first be prepared to face (with all that this implies) the full extent of the crisis of its discipline. This crisis is in many ways a symptom of the larger crisis of western society, in which the revolutionary idea of change, organic and dialectical concepts of evolution, and the liberal and humanist traditions of progress are all, in various degrees, affected. In recent years the consciousness of this wider background of crisis seems once more to be gaining ground, and perhaps the conjecture may be hazarded that a new interest in historical method can only benefit from an awareness of its present background. Such awareness may indeed facilitate the first steps towards re-opening, in the realm of literary history, the

* This paper uses and develops further the theoretical assumptions that govern the present writer's previous work, especially *New Criticism und die Entwicklung bürgerlicher Literaturwissenschaft* (Halle, 1962) and *Shakespeare und die Tradition des Volkstheaters* (Berlin, 1967). Some of these assumptions have also gone into several articles, of which two are accessible in English: "The Soul of the Age: Towards a Historical Approach to Shakespeare," *Shakespeare in a Changing World*, ed. Arnold Kettle (London, 1964), pp. 17-42; "Shakespeare on the Modern Stage: Past Significance and Present Meaning," *Shakespeare Survey*, 20 (1967), 113-20. Since this essay was first published, I have rewritten and collected my studies in the theory and history of literary history under the title *Literaturgeschichte und Mythologie: Methodologische und historische Studien* (Berlin, 1971).

question of method and purpose from an angle which defines itself, at the outset, beyond the assumptions of formalist criticism.

Among the recent forces of adversity which the historical study of literature saw itself confronted with, the New Criticism was certainly not the least important. But while the anti-historical direction of its influence can scarcely be doubted, this does not mean that its critique of literary history did not raise a number of very important questions. Now that the New Criticism has itself become part of the history of criticism, the neohumanist and formalist revolt against positivism, as well as its consequences, can more nearly be seen in perspective. At this date we certainly cannot go back to the nineteenth-century tradition of historical philology. But for all those who have felt that the theory and practice of formalism do not offer any valid alternative, the demise of positivism can never mean the end of literary history. A new method of literary history will reject the uncritical study of sources, influences and biographical data as an end in itself; but it will also refuse to accept the New Critical indictment of the "extrinsic" approach, precisely because the much recommended "intrinsic" study of literature has shown itself equally incapable of coping with the challenge of literature as a process in time.

Any serious re-appraisal of the aims and methods of literary history, then, would have to dispense with antiquarian as well as formalist assumptions. It would have to pursue a more dialectical method, for which the work of art, even when it imitates reality, is seen to be more than merely the reflection or expression of a past age or society. There would still be room for an approach to literature as past mimesis, but not at the cost of present morality. Thus, the customary distinction between the "extrinsic" and the "intrinsic" approaches would appear to be almost as irrelevant as the similar one between the pastness of the work and its present "autonomy." From this angle, history would then be seen as a comprehensive process which includes the present as well as the past; a process which is a continuum and as such as indivisible as the aesthetic experience, which appeals to the whole nature of man as a historical being. In this *process* and in this *nature* both the extrinsic and the intrinsic interact: change and value constitute a relationship which corresponds to a similar tension, in the work of art, between what is past and what is present. Literary history has to embrace this necessary tension, and conceive of its object in terms of both the unity and the contradiction of mimesis and morality, of past significance and present meaning.

I

As indicated, a new approach to the historical study of literature cannot pass by, and indeed must not underrate, the theoretical positions from which the New Criticism has challenged the methods of traditional literary history. This is not the place for a full survey of new critical opinion on the subject, but perhaps a few illustrations will suffice to bring out its main direction and emphasis. Even when, with some effort, the New Critics would retain a grudging modicum of respect for the "intense and precise labors of the Victorian philologists in the service of authenticity and other forms of factuality,"[1] their rejection of historical antiquarianism was as consistent as it was complete. If this had entailed a formulated alternative in historical method, there might have been more to be said for their polemics, especially for their attacks on the academic accumulation of unrelated historical facts, and even their scarcely concealed scorn for those mechanistic "exercises relating literature to various kinds of influence — social, political, economic, climatic, national, regional, traditional, psychological, and genealogical."[2] Such polemics, of course, were almost as vigorous in Britain and Europe, as in F. R. Leavis' protests against "the usual compilation . . . — names, titles, dates, 'facts about', irrelevancies, superficial comments, and labour-saving descriptions."[3]

These attacks (which were also aimed at "the verbose inanities of tendencies," historical *Zeitgeist*, etc., and which were echoed by a good many liberal critics) are too well-known to call for further documentation. They were all more or less explicitly based on certain theoretical assumptions which, reduced to their common denominator, can perhaps best be phrased negatively : they saw "the great mistake of the scientific-historical scholarship" in the fact that it "had allied itself with the physical sciences of the nineteenth century."[4] The most disreputable symptoms of such *mésalliance* were diagnosed in "the whole underlying assumption that literature should be explained by the methods of the natural sciences, by causality, by such external determining forces as . . . *race, milieu, moment.*"[5] Such "scienticism,"

1 William K. Wimsatt, Jr, and Cleanth Brooks, *Literary Criticism: A Short History* (New York, 1957), p. 537.

2 *Ibid.*, p. 543.

3 F. R. Leavis, "Criticism and Literary History," *The Importance of Scrutiny*, ed. Eric Bentley (New York, 1964), p. 12.

4 Lionel Trilling, "The Sense of the Past," *The Liberal Imagination*, Mercury Books edn. (London, 1961), p. 182.

5 René Wellek, "The Revolt Against Positivism in Recent European Literary Scholarship," *Concepts of Criticism*, ed. Stephen G. Nichols (New Haven and London, 1963), p. 256.

it was argued, was behind both the "study of causal antecedents and origins" and the use of "quantitative methods of science: statistics, charts, and graphs."[6]

Again, this is not the place to open the vast question of the relation of historical scholarship and natural science, and in any case an answer to this question would have to show, as many scholars and critics have done, that literary criticism is not an exact science. But even though the early battle in "the revolt against positivism" was in many ways justified, later new critical polemics tended both to complacency and to ingenuousness. Even while the enemy was routed, the attacks continued to be directed at a straw man who supposedly still believed in the methodological identity of history and mechanical physics. Although positivism was dead, its spectre was not allowed to find rest. These polemics, which served as a comfortable *alibi* to the anti-historical bias of the newer criticism, were questionable in several respects.

In the first place, the attack against the mechanistic aspects of nineteenth-century literary scholarship never paused to consider that the tradition of historical inquiry was much older than, and never solely identical with, the pseudo-scientific pose of some latter-day philologists. The rise of historical criticism can (roughly) be traced in the decline of the social and theoretical presuppositions of natural law, and dates from, say, Vico's *La Scienza Nuova* (1725), the work of Leibniz, Shaftesbury, the French enlightenment and, in its fully developed form, from Herder's *Ideen zur Philosophie der Geschichte der Menschheit* (1784/91). It finds its mature expression in Goethe's own "sense of the past and the present as one," for him a "powerful and overwhelming feeling," which could hardly "be expressed wonderfully enough." ("Ein Gefühl aber, das bei mir gewaltig überhand nahm und sich nicht wundersam genug äußern konnte, war die Empfindung der Vergangenheit und Gegenwart in Eins. . . ."[7]) This is a·poet's statement which corresponds to Schiller's attempt, in his theory of *Universalgeschichte*, "to connect the past with the present": "das Vergangene mit dem Gegenwärtigen zu verknüpfen."[8] From here, through Hegel, this tradition of historical thought branched off in two directions. On the one hand there was the *geisteswissenschaftliche* idealism of Dilthey and the later historians of *Historismus*, Ernst Troeltsch and Friedrich Meinecke, whose philosophy of history cer-

---

6 *Ibid.*, p. 257.

7 J. W. Goethe, *Dichtung und Wahrheit* (14.Buch); cf. *Werke* ("Jubiläums-Ausgabe"), xxiv, 213.

8 Friedrich Schiller, *Was heißt und zu welchem Ende studiert man Universalgeschichte?* 2. Aufl. Jena 1790 (repr. 1953, ed. F.·Schneider), p. 36.

tainly contained elements of irrationalism, but not of mechanism. On the other hand it was, in the context of revolutionary materialism, carried on by Engels and especially Marx, who in his well-known comment on classical Greek art argued that certain great works of art can only arise at an early or undeveloped stage of social development, and that "the charm of their art for us" is not opposed to their historical origins; so that the true "difficulty" of the historian's task lies not in the fact that "the Greek epic and Greek art are connected with certain social forms of development," but rather that these works of art "still offer aesthetic pleasure to us and in some respect serve as norm and unattainable standard." ("Aber die Schwierigkeit liegt nicht darin, zu verstehn, daß griechische Kunst und Epos an gewisse gesellschaftliche Entwicklungsformen geknüpft sind. Die Schwierigkeit ist, daß sie für uns noch Kunstgenuß gewähren und in gewisser Beziehung als Norm und unerreichbare Muster gelten."[9])

It was an illusion, therefore, to assume that the indictment of philological positivism could refute the tradition of historical inquiry at large. At the time when Hippolyte Taine was developing his determinism in terms of the *moment*, the *race* and the *milieu* (1863), the more dialectical concepts of historical criticism were perhaps overshadowed by what Nietzsche contemptuously called the reign of "that blind force of facts" ("jene blinde Macht der Fakta"[10]) but they certainly had not ceased to be available. There was, from the point of view of method, a tradition in which "the past and the present" could be considered "as one" and in which the present "charm" (and meaning) of great art, its norm and standard, might well be reconciled with a thorough understanding of its past genesis.

If it was undiscriminating to charge the historical approach with the abuse of "the methods of the natural sciences," then it was no less questionable, in the fourth decade of the twentieth century, to conceive of these methods solely or mainly in terms of nineteenth-century ideas of causality and such mechanistic assumptions as "that the world was reflected with perfect literalness in the will-less mind of the observer."[11] Again and again the literary historian was warned to keep away from the methods of science — but of a science which was hopelessly out of date. Nor was there, on the side of the critics, any curiosity as to whether the method of historiography itself had not (like that of modern science) developed considerably. By now to

9 Karl Marx, "Enleitung zur Kritik der politischen Ökonomie," in Marx and Engels, *Werke* (Dietz edition), XIII, 641.

10 Friedrich Nietzsche, *Vom Nutzen und Nachteil der Histoire für das Leben*, Kröners Taschenausgabe, XXXVII (Leipzig, 1933), p. 70.

11 Cf. Trilling, *The Liberal Imagination*, p. 182.

condemn the writing of history on the charge that it adopts the methods of the natural sciences (*which* "natural sciences"?) has become meaningless, if not downright complacent. At any rate (and this is not the place to say more) it ignores a great deal in modern physics; for instance the tendency among physicists in recent years to speak of their science in terms which (as a distinguished historian notes) suggest an "identity of aim between scientists and historians" and even "more striking analogies between the physical universe and the world of the historian."[12] It may be that in the light of such statements and recent insights into the nature of "the two cultures" (and how "dangerous" it is "to have two cultures which can't or don't communicate"[13]) the responsible literary critic will have to be more and more wary of stressing the irreconcilability of the two disciplines.

To say this is not to minimize the basic differences in method, and is emphatically no apology for positivism, but it may help us to recover a more sober perspective, from which the nineteenth century's "serene unification of scientific conscience" can be viewed with less ambiguity (than Cleanth Brooks betrays in the context of this phrase). Whatever its shortcomings, historical philology was intellectually the most coherent movement in nineteenth-century scholarship, and it is with some feeling of respect that one would wish to see *the necessary criticism* to be based on more facts and less arrogance. It would take more detailed investigation into the method and practice of nineteenth-century literary history to assess the degree to which the attempts at historical syntheses were actually thwarted by the pseudo-scientific pose. Not that the "blind power of facts" (Nietzsche) can ever be admired again, but on the basis of a recent study of traditional literary history in America[14] one is inclined to think that the really important works are less seriously affected by the mechanism of uncritical research than is commonly assumed by the critics of positivism. A sober re-assessment of these works (some of which, by

12 E. H. Carr, *What Is History?* (London, 1962), pp. 80, 66. Contrasting modern and nineteenth-century assumptions of method, Carr writes (pp. 77-78): "Nowadays both scientists and historians entertain the more modest hope of advancing progressively from one fragmentary hypothesis to another, isolating their facts through the medium of their interpretations, and testing their interpretations by the facts; and ways in which they go about it do not seem to me essentially different."

13 C. P. Snow, *The Two Cultures: And A Second Look*, Mentor edn. (New York, 1964), p. 90. Snow raises a vast question which has been asked, independently, in the distinguished work of Jacob Bronowski (see, e.g., *Science and Human Values* [London, 1961], pp. 50, et passim), in the writings of A. N. Whitehead, G. H. Hardy, et al.

14 See "Wanderlungen und Krisen amerikanischer Literarhistorie" in my *Literaturgeschichte und Mythologie* (pp. 218-80), where the traditions of Moses Coit Tyler and Vernon Louis Parrington are discussed.

the way, are eminently readable) would, among other things, reveal a startling contrast to the much more analytical and experimental prose of the New Criticism.[15]

If the new critical attitude towards historical scholarship was somewhat ambiguous, it was also, of course, not uniform. The various critics reacted rather differently, and there were quite a number of protests (some of them undoubtedly sincere) "that the literary historian and the critic need to work together" and that both functions should, ideally, be united "in one and the same man."[16] But, as the main works in the tradition of historical inquiry were generally treated with more condescension than knowledge and as their results were, in the practical business of criticism, usually ignored, such protests often rang hollow. So whereas the critics did not offer any theoretical alternative, there developed and spread a climate of critical opinion in which historical scholarship seemed *per se* hostile to critical evaluation; likewise, the genetic approach seemed *per se* to be an expression of relativism; the study of the writer's background and biography seemed *per se* to be a symptom of the "intentional fallacy"; etc. As in the forties and early fifties the New Criticism reaped its academic triumphs and one scholarly journal after the other thinned the volume of its historical contributions, it must have appeared to many that the study of literary genesis could only detract from and never add to the critical approach to literature as a serious art form. Small wonder, when even the most thoughtful observers approached the relations of "History and Criticism" as "something unavoidably problematic, part of a troublesome opposition which runs through all our experience."[17] Such an opposition was in many quarters not merely taken for granted; it was justified by, and elaborated into, the theory of "absolute" criteria of evaluation. It was an "absolutism" by which the (undoubted) "relativism" of the traditional literary historian was, unfortunately, not overcome but relegated to a series of opposites, among which change and value, development and order,

15 Ironically it "was precisely this scientific pose, conscious or unconscious, that constituted one of the main strengths of the New Criticism" (J. H. Raleigh, "The New Criticism as an Historical Phenomenon," *Comparative Literature*, XI [1959/ 60], 23). The irony of it was noticed by at least one critic who — finding in Allen Tate's work "a rage, so deep a hatred of Science and positivism, not to say democracy" — saw "a certain irony in his position, since the very textual analysis he defended was an aping of scientific method and rigor" (Alfred Kazin, *On Native Grounds*, [New York, 1942], p. 361).

16 Cleanth Brooks, "A Note on the Limits of 'History' and the Limits of 'Criticism,'" *The Sewanee Review*, LXI (1953), 132.

17 W. K. Wimsatt, Jr, "History and Criticism: A Problematic Relationship," *The Verbal Icon: Studies in the Meaning of Poetry* (Lexington, Ky., 1954), p. 253.

history and aesthetics, past significance and present meaning, appeared more irreconcilable than ever before.

II

However, it would be a gross over-simplification to imply that the New Critical critique of traditional literary history was entirely based on a series of formalist fallacies. Nor would one wish to minimize the extent to which the virtue of close textual analysis can survive the decline of the dogma of the autonomy of literature, thereby making a very considerable contribution to the more recent *rapproachement* of literary criticism and historical scholarship. And in the work of critics such as F. R. Leavis, Yvor Winters and Kenneth Burke, these possibilities reach as far back as the thirties and forties. For whatever the degree of the failure of the New Criticism in the field of literary history, even in its heyday a number of serious issues were raised and several very penetrating questions were asked, which a new approach would not wish easily to dismiss.

Among them, the question of relevance was foremost. Inspiring the attack on historical antiquarianism, it asserted the need for a new consciousness of "the relation between antique fact and poetic value."[18] The simplest and the most straightforward form in which the problem was posed was one in which the purpose of literary history was defined from the angle of the present. A history of English literature, F. R. Leavis wrote, "will be undertaken because the works of certain poets are judged to be of lasting value — of value in the present."[19] From this position, which may be said to stress one aspect of one basic truth, the need for evaluation was articulated with a new sense of urgency : if the criteria for a history of literature somehow correspond to a living system of values, then an awareness of these values would indeed seem to be *one* prerequisite for historical studies. F. R. Leavis (without bothering much about the emphasis carried by our cautious italics) put this quite bluntly: "Such a history, then, could be accomplished only by a writer interested in, and intelligent about, the present. It would, for one thing, be an attempt to establish a perspective, to determine what of English poetry of the past is, or ought to be, alive for us now."[20]

The strength of this position consisted in the fact *that* (not in the method *how*) the literature of the past was related to what was felt to

18   Wimsatt and Brooks, *Literary Criticism*, p. 537.
19   Leavis, "Criticism and Literary History," p. 13.
20   *Ibid.*, p. 14.

be "alive" in the present. When the interests of contemporary literature can find an echo in the literature of the past, then there needs
must exist some community of poetic values (and, we should add, of
historical moments). Even when this community was defined solely
in terms of "modern" values, it comprised, and had to be defined in
terms of, a sense of tradition. But then, again, "tradition" was taken
as a mode of relating (rather than *correlating*) past poetry to present
practice. F. R. Leavis and most of the new critics still behaved as if
their literary history virtually had the choice between past significance
and present meaning – *their* choice being, of course, in favor of the
latter.

The result, even though it satisfied current aesthetic assumptions,
was not very helpful in establishing criteria by which a new approach
to literary history might have prospered. F. R. Leavis' *The Great
Tradition* (1948), just as Cleanth Brooks' *Modern Poetry and the
Tradition* (1947), yielded the proof that by and large the historical
community of values had been defined solely in terms of "modern"
meaning. Here were two accomplished critics, both of them certainly
"interested in, and intelligent about, the present," and both venturing
into literary history, but with a result that somehow defeated the very
aims and functions of this discipline. To be sure, neither critic had
intended to write anything like a history of the English novel or a
history of English poetry — as they are "or ought to be, alive for us
now." But the historical elements of tradition which they recommended, were so much at odds with the history of English literature
as an actual process of possibilities (a process, that is, of both developments *and* values), that not even the rudiments for a future synthesis
of history and aesthetics were laid. (In this, Leavis and Brooks followed the critical theory and practice of T. S. Eliot, who however —
interestingly enough — had defined the idea of tradition much less
exclusively and more "historically," when he said that tradition
involves "the historical sense" with its "perception, not only of the
pastness of the past, but of its presence.")[21]

To take up only one example, the criteria by which Leavis defined
the great tradition of the English novel were not merely narrow and
exclusive, but also confusing. To dismiss, usually in form of a foot-
note, Defoe (without mentioning *Robinson Crusoe*) as well as Thackeray, Scott and Hardy may perhaps be legitimate for one who wishes
to bring out the undoubted greatness of George Eliot, Henry James
and Joseph Conrad. But in this context to introduce such concepts as
"historical importance" or "the important lines of English literary

21   T. S. Eliot, "Tradition and the Individual Talent," *Selected Essays: 1917-1932*
(London, 1932), p. 14.

history" is entirely to beg the question not merely of literary history, but of a workable synthesis of criticism and history. If Leavis states his "reason for not including Dickens in the line of great novelists" and then proceeds to assure us that he is "a great genius and is permanently among the classics";[22] if he gives a mere "note" to Emily Brontë "because [her] astonishing work seems to me a kind of sport," and then continues to say that "out of her a minor tradition comes . . .";[23] if Fielding is rejected as "simple" and then is said to have "made Jane Austen possible by opening the central tradition of English fiction";[24] – then there must be something wrong with a criticism which conceives of "tradition" not historically, not as a process of both developments *and* values, but in terms of three or four major modern novelists. Again, the complex relationship between past significance and present meaning is overlooked. It is ignored or replaced by a concept of tradition which can conceive of no unity and of no living interplay between the past world of the English novel and its present reception, but which judges everything in terms of "the significant few" major novelists. (Leavis touches on the real problem, which he prefers not to go into, when he says: "To be important historically is not, of course, to be necessarily one of the significant few."[25])

But to raise these objections is not to dispute the relevance of a concept of value, which (for Leavis) is seen "in terms of that human awareness . . . of the possibilities of life."[26] Nor can such a concept of value be anything but critical. That is to say that it will evaluate the literature of the past not "as a record of past customs, past habits, past manners, past fashions in taste,"[27] or anything which is in the nature of a museum. If, as the New Criticism was perfectly justified to insist, literature is properly understood as literature and not as a medium of sociological reference and exemplification, then indeed

---

22   F. R. Leavis, *The Great Tradition*, Penguin edn. (Harmondsworth, 1962), p. 29.

23   *Ibid.*, p. 38.

24   *Ibid.*, p. 11.

25   *Ibid.* There seems to be a similar contradiction, of which Cleanth Brooks is probably unaware, when he says "that we need to revise drastically our conventional *estimate* of the *course* of English poetry." ("Criticism, History, and Critical Relativism," *The Well-Wrought Urn*, Harvest edn. [New York, 1947], p. 224; my italics.) At any rate, this is too facile a way of correlating value ("estimate") and development ("course").

26   Leavis, *The Great Tradition*, p. 10.

27   Cleanth Brooks, "The Quick and the Dead: A Comment on Humanistic Studies," *The Humanities: An Appraisal*, ed. Julian Harris (Madison, Wisconsin, 1950), p. 5.

the poetic value of a work of literature is not easily to be abstracted from its ideological or biographical significance. To elucidate the latter is not in itself identical with an awareness of the former. And to achieve this awareness, it is certainly not enough to assume "that the specific problem of reading and judging literature is completely met in the process of learning the meaning of words, the political and philosophical allusions, the mental climate in which the poem originated, etc. etc."[28]

The most valuable contribution of the New Criticism, then, was to raise (if not to answer) the question as to the function and the criteria of literary history. To stress the need for evaluation involved an awareness of both, the necessity of selection and the importance of achieving a point of view from which to select and hence to evaluate. In the words of W. K. Wimsatt: "We are bound to have a point of view in literary criticism, and that point of view, though it may have been shaped by tradition, is bound to be our own. . . . Our judgments of the past cannot be discontinuous with our experience or insulated from it."[29] The realization of one's own point of view as both distinct from, and shaped by, the past finally called for a recognition that the object of evaluation was (just as its "subject," its ego) part of a more comprehensive process of tradition and experience. Such an approach could conceive of history not only "in its several antecedent or causal relations to the writing of literature" but it could also raise the question "whether antecedents themselves, if viewed in a certain light, do not become meanings."[30]

But to answer this question already involved a break with the formalist dogma of the autonomy of the work of art. This paved the way towards the more recent synthesis between literary criticism and historical scholarship which reveals the extent to which the virtues of close textual analysis can survive the decline of formalism. The inevitable compromises so characteristic of the late fifties and the sixties, need not detain us here. Obviously there are plenty of ways and means through which historical concepts such as, say, the author as "The Necessary Stylist" (Mark Spilka) can be re-introduced, and the whole question of rhetoric can be smuggled into the discussion of the purists. Once the "implied author" is conceived as a "core of norms and choices," a "choosing, evaluating person" who attempts "consciously or unconsciously to impose his fictional world upon the reader," the "strategy of point of view" (Percy Lubbock) can no longer be

28 Cleanth Brooks, "Literary History vs. Criticism," *The Kenyon Review*, II
30 *Ibid.*, p. 254.
29 Wimsatt, "History and Criticism," p. 258.
(1940), 407.

divorced from the world of history and sociology. This is a far cry
from the formalist ghost of "the affective fallacy"; and even though
The Rhetoric of Fiction still neglects the "social and psychological
forces that affect authors and readers,"[31] it again points to what
is potentially the historical meaning in the narrative structure of
point of view. Similar tendencies have for some time been noticed in
the interpretation of imagery, another domain of formalist interpretation, where there is a tendency to widen the scope of the term image
and to stress its subject-matter or "tenor" as opposed to its "vehicle,"
the real subject of the discourse as opposed to the adventitious and
imported image.[32] It surely is a sign of the times, when a critic of the
stature of W. K. Wimsatt produces a historical monograph on the
portraits of Alexander Pope, or when Cleanth Brooks, former explica-
tor of "paradox" and "irony," now at great length writes on the
geographical theme and background of Yoknapatawpha County. To
recognize "that a writer's choice of a subject is an aesthetic decision"[33]
prepares the way for a deeper understanding of history as part of the
literary theme. The renewed interest in thematics, like that in poetic
personality and rhetoric, is an indication of far-reaching transitions
and changes in critical doctrine. Themselves part of history, they
re-open the neglected dimensions of change and society by which
literary history can now be discussed more profitably in terms of what
it can and what it cannot accomplish.

III

A dialectical approach, which is conscious of its own social function,
will wish to consider the problem of literary history from an angle
where literature *is* history, and history is an element of literary structure and aesthetic experience. What is needed is not simply an act of
combination between the literary historian's approach ("A is derived
from X") and that of the critic ("A is better than Y"). It is not good
enough to have — in F. W. Bateson's sense — a "more intimate co-op-
eration" of their efforts, or anything less than an integration in

31 Wayne C. Booth, *The Rhetoric of Fiction* (Chicago, 1961), p. 74 and p. ix.
See also Mark Spilka, "The Necessary Stylist: A New Critical Revision," *Modern
Fiction Studies*, VI (1960/61), 285.

32 See the discussion of theories of metaphor in my *New Criticism*, pp. 220-277;
there is a much shorter French version in *Recherches internationales*, VIII (1964),
no. 43 (maijuin), 201-11.

33 Harry Levin, "Thematics and Criticism," *The Disciplines of Criticism*, ed.
Peter Demetz et al. (New Haven and London, 1968), p. 145.

method and purpose. To say that the historian is concerned with a task like "A is derived from X" is in itself a somewhat superficial formula; but even if this is read as a symbol of the genetic approach, it will not do merely to combine or to *link* the study of genesis with the critical evaluation of the art work. One has to be contained in the other, and the historical sense of the critic needs to be quite indistinguishable from the critical sense of the historian.

A postulate like this may sound presumptuous and, perhaps, over-optimistic, but really the object and the function of literary history can demand no less. Let us for a moment ask the question: What *is* the object of the literary historian as critic? Is it the work of art as it is experienced today? Or is it the work of art in *statu nascendi*, in the contemporary context of its genesis and original audience? To ask the question is to draw attention to both the unity and the contradiction of the past world of the art work and the present world of its reception; or, in other words, to suggest that the historian's task (and the pastness of the work) cannot be separated from the critic's task (and the work of art as a present experience). Obviously, we cannot afford to isolate these two necessary aspects: merely to do the former is to fall back into some kind of antiquarianism; merely to do the latter is to run all the risks of misunderstanding and distortion that the New Criticism was guilty of so often. The one alternative will finally reduce literary history to a study of origins and influences, a mere *Entstehungsgeschichte*; the other reduces the discipline to a series of modern appreciations, a mere *Wirkungsgeschichte*. Neither is (as an alternative) acceptable: in the last resort, for literary history to study past significance makes no sense without an awareness of present meaning, and an awareness of present meaning is incoherent without the study of past significance.

Thus the object of the literary historian as critic is necessarily complex. It involves both genesis and value, development and order, the work of art as a product of the past and the work of art as an experience in the present. To stress these two dimensions of the work in terms of their interrelationships is to argue for more than just expediency (in the sense that an awareness of history might prevent us from making a mistake or overlooking an anachronism in interpretation). The point that has to be made is not that the historian (or the critic) had better do his job thoroughly. The point is that these two dimensions are *inherent* in the work of art, and that the study of genesis and the pursuit of evaluation find an equivalent in the similar relationship, which is a historical *and* an aesthetic one, between the mimesis and the morality of the work of art itself. Or, to make this point from a somewhat different angle, one might refer to two basic functions of literature: on the one hand the work of art as a product of its time, a mirror of its age, a historical reflection of the society to which both the author and original audience belonged. On the other hand, it is surely no idealism to assume that the work of art is not merely a product, but a "producer" of its age; not merely a mirror of the past, but a lamp to the future. Incidentally, it was Karl Marx who pointed out that art is one of the "besondre Weisen der Produktion"[34] — the "special forms of production" — as in the sense that the work of art can produce its audience, and influence their attitudes and values.

In order to distinguish these two basic functions of literature one might call them, although this is to over-simplify, the mimetic and the moral. (The over-simplification does not reveal that each is, indeed, correlated with the other : the moral element is implicit in *mimesis* as representation, just as the sensuous nature of representation and imitation points to the only process through which morality can be translated into art.) But if we, for the present purpose, accept this convenient distinction of terms, it may be said that the twofold function of art calls for a corresponding activity of the historian as critic and of the critic as historian. Once the work of art is seen as both imitation and creation, it must be conceived as not merely a product of the past, but also as a "producer" of the future. And while the former function is involved in the genesis (and is rooted in the past world of the artwork), the latter function is realized in both the past world and the present world of its reception: it is rooted in a creative capacity for "production," which transcends the very time and age that are the object of the *mimesis*. Thus, the "mimetic" (the historical) and the "moral" (the ever present) functions interact: the literary historian as critic approaches an object in which *Zeitlichkeit* and *Überzeitlichkeit*, time and "timelessness," can be fused into one.

This is the very stuff that literary history is made of. The past significance of the work of art, its background and origins, is in the last resort indivisible from its present meaning and its survival into the future. The literary historian is confronted with more than the coexistence of these aspects: he has to face both their contradiction and unity. But to say this is not to make a new and particularly sophisticated demand on the historian of literature. Eventually, this is the same problem that, some 350 years ago, Ben Jonson faced, when he paid his highly complex tribute to his dead rival's work as "a Moniment, without a tombe"; Shakespeare's work, he said, was "for all time," but at the same time (or even before this) he also remarked that Shakespeare was the "Soule of the Age."[35] Jonson's epitaph can

---

34   Marx and Engels, *Werke*, Ergänzungsband I, 53f.
35   I use the text in E. K. Chambers, *William Shakespeare: A Study of Facts and Problems* (Oxford, 1930), II, 208f.

hardly be said to anticipate the systematic approach of a modern literary history, but the basic problem, which is a dialectical one, is there quite clearly. It is the problem of origin and survival or, in a different light, of a great work as the product of its age and the "producer" of its future. For the modern literary historian to grasp the dialectics of *Zeitlichkeit* und *Überzeitlichkeit* calls for an awareness of the art work as having both a past and a present dimension (as well as a present and a future existence). And it calls for a perception from this awareness, that these dimensions are, as an object of literary history, simultaneous in their interaction and tension.

The task of the literary historian, consequently, cannot be abstracted from either the genetic or the functional aspects of literature. For the historical study of origins helps to assess the continuity of, or the degree of change in, its social functions; while the study of its present functions can, in its turn, help us to appreciate the potential richness of the constellation presiding at its origin. In this sense, history can be studied as meaning: the structure of the work of art is potentially inherent in its genesis, but in society it becomes functional only through its affect in terms of a human and social experience. Structure is intimately linked up with, though not determined by, either its genesis or its affective relations. It is correlated to both its past genesis and its present functioning; for the critic to understand the full measure of this correlation is to become conscious of the necessary complexity of structure as history.

IV

But to discuss this correlation in terms of history and aesthetics yields only very general results which do not by themselves suggest a more practical application of theory. In order to illustrate some of the issues involved, we propose to raise the problem in the more practical context of the historical, critical and theatrical interpretation of Shakespearean drama. Although here the gulf that separates the critical and the historical approaches has in recent years been considerably narrowed, there still exists an astonishing number of conflicting assumptions as to what are the aims and methods of literary inquiry into a great work of the past. Among these, the unresolved tension between past genesis and present function looms large, although as a problem of method it has hardly been perceived or discussed.

At the risk of repetition, the basic problem may perhaps again be phrased in terms of the question which we have asked above : What is the object of a historical and critical approach to Shakespeare? What does the literary historian as critic mean when he refers to *Hamlet*?

Presumably the answer would still be quite different according to whether the person in question would wish to stress the importance of historical research or the priority of critical judgment. On the one hand (in terms of historical research) the answer would preferably be: the Renaissance play. Hamlet, according to this approach, will be a historical figure, the play's message an Elizabethan one in the sense that its past significance is to be explored without (explicit) reference to its modern meaning. On the other hand (and this would be the more critical approach) the answer would involve a different object which is primarily related not to the Elizabethan theater or even the Elizabethan text, but to the modern sensibility that it is meant to evoke. From this angle, an interpretation (or a theatrical production) would be authentic as long as it achieves the tone and tenor of our own age: Hamlet will be a modern symbol and the play's message a contemporary one in the sense that in the last resort its present meaning has priority over its past significance.

Actually, the two points of reference may not be so diametrically opposed, but the contradiction involved is an objective one. No matter what the approach is, there remains a historical text for modern readers (or actors); on the one hand there is the Elizabethan context and meaning, on the other, the modern understanding and interpretation. There is no getting away from this inevitable tension between the historical and the modern points of view, and no one-sided solution is feasible. The most learned and historically-minded scholar cannot physically become an Elizabethan; he cannot recreate the Globe or visualize the original production. Even if he conceived of Shakespeare's drama as being enacted in the theater, he would still be influenced by his own experience of the modern stage, its twentieth-century audience and actors and their social relationships that are quite different from those which, in Shakespeare's Globe, then constituted part of the play's meaning.

The underlying contradiction is not an academic one, and the more we think of it in terms of practical interpretation (including the theatrical interpretation of Shakespeare on the modern stage) the clearer the theoretical implications will emerge. Since today it is just as impossible to understand Shakespeare without a modern interpretation as it is to have an interpretation without Shakespeare, we cannot proceed from either a genuine Elizabethan production (and this already contained an interpretation of the text) or from one which makes us believe that *Hamlet* is a modern play. Today *any* Shakespeare interpretation has to come to terms with the tension between historical values and modern evaluations. But this contradiction is not necessarily frustrating, and the way it is solved constitutes the most essential decision of both historical criticism and serious theatrical interpretation. Viewed from the angle of the drama as a work of the theater, this contradiction involves an inevitable tension between the mimetic (or expressive) and the affective aspects, between the significance of what Shakespeare's work reflected (or expressed) in plot and character, and the changing impact of this on the contemporary spectator. Now to recreate the mimetic and the expressive dimensions is impossible without reference to Shakespeare's world and his intentions; to reassess their affective and moral effects is impossible without reference to our audience and our world.

For the literary historian and critic the question, then, is not *whether or not* to accept both worlds as points of reference, but rather *how* to relate them so as to obtain their maximum dimensions. To put it like this may appear provocatively superficial, but to resolve the contradiction one cannot minimize the conflicting elements when each is — in its different world — so inevitable and necessary. The "maximum dimensions" then, can mean no more and no less than this: to have as much of the historical significance and as much of the contemporary meaning merged into a new unity. Of course there is no easy formula as to how this synthesis of historical values and modern evaluations can be achieved. But in order to grasp its dialectic, it is well to remember that it is not entirely a case of opposites. On the contrary, it would be a grave mistake to overlook those many points of contact and identity, where, say, Shakespeare's Renaissance values can today be considered valid. This area of identity or interaction, however, is not simply given; it will be enlarged from a contemporary point of view which can conceive its own social direction as historical in the sense that it affirms both the revulsions and the links of contact between the past and the future. In the last resort this relationship involves a social and a methodological position from which both the change and the continuity can be accepted as part of a meaningful movement in history. In the present reception of Renaissance drama, therefore, the area of identity will radically differ between, say, a Marxist interpretation and one based on the premises of Jacques Maritain's neoscholasticism. Where the Renaissance heritage is not repudiated, there is bound to be a wide range of living contact, in which the "historical" element can be viewed as part of a wider configuration in which the present reproduction of past art is one way of bringing about a meaningful future.

Nor is this area of identity, which of course is also one of humanity and derives from man's anthropological status, confined to the Renaissance tradition. We are all, the great dramatists of the past, their contemporary producers and critics, characters in history; our own points of reference are, like our predecessors', products of history. In this, our present values emerge from the same historical process which is both reflected in, and accelerated by, Shakespeare's contribution. This is quite obvious in the history of literature which can only be written in reference to a scheme of values that (among other things) has to be abstracted from its great objects, including Shakespeare's dramas. Their greatness has been confirmed by the very contribution they have made for furnishing us with criteria by which to judge, and to judge not only modern plays but also the history of the drama as a whole.

Since such area of identity may be accepted as given, the relationship between Shakespeare's vision and its modern perspectives cannot simply be described as one of conflict or opposition. The difference between his world and ours is obvious enough, but it does not exclude some kind of concurrence. As Arnold Kettle has remarked, "the best way to emphasize the value of Shakespeare in *our* changing world is to see him in *his*, recognizing that the two worlds, though very different, are at the same time a unity."[36] This unity is at the basis of all our veneration for Shakespeare; without it, the impact of his work would not be possible. At the same, this unity does not preclude a contradiction which is at the basis of all our conflicting interpretations. In very much oversimplified terms: the unity creates the need of our interpretations of *Shakespeare*; the contradiction accounts for the need of our *interpretations* of Shakespeare. But actually each is contained in the other, and the interpretation as a whole can only succeed when these two aspects are inextricably welded into one. (By himself the modern historian can, as we have seen, either enhance or reduce the sphere of unity or the area of contradiction, but he can never entirely annihilate either.)

Once this relationship (although here still oversimplified) is understood more deeply, the historical study of literature has gained at least two negative standards of evaluation, but they may have some practical use for judging not only the literary but also the theatrical interpretation of the great drama of the past. For in the theater as elsewhere, the modernized classic is no more acceptable than the museum version. This may not be saying anything new, but perhaps it helps to recover certain assumptions which might prove practicable to both the theater director and the historical scholar. If the rift between them could thus be narrowed, the present theatrical reception of Shakespeare need be neither academic nor irresponsible. In modern Shakespearean productions, then, Hamlet need not become a hippy in order to convince, nor would it be necessary, as Martin Walser thinks it is, to produce "the old play" in order "to show us what things were like formerly" ("um uns zu sagen, wie es früher war"). If the past can be conceived, neither in its identity with, nor

36 *Shakespeare in a Changing World*, ed. Arnold Kettle (London, 1964), p. 10.

in its isolation from, the present, a historical perspective could evolve which might be both theatrically effective and convincing to the scholar. No topical effects are wanted, but a sense of history which can discover permanence in change but also change in seeming permanence; the past in the present but also the present in the past. Hence the "timeless" would result through a sense of time and history. It is in this sense that Shakespeare is "for all time" precisely because he was the "Soule of the Age." In this view, a historical vision can be made to yield a contemporary meaning. Its past significance was achieved because, at the time, it was contemporary and *then* incorporated the experience of the present. The meaning of literary history today can best be discovered through this past present, or that part of it which — although past — is still present and meaningful in a contemporary frame of reference. Thus, past significance and present meaning engage in a relationship which, in its interdependence, may illuminate either — the past work as against its present reception, and the contemporary interpretation against the historical significance of the work of art.

3

Some Observations on Method in Literary Studies

D. W. Robertson, Jr

A WORK of literature, or, indeed, a work of architecture, a statue, or a painting is usually approached in either of two ways. It may be presented as a "work of art" embodying elements that appeal more or less spontaneously to the student. Its relevance may be explained on the basis of the insights of the teacher regarding form, structure, and techniques that are thought of as belonging to the province of all art. On the other hand, the student may be led to examine sources, traditions, historical information of relevance to the work in question, and other matters thought to have a subsidiary value in appreciating the work of art. Roughly, those who employ the first approach are called "critics" while those who employ the second are called "scholars." This difference has led to a great deal of debate.[1] To avoid the unpleasantness arising from controversy, and perhaps, with some sense of creating a kind of Hegelian "higher synthesis," many scholars now like to be thought of as "scholar-critics," and critics have in some instances made certain concessions to scholarship. Usually, the "scholar-critic" agrees with the critic that human nature is a constant and that there are qualities of art that may be said to have a universal appeal. The deliberate cultivation of exotic art, either as "primitive art" or as art from geographically remote places, during the early years of this century, together with an increasing interest in humanity for its own sake, regardless of its specific cultural traditions,[2] has given a tremendous impetus to the study of all forms of human expression. Most recently, it has become fashionable to reduce works of art, literary or visual, to their elemen-

---

1 At a recent conference of humanistic scholars held at Princeton in connection with the series *Humanistic Scholarship in America: The Princeton Studies* the divergence between "critics" and "scholars" or their equivalents in a variety of fields became surprisingly evident. The "critics" seem in general to have fared better than the "scholars" on this occasion.

2 For an interesting discussion of this phenomenon, see Luis Díez del Corral, *The Rape of Europe* (New York, 1959), esp. Ch. vii.

tary structures, regardless of content. These structures are felt to be somehow valuable in themselves, especially as "aesthetic" manifestations of a kind of universal human reality.

There is some evidence of a growing uneasiness with this posture. In the first place, an ingrained historical optimism has led many persons to assume that privileged men of the past "transcend" their time in such a way that they are able to "look forward" to ideas and attitudes we now think of as being more or less self-evident. The scholar has frequently adjusted his "history" in such a way as to make possible accolades of "great artists" in the past as prophets, and the critic has welcomed such interpretations as confirmation of universal human realities. Each new critical school has been quick to adopt all the more admirable artists of the past as worthy predecessors of its own views and attitudes. However, rapid changes in attitude since the early years of this century, in spite of the continuity of a certain substratum of opinion, make it clear that what was "self-evident" in 1920 is no longer "self-evident" today. Are the attitudes "self-evident" to Chaucer, Shakespeare, or Pope the attitudes of 1920 or those of 1968? It is clear that they cannot be both, and it is increasingly obvious that they cannot be either, and that, moreover, Chaucer, Shakespeare, and Pope did not share the same attitudes. Meanwhile, we have learned a great deal since 1920 about history, so that much of the historical reconstruction of the scholar-critics of a generation ago now seems naive and factually unacceptable. Not only that, but "aesthetic" ideas have changed as well, so that what appeared to be "universal art" in 1920 must now be made "universal" on quite other grounds, if, indeed, it is possible to formulate any such grounds at all.

Perhaps the first coherent solution to the problem was that advanced by historians of the visual arts, who have developed, chiefly under the guidance of Heinrich Wölfflin, a concept of "stylistic history".[3] The aims of stylistic history were at first rather modest: to study changing modes of apprehending the visual world. However, it was realized at the outset that these modes of vision imply "the bases of the whole world picture of a people," and it has become apparent that stylistic history does not lose its validity when the visual arts themselves abandon the "visual world" as it is ordinarily understood entirely. It became clear that what is "good" in terms of one artistic style is not necessarily "good" in terms of another, and, further, that each style representing the tastes of a given population at a given time has an appeal peculiar to certain specific attitudes and ideals, which are much more "basic" than the visual styles seem to be when we regard them

3 Wölfflin's seminal study, available in English as *Principles of Art History*, was first published in 1915.

in isolation from their cultural contexts. In so far as literary studies are concerned, various efforts have been made to demonstrate parallels between styles in the visual arts and styles in literature, but since the whole subject of stylistic history is still new, and since appropriate descriptions of specific stylistic periods are not always available, a great deal of work still needs to be done.[4]

A new impetus to sharper historical perspectives has arisen in two disciplines unrelated to art history. The fact that these disciplines seem at first unrelated to literary studies should not deter us from paying careful attention to their conclusions, since these conclusions will undoubtedly exert a profound effect on such studies in the future. In the first place, certain psychologists, who belong, roughly, to the "phenomenological school" in Europe, most notably Dr. J. H. van den Berg,[5] have developed a concept of "psychological history." Much of their work has a very sound basis in observation, and it is by no means necessary to be a disciple of Husserl in order to appreciate the value of some their conclusions. Having observed that different social structures in the modern world profoundly affect the psychic constitutions of those who participate in them, these psychiatrists have reached the very plausible conclusion that historical changes in social structure produce marked alterations in "human nature." That is, "human nature" in one kind of social environment is likely to be very different from "human nature" in a second social environment differing significantly in structure from the first. This general conclusion has already influenced a number of historical studies.[6] Techniques for employing it vary among scholars, and the results have not always been convincing. Nevertheless, it is evident that the idea, here stated only in a very simple form, has enormous possibilities for development, and that its disciplined application will profoundly affect our attitudes toward the literature of the past.

Beginning with far different assumptions, largely derived from

4 No adequate history of the Baroque style is as yet available. For the Rococo, there are suggestive observations in Arno Schönberger and Halldor Soehner, *The Rococo Age* (New York, 1960). Literary materials are used effectively in connection with the nineteenth century by Werner Hofmann, *The Earthly Paradise* (New York, 1961). Efforts to distinguish the effects of Romanesque and Gothic styles in literature appear in Paul Zumthor, *Langue et techniques poétiques a l'époque romane* (Paris, 1963), and in the present author's *A Preface to Chaucer* (Princeton, 1962). There are highly suggestive materials in the recent works of Marshall McLuhan.

5 Dr. van den Berg's most famous work, *The Changing Nature of Man*, is available in English (New York, 1961). Certain of his other studies, notably *Het menselijk lichaam* (Nijkerk, 1959), are also relevant.

6 See the review article by R. van Caenegem, "Psychologische Geschiedenis," *Tijdschrift voor Geschiedenis*, LXXVIII (1965), 129-149.

theories of "structural linguistics" first announced in Prague in 1928, anthropologists like Professor Lévi-Strauss and philosophers like Michel Foucault,[7] have sought to show that careful "synchronic" studies, or studies in depth of a given culture at a given time, reveal adequate and reasonable "universes of discourse" suited to the structures of earlier or more primitive societies that should not be naively criticized from the point of view of our own, and, at the same time, that historical change is something far more complex than we had ordinarily assumed it to be. Again, the results of these studies may be appreciated even by those who do not share all of the assumptions upon which they are constructed. That is, the conclusions are not necessarily offensive to linguists trained in the school of the "Young Grammarians" who have learned to reverence scholars like Streitberg, Meillet, and Kieckers. The new studies have shown that a given idea or institution may play a far different rôle in one society than it does in one immediately preceding it or in one immediately following it in time. This fact becomes more apparent when a society is viewed as a "system," not, that is, as a rigorous artificial structure, but as an integrated whole in which the various "parts" are sufficiently interdependent so that a change in one implies concomitant changes in all the others. The metaphor "organic structure" has sometimes been used in this connection, but, although it may be revealing and helpful, it should be considered as a tool rather than as a descriptive epithet. Perhaps it is significant that these ideas are contemporary with "systems analysis" as it has been developed in other fields. In any event, the old attitude toward the "history of ideas" frequently oversimplifies or distorts the actual situation before us in the historical evidence, since it tends to neglect the shifting position of the ideas being studied within the social structure as a whole.

Disturbed by the usual naiveté of diachronic studies in this respect, Professor Foucault has developed a concept of historical "archaeology." That is, he has set out to show, specifically on the basis of attitudes toward language and money, that a substratum of common assumptions underlies apparently divergent opinions set forth contemporaneously in a given society, and that this substratum undergoes radical shifts at certain periods in the course of history. Although

7 For a brief account of the early development of structural linguistics, see Emile Benveniste, *Problèmes de linguistique générale* (Paris, 1966), Ch. viii. Professor Lévi-Strauss is best known to English readers for *The Savage Mind* (Chicago, 1966). The book reveals a fondness for outmoded Marxist polarities and is tinged with romantic neo-primitivism. Its author dislikes stylistic history. Nevertheless, some of the results are extremely useful. Foucault's relevant work is *Les mots et les choses* (Paris, 1966). His earlier work on madness tends to be sensationalistic and the scholarship is unreliable.

the evidence adduced is sometimes rather fragmentary, especially in the treatment of the Renaissance, and Professor Foucault is not always aware of the background of some of the ideas he adduces (like that, for example, of *convenientia*), the results are extremely impressive in a general way. He makes it obvious that "truths" concerning language and money in the nineteenth century are not the "truths" concerning these matters in earlier societies, and that we have no justification for projecting nineteenth-century "truths" about these matters on the Baroque or Renaissance past. Meanwhile, although he did not employ the evidence of stylistic history in any systematic way, the "periods," or chronological divisions of relative stability in the substratum of thought, that he proposes are roughly the same as those used by stylistic historians in the study of the visual arts. At the same time, with minor exceptions, they are generally consonant with conclusions we should expect from studies in "psychological history." That is, scholars interested in stylistic changes, alterations in "human nature," and shifts in the substratum of thought are occupied with what are essentially similar phenomena. In this connection, it is highly significant that similar conclusions have been reached on the basis of very different kinds of premises and working methods. It is obvious that, leaving aside all quarrels about premises, definitions, and other features of what might be called the tools of investigation, we shall, in the future, need to be much more thorough in our synchronic studies of cultural structures in the past. The integrity of past structures must be respected, and histories of isolated classes of phenomena must be written with a careful eye to the shifting position of those phenomena within the structures that produce them. Above all, it seems obvious that we shall need to exhibit far greater reluctance than we have usually shown to impose our own formulations about ideas and institutions on the structures of the past as though they were universal truths.[8]

Perhaps the key to any helpful understanding of earlier cultural structures is the realization that human formulations and institutions, including our own, are contingent phenomena without any independent reality of their own. For example, language exists only in the

8 In 1950 in "Historical Criticism," *English Institute Essays, 1950* (New York, 1951), I wrote that the historical critic "looks with some apprehension on the tendency of the literary critic to regard older literature in the light of modern aesthetic systems, economic philosophies, or psychological theories. He feels that such systems . . . do not exist until they are formulated." This statement was inspired by a reaction to some remarks by P. W. Bridgman in *The Nature of Physical Theory* (Princeton, 1936), and was felt to be harmonious with views acceptable in the field of "general semantics," a subject that was then popular. However, the statement has frequently been deplored. I have not abandoned it, and the present essay may serve to make it more comprehensible.

presence of one human being addressing either another human being, himself as though he were another human being, or an imaginary audience, including any inanimate objects to which he may choose to speak. It has no reality beyond one of these situations, and it has no "nature" independent of the nature imposed on it by the speaker and his audience, real or imaginary. The sounds that are the vehicle for language do not constitute its nature, since they have no significance as language except by virtue of a common understanding between the speaker and his audience, real or imaginary. If, as the psychological historians insist, human nature undergoes changes, it is clear that language must undergo changes also, not only of the kind usually discussed under the heading "linguistic change," but also more profound changes in its nature. Again, the nature of language in one society may be quite different from its nature in another society. In connection with this last consideration, Foucault seeks to show that Baroque language was essentially "representation," but that in the nineteenth century language became "expression." The only sane answer to the question as to whether language *is* "representation" or *is* "expression" must be that language was "representation" for speakers during the Baroque period and was "expression" for speakers during the nineteenth century. To say that language *is* expression and has always been expression, or, as more recent linguists are likely to say, language is "a system that embodies a reproduction of reality," is to posit an independent existence and nature for something merely contingent. It is also true that the assumption of any absolute stand on the nature of language will inevitably prevent us from understanding the language of the past as it survives in literary and other documents. This is not to say that formulations of the kind "Language is a system" are not useful. They may be very useful indeed so long as they are regarded as tools and not as absolutes. But in our studies of Chaucer, Shakespeare, or Pope (each of whom used a language appropriate to his time and place), we should constantly keep before us the fact that the language employed by any one of them is not "the same thing" as the language we employ today. The tendency to read literary texts from the pre-nineteenth-century past as though the language in which they were written was essentially "expression" has given rise to enormous distortions in our criticism.

This caution concerning language should be extended to other ideas and institutions as well. For example, the Oxford neo-positivists have frequently adduced ideas from Hume, Kant, Hegel or other earlier philosophers as though those philosophers were writing today. This procedure simply fails to recognize the fact that a statement by Hume means quite a different thing taken in isolation today from what it meant in the context of the society to which Hume addressed himself. What is worse, the same neo-positivists have not infrequently subjected the terms used by earlier philosophers to semantic analysis in an effort to show that they are meaningless. It may be quite true that a term used by Hume or Kant has little meaning in the stylistic environment in which we move, but this does not imply that the term was meaningless at the time it was used. That is, a statement may be valid at one time and meaningless at another. Again, as I have sought to show elsewhere, the system of "principal vices" popular during the late Middle Ages may be largely irrelevant in the society of today, but it played a functional part in medieval society, where it had a genuine operational validity.[9] The same kind of considerations apply to more complex institutions like marriage. It is obvious that the institution of marriage plays an entirely different part in our society with its egalitarian ideals, where the sacramental value of the contract is usually merely formal and its function is largely personal, from that it played in an hierarchical society organized in small groups like that of the Middle Ages. Nevertheless, scholars have not hesitated to attribute "modern" attitudes toward marriage to Chaucer, who lived in a society where such attitudes would have been absurd.[10] The initial assumption that marriage is "the same thing" in the fourteenth century as it is today is, of course, erroneous.

Generally, the categories by means of which we analyze our own society may sometimes appear in earlier societies. When such coincidences occur, as they do in the examples cited above, we should be willing to recognize the fact that their significance in the past may be very different from their significance in the present, and, moreover, that their significance in the present will undoubtedly change in the future with changes in the structure of society and concomitant alterations in "human nature." That is, unless we take into account changes in the positions of institutions within the social structure in the course of time, our studies of subjects like "the history of marriage" are bound to be misleading. The common assumption that institutions, attitudes, and ideals display a "linear development" in the course of history has no justification in the evidence of history itself. And the further assumption that the present represents a kind of glorious fruition of linear developments amounts to nothing more than what might with some justice be called "historical anthropomorphism" inherited from romantic philosophers like Hegel.

In addition to preserving old categories, but in altered form, new

9 *Chaucer's London* (New York, 1968), pp. 5-8, 68-69, 218-20.

10 The claim for Chaucer's "modernity" in this respect is usually made in connection with "The Franklin's Tale." But as I shall seek to show in a forthcoming article, to appear in *Costerus*, this interpretation rests on dubious premises.

societies construct new categories of their own. These new formulations are likely to appear in fairly large numbers at about the same time, and their appearance on a large scale is accompanied by "changes in style," or "changes in human nature," or, to put it in another way, "changes in the substratum of thought." Such changes occurred, for example, in the mid-twelfth century, in the fifteenth century, in the early seventeenth century, in the later eighteenth century, and at the beginning of the nineteenth century. It is possible, of course, and sometimes desirable to subdivide the "periods" thus established still further. Sometimes these periods coincide with periods of linguistic change as such change is described by historical linguists, although the significance of this coincidence has never been explored. The new categories developed during these periods of change are concomitant with changes in social structure and have little relevance to social structures preceding them. For example, the later eighteenth century developed a concept of "art" and "the artist" that has been continued and modified since. But neither the eighteenth-century concept nor its subsequent modifications have any relevance to earlier societies where "art" meant something entirely different and where the "artist" in the eighteenth-century sense did not exist. Thus, for example, one student of the Gothic cathedral has seen fit to explain at some length that the cathedrals do not constitute what we call "art."[11] The same period witnessed the development of an idea of "personality," which was deepened and strengthened in the nineteenth and twentieth centuries, but this, too, was an idea suited to life within a new kind of social structure without relevance to life as it was lived in earlier centuries.[12] The usual assumption that "art" as we understand it, or "personality" has "always existed" even though people did not "talk about it" in earlier times makes an unwarranted universalization of purely contingent phenomena.

In general, new categories should not be imposed on the past. Freudian psychology, for example, represents a series of generalizations based on the effects of a kind of social structure that developed during the course of the later nineteenth century. The relevant social conditions together with certain concomitant attitudes toward sex did not exist in the eighteenth century, and are now rapidly disappearing. Hence efforts to analyze earlier cultural phenomena in Freudian terms inevitably lead to false conclusions. This is not to say that Freudian psychology is or was "wrong," but simply that its truths have a date and locale attached to them. To put this in another way, Freudian psychology is a part of a "universe of discourse" with a

---

11 See Jean Gimpel, *The Cathedral Builders* (New York, 1961), pp. 95-97.
12 Cf. *Chaucer's London*, pp. 5-7.

nexus of relationships to other elements in that "universe." To insert it into an earlier universe of discourse where no such nexus exists is to create absurdities. That is, Freudian "complexes" have about as much place in discussions of Shakespeare as have carburetors or semi-conductors. It cannot be emphasized too urgently that any age in the past can be understood only when we analyze it in so far as is possible in its own terms. If we can begin to understand those terms in their own context, we can begin to understand the age, but if we impose our own terms on it, we might as well be studying ourselves rather than the past.

Changes in the structure of society and the nature of language frequently imply changes in very basic attitudes toward reality, toward the location of reality, and toward its relation to space and time.[13] Since the early nineteenth century, for example, there has been a very marked tendency to locate reality within the individual. Croce's "intuition," Ortega y Gasset's position that "Reality is my life," and Bishop Robinson's desire to locate God "in the depths of the personality," to cite only a few random examples, are all manifestations of a common "stylistic" or "archaeologically discernible" mode that is a more or less natural concomitant of a society in which the individual is isolated in a complex of large group structures. This mode, with its emphasis on inner reality, is at the same time conducive to expressionistic attitudes toward thought, language, and art, to subjective evaluations of space, and to a mistrust of the "past" and the "future."[14] But to impose various facets of this mode or its logically felt consequences on the past, as though it were generally characteristic of all humanity, is to invite serious misapprehensions concerning both ourselves and our ancestors.

In the course of the above discussion I have used "the past" simply as a convenient expression. Actually, we know very little about the past beyond the dubious evidence of our memories, which are always colored by the present. What we as students have before us instead of the past itself is a series of monuments, artifacts, and documents existing in the present, which are just as much a part of the present as are automobiles, neutrons, or cola beverages. The historian or the student of literature concerns himself with the order and significance of the

13 For changing attitudes toward time, see Georges Poulet, *Studies in Human Time* (New York, 1959). There are useful observations in Foucault, and in some of the writings of stylistic historians. Historians of the visual arts frequently treat changing attitudes toward space.

14 Modern thinkers often seek to objectify what are essentially subjective evaluations of space, as Heidegger does in *Being and Time* (New York, 1962). On attitudes toward the past and the future, cf. Hofmann, *The Earthly Paradise*, p. 50, and *Chaucer's London*, p. 120.

detritus of the past in the present, not with the past itself, which is
unapproachable. The works of Chaucer, or Shakespeare, or Milton
exist today in libraries, in homes, or in the rooms of students. Why
not treat them as though they were written within our own generation? The critic, or even the scholar-critic, often shows a marked
inclination to do this, either by stating, in terms of some currently
fashionable critical doctrine, that great art is universal, or by seeking
to interpret the evidence of the past in such a way as to make it
conform to the conventions of the present. If modern audiences
cannot appreciate the music of Bach played in a Baroque manner on
Baroque instruments, why not present symphonic arrangements of
Bach that make Bach sound like Tchaikowsky?

There are a number of valid answers to this question, some of them
quite simple. To begin with a simple one, it is fairly obvious that
Tchaikowsky wrote much better music in his own style than Bach
could, and that the efforts of an arranger of Bach are unlikely to equal
the efforts of Tchaikowsky himself. If one wishes to listen to music
in the style of Tchaikowsky, he would do much better to listen to
Tchaikowsky's own compositions. The idea that Bach's music transformed for a modern symphony orchestra has a "cultural value" is,
therefore, specious. Moreover, the unpleasant prospect looms that we
shall some day hear Bach in the style of Webern, or the later Stravin-
sky, or even Stockhausen, as Bach keeps up with the times. Much the
same criticisms may be made of Chaucer, or Shakespeare, or Milton
transformed in the classroom into "modern" authors. They are less
good at their newly imposed task than are modern authors themselves,
and their "cultural" value becomes negligible. More seriously, the
literary critic who customarily employs tools first created during the
romantic movement now modified by Crocean aesthetics in its various
modern forms, frequently commits historical blunders that are obvious
to persons of no very great sophistication.[15] Crocean aesthetics is,
actually, little more than a rationalization of the expressionistic style
which seeks to turn all art into a lyrical expression of intuitively
recognized inner truths. Although it is well suited to works produced
in this style, it has no relevance to earlier styles consonant with social
structures wherein the conditions necessary to produce expressionistic
attitudes did not exist. If we are to compose valid criticism of works
produced in earlier stylistic periods, we must do so in terms of conventions established at a time contemporary with the works themselves.
If we fail to do so, we shall miss the integrity of the works we study,

15 The romantic origin of the fundamental attitudes of modern criticism has
been amply demonstrated by M. H. Abrams in *The Mirror and the Lamp* (New
York, 1958).

not to mention their significance, frequently profound, for their original audiences.

What we call the past is, in effect, a series of foreign countries inhabited by strangers whose manners, customs, tastes, and basic attitudes even partially understood widen our horizons and enrich our daily experience. Concealed self-study through the inadequate medium of the past only stultifies us within the narrow confines of our own naively envisioned perspectives. The specious and easy "relevance" achieved by positing "universal humanity" and then imposing our own prejudices on the past is not merely detrimental to understanding. It will soon become absurd in the light of a growing awareness of the complexity of historical processes. Finally, it is barely possible that the recognition of valid realities established by earlier generations may lead us at least one small step away from that rancid solipsistic pit into which the major tendencies of post-romantic thought have thrust us.[16]

Specifically, there are a number of ways in which literary studies might well be improved in the light of the above considerations. In the first place, the usual "diachronic" courses now offered in colleges and universities — courses in the history of the epic, the drama, the lyric, or other "genre" histories — should be recognized as being extremely artificial and misleading. The "lyric" is one thing in the thirteenth century and quite another in the nineteenth century. To present students with a "definition" of the lyric and then study its "history" from the thirteenth century to the present is to engage in a completely artificial exercise that has almost no educational value except that accidentally achieved by the presentation of occasional works that one student or another may, for a short time, enjoy. Similarly, to concoct a "definition" of tragedy, an exercise for which Aristotle offers an unfortunate precedent, and then to make all "tragedies" — Greek, Elizabethan, romantic, and modern — conform to the definition is not only to limit the understanding of the student but to distort the evidence of the past within a framework that has no intellectual respectability. If we are to make literary courses significant, genuinely stimulating, and indeed comparable in sophistication with courses now being offered by some historians of the visual arts, we shall need to emphasize "period" and "author" courses a great deal

16 The fact that empirical attitudes, for all their vaunted objectivity, imply the reality of the nervous system of the observer rather than that of anything observed is more often felt than faced squarely. The emphasis on the inner reality of the artist in modern art needs no special elaboration, since it is fairly obvious. However, for significant observations on the subject, see, for example, Wallace Fowlie, *The Age of Surrealism* (Bloomington, 1960), pp. 29-30; Marcel Brion, *Art abstrait* (Paris, 1956), pp. 25, 27, 93-94, 139.

more, and to enrich these courses with more thorough and intellectually respectable considerations of relevant monuments from the visual arts, with descriptions of social institutions, and with efforts to evaluate the works being studied in a way that would have been comprehensible to their authors and their original audiences. The usual "genre" courses do not provide sufficient time for the development of an adequate background in the various styles encountered.

Diachronic studies of relatively brief periods in detail can be extremely helpful, since they reveal the gradual changes in attitude that culminate in more pronounced changes in style. However, such studies should not assume any kind of "progress" except that in time. As social institutions change there are concomitant changes in thought, language, and ideals, as well as changes in style. But these changes are better regarded as adaptations within a system than as illustrations of linear progress. Ideas and forms of expression appropriate to a later generation are not necessarily appropriate to an earlier generation, so that there are little grounds for thinking of them as "improvements." But such studies can show very clearly the interaction of various elements in a society that accompany changes in literary conventions. Studies of more extensive periods broken by major stylistic shifts, like the eighteenth century, for example, can serve to illustrate the kind of dramatic contrasts that may appear in the juxtaposition of two very different styles. Undergraduate "survey" courses afford a striking opportunity to present in a simplified fashion the integrity of various stylistic conventions and at the same time to clarify the essential peculiarities of the stylistic modes to which we are accustomed today. But in order to be effective, such courses need to concentrate on a few selected literary texts and to make far more use of the visual arts, music, and relevant historical sociology. Stylistic features are frequently more apparent in the visual arts than they are in literature, since it is always possible to read a text naively in terms of one's own stylistic attitudes.

All this implies, of course, a new professionalism in graduate training. Too frequently graduate students today are treated as though they were potential poets or novelists whose "sensibilities" need cultivating. There is undoubtedly a place for creative arts courses in a modern university, and certainly no one objects to cultivated sensibilities. However, if graduate schools in English are to be professionally effective, they must provide a more thorough grounding in period studies, with emphasis on primary sources in variety, and the cultivation of the kind of imagination that involves skepticism concerning accepted secondary formulations, the ability to see new relationships among primary materials, and the impulse to formulate relevant relationships between those materials and literary texts. The old system that required little more than the learning of a long series of secondary conclusions by rote, regardless of their value, is now long out of date, and its futility is obvious, even to the students themselves. It has led to academic conservatism of a most undesirable kind and to the unthinking repetition and transmission of outmoded generalizations on a large scale. Literary scholars must learn to welcome the prospect of new approaches and new ideas. At present no group of university men is more resistant to change or more antagonistic to new developments that do not serve to confirm attitudes previously learned than that made up of teachers of what are called the humanities.

The task of understanding a literary text from an earlier generation as it was initially presented is formidable. We cannot, on the basis of the evidence available, reconstruct completely any period in the past, and our understanding will always be impeded to a certain extent by the conventions of our own times, which change continuously, but from which no one can escape entirely. But this fact should act as a stimulus rather than as a deterrent, since it means that there will always be something more to be done. The frontiers before us have no limit. And we may be consoled by the fact that the more accurately we can describe the detritus left to us by the past, the better able we shall be to understand ourselves. And if the "humanities" — a nineteenth-century invention — can help us in this task, they will serve a useful and beneficial function in our society. Meanwhile, the realization that our own attitudes are, like those of the past, largely contingent may help to induce a certain equanimity and detachment. If literary studies are divorced from the larger concerns of cultural history they will eventually wither away.

4

The Life and Death of Literary Forms

Alastair Fowler

I. Forms and the Literary Model

THE SUBJECT proposed is the "life" and "death" of literary forms, not of literary works (a different subject). We say that the mock epic form has died out but *The Rape of the Lock* in some sense lives on, that the sonnet continues viable though Constable's *Sonnets* are moribund, that pastoral persists in fresh guise, even if Googe's *Eclogues* do not. The historical duration of works need not coincide with the duration of the forms they use.

However, I must not take this as axiomatic, since for certain meanings of *form* it would be untrue. If forms meant personal configurations —as in Buffon's *le style est l'homme même*—they might be coterminous with individual literary works. And a Crocean idealist who thought of form as "expression-intuition" would not even want to distinguish it from the internal event of the work;[1] for him, each work is formally unique, the diachronic propositions of literary history meaningless. Best begin, then, by specifying a literary model.

The theoretical model currently useful is likely to be based on recent ideas of the substrate, and consequently to draw on post-Saussurean linguistics and on information theory. Thus we may define a literary work as the record of a specialized speech act. An author makes and communicates it, much as speakers express themselves, through a system of shared grammatical rules—Saussure's *langue*—supplemented by other more specialized systems of conventions.[2] His individual speech act, however, is *parole*, a unique contingent communication, which,

---

1 See René Wellek, *Concepts of Criticism*, ed. S. G. Nichols (New Haven and London, 1963), p. 56.

2 Here I follow F. W. Bateson's extension of the concept *langue* in "Modern Bibliography and the Literary Artifact," *English Studies Today* (Bern, 1961); see esp. pp. 74-76. Cf. E. D. Hirsch, *Validity in Interpretation* (New Haven and London, 1967), p. 134.

though it depends on previously shared conventions, may also modify them to initiate new conventions. These in turn become *langue* for subsequent *paroles*. As for the difference between everyday and literary communication, it seems to lie in the latter's more elaborate *langue*, which may include not only rules of spoken or written grammar but also many sorts of conventional types, such as modes, genres, motifs, topics, narrative devices, symmetries of structure, rhetoric, and meter. Literary forms, in short, are precisely what distinguish literature from ordinary communication.

Reflection finds a difficulty here, in that some literary forms occur in *paroles* outside decent literature, even outside writing altogether. Figures of speech may figure in speech, and verse was sometimes used for technical treatises during the Middle Ages. To account for this, one supplements the linguistic with the information theory model. In information theory, oral and written conventions work as signal systems, by which communications are constructed from series of signals. The signal system may work together to optimize construction of the correct message, through an arrangement of noise-combating codes called redundancy: " 'redundancy' may be said to be due to an additional set of rules, whereby it becomes increasingly difficult to make an undetectable mistake."[3] Now literary works, since they often deal with elusive or hard ideas, and since they communicate themselves across "noncooperative links" (reception can't usually be checked by questioning an author) need a high degree of redundancy. Perhaps, then, what distinguishes literary communication is not any particular form or signal system, but rather the redundancy available. In short, the unity of mutually confirming structures. Thus, if ordinary speech achieves a high degree of redundant integration it may become memorable, pass into the literature and be reckoned a "saying."

Redundancy of literary forms tends to prolong the possibility of constructing the work (or something like it) even after some of its many signal systems have fallen into oblivion. That is how literary works sometimes survive even their own genres. In a similar way redundancy makes it possible to construct very novel communications, such as *avant-garde* experiments. And it is the same all-important conception of information theory that guarantees validity of interpretation and determinacy of meaning.

Validity of interpretation in E. D. Hirsch's sense[4] can only be defended against subjectivism on the ground that a work remains inaccessible to

---

3   Colin Cherry, *On Human Communication* (New York, 1961), p. 185; see also Monroe C. Beardsley, *Aesthetics* (New York, 1958), pp. 215-17.

4   *Validity in Interpretation*, pp. 3-6, 10.

interpretation, free or otherwise, until it is constructed. Since construction depends on identification of signals in terms of systems shared with the author, no reader can claim the freedom to interpret as he pleases. For signals themselves are meaningless. And if a reader identifies them according to inappropriate signal systems, or in disregard of redundancies, the communication he constructs is not the one to be interpreted.

As for determinacy of meaning, Hirsch's genre logic guarantees it *in potentia*. In practice, however, the generic rules which sharing of types depends on may remain inaccessible. Only by recourse to the conception of redundancy, can we understand how meaning continues determinate in practice in certain instances, even after some of the generic forms involved have long been smoked over by time's tenebrosity.

Still, "genre ideas have a necessary heuristic function." [5] Hirsch refers to his broad category of "intrinsic genre," but the same is true of genre in a more conventional sense. Traditional genres and modes, far from being mere classificatory devices, serve primarily to enable the reader to share types of meaning economically. Moreover, his subsequent understanding is also genre-bound: he can only think sensibly of *Oedipus Tyrannus* as a tragedy, related to other tragedies. If he ignores or despises genre, or gets it wrong, misreading results. Johnson's blunder over *Lycidas* and the more recent and even more spectacular critical error of taking *Paradise Lost* as classical epic with Satan the hero are dreadful examples. Clearly, generic forms must rank among the most important of the signal systems that communicate a literary work.

By forms, then, I mean all the conventional elements of literature, from modes to metrical patterns. Archetypes, however, though closely associated with conventions by Northrop Frye, [6] and indirectly involved as we shall see in every full description of a genre, I exclude. For they appear just as much in other fields of discourse, so that they must be reckoned psychological rather than literary types. I also differ from Frye about the relative importance of forms. To "commentary," or structural analysis of an individual work, he prefers "identification," a superior kind of criticism that follows "an inductive movement towards the archetype," away from verbal texture, through imagery and larger conventions, to mythic archetypes shared with other works. [7] I think

5 *Ibid.*, p. 78.

6 See, e.g., *Fables of Identity* (New York, 1963), p. 123, and cf. W. K. Wimsatt, "Criticism as Myth," *Northrop Frye in Modern Criticism*, ed. Murray Krieger (New York and London, 1966), p. 87 n.

7 *Fables*, p. 13; Wimsatt, p. 87.

that the *Hamlet* criticism of superior interest to all except theoreticians
and anthropologists is likely to consist of statements about what is
peculiar to Shakespeare's play, not what it shares with *Samson Agonistes*
or ancient Greek myths. About intrinsic genres and individual *paroles*[8];
not archetypes, or even genres. Since, however, literary works can only
be communicated through generic forms, these may be of great, though
subsidiary, critical interest, according to the individual case. Historically, too, the interest of any form is liable to fluctuate over any considerable period. It may even lose significance altogether. Then either it
will become a mere habit without value *qua* signal (as with some Romantic poets' use of stanza forms long after interest in their proportion
had declined); or it will cease to be used altogether (pastoral eclogue,
poulter's measure, epic). Of all literary forms the class whose continu-
ance probably matters most is genre.

II. Interpretation and Genre

By genre I mean a better defined and more external type than mode.
Genres each have their own formal structures, whereas modes depend
less explicitly on stance, motif, or occasional touches of rhetorical tex-
turing. However, some types can function both as genre and as mode.[9]
Thus epic (Dryden's *Aeneis*) is written side by side with heroic tragedy
(*Aureng-Zebe*) and heroic satire (*Absalom and Achitophel*). Borderline cases inevitably occur: some critics have treated *Absalom and
Achitophel* as satiric mock-epic. And mixtures abound: eclogues ming-
ling pastoral and satire, epics embracing many modes or even contain-
ing inset passages in other genres. Nevertheless, we can usually identify
broad generic and modal types with a fair degree of validity.

Recognition of genre depends on associating a complex of elements,
which need not all appear in one work. But invariably external forms
will be among the indicators: structure, or formal motif, or rhetorical
proportion. We know epic by, among other things, its high style, formulae, episodes and similes. And we know picaresque by its large-scale

---

8   Hirsch (pp. 103, 111.) defines intrinsic genre as between *parole* and *langue*.

9   Apparently only broad major genres have corresponding modes. Epithalamium,
e.g., has none, unless one were to count such passages as *Paradise Lost*, VIII,
510-20. Puttenham is probably right in considering epithalamium a sub-genre of
the triumphal: see *The Art of English Poesy*, ed. Gladys D. Willcock and Alice Walker
(Cambridge, 1936), p. 46. Triumph itself, however, had a very flourishing equivalent
mode in Elizabethan literature, of which a good example would be *The Faerie Queene*, III,
xi-xii. See my *Triumphal Forms* (Cambridge, 1970), Ch. iii.

rhetorical proportions, such as the relative frequency of episodes and changes of scene, or the prominence of narrative and the relative unimportance of plot, character and description. Motifs are particularly interesting as indicators, since they seem to reveal the ultimate relation of literary types to archetypes. And adequate description of pastoral eclogue—adequate enough, for example, to distinguish it from town eclogue and piscatory eclogue—is bound to deal with substantive motifs, such as climate and occupation, that can legitimately be related to Golden Age archetypes. However, it may be a mistake to identify genre primarily with thematic motifs,[10] since these often occur in more than one genre. Strictly speaking only motifs with a formal basis, such as the singing contest, are securely genre-linked. Usually there are so many indicators, organized into so familiar a unity, that we recognize the generic complex instantly. But recognition still depends on correlating individual signals, any of which is liable to change its value or cease to function. Conversely, if a genre becomes obsolete, its characteristic forms lose significance.

Some regard all genres as obsolete. They imagine them as sets of old rules, irrelevant to post-Romantic literature. But all literature may in fact be genre-bound, without this being consciously realized. Indeed, the operation of genre has always had a large unconscious element: no one could ever be simultaneously aware, for example, of all he meant by epic. But such scruples need not inhibit critical approximations. The first mock epists might have been hard put to it to assign their poems to a genre now really obvious to us at a remove from the creative moment. And similarly modern fiction, itself not exactly uninstructed by critical precept, is necessarily communicated by modulation of at least potentially recognizable genres. (Even the novel is far from being the "open" form, different from all others, that Alan Friedman calls it.) Thus Calder Willingham's *Eternal Fire* burlesques southern gothic; Thomas Mann's *Doktor Faustus* combines *Bildungsroman* with novel of ideas; and Pat Highsmith's *They Who Walk Away* departs from the crime in the direction of the psychological novel. Justifying any precise generic identification calls for lengthy critical demonstration; for it is naturally hard to define emergent sub-genres in explicit detail. But much contemporary criticism in effect attempts just this endeavor. Since new works often seem to mix existing types—successfully or unsuccessfully—many critical evaluations have to be in generic terms. We say that Burgess's *Tremor of Intent* vacillates uncomfortably between straight and burlesque espionage thriller; or that uncertainty of

10 As Frye tends to do: see, e.g., *Anatomy of Criticism* (Princeton, N. J., 1957), pp. 44-45.

genre helps to account for the failure of Mailer's *Barbary Shore.*

It is not merely that old forms survive and new forms go on being generated. More fundamentally, genre operates in all interpretation, every meaning communicated being a type. The unique intrinsic type may be poles apart from such rigid extrinsic types as the traditional genres. Still, some sense of these must precede that grasp of the intrinsic type on which true reading depends. Hirsch's conception of generic types is more flexible and elusive than Rymer's; and no doubt only a very elastic conception indeed—stretching from types as broad as poetry and fiction down to minute variations of subgenres and even to grammatical forms—can accommodate the variety of actual literary communication. But to say this is not to abrogate conventional distinctions of genre, which continue to be of historical and heuristic value. Recognizing obvious epic forms in Joyce's *Ulysses* (e.g. formulae) sets the reader to noticing others more arcane (e.g. encyclopedic schemes).

However this may be, the obsolescence of a genre is certainly a critical event historically. For it alters the whole balance of significant forms, even making some of them insignificant; so that not only literary works embodying the generic form-complex, but also those in other genres may become more difficult. The discontinuation of the allegorical morality play, for example, has made obscure certain non-naturalistic passages in Shakespearean plays belonging to other kinds. In *Measure for Measure*, unfamiliarity with the Severine motif deprives many of the pleasures of surprise at Vincentio's clemency.[11] Changes of balance among significant forms affect readers' responses to constituents in a sweeping fashion comparable to that whereby color in impressionist painting took the place of linear definition in the older schools. It is no exaggeration to assert that during the last two centuries interest in rhetorical schemes and in structural proportion has almost completely given way in increased interest in rhetorical tropes and in tonal effects.

Obsolescence is the most noticeable change a genre may suffer. But really it is only one—and not necessarily the last—of a series of changes that generic forms continually pass through. This flux has somehow to be accommodated in any adequate theory of reading. For we must not think of extrinsic types as fixed and constantly available. On the contrary, valid interpretation will often involve laboriously chronicling a work's moment in its genre's history. Only relevant states of the form, not subsequent modifications or primitive antecedents, lead to the meaning; though a critic assessing significance may take the genre's whole time-worm into account. In other words, genre theory needs

11   On the motif of the disguised ruler, see Mary Lascelles, ed., *Shakespeare's Measure for Measure* (London, 1953), p. 101.

radical revision before it can be considered to provide a literary model with historical dimension. For example, it will not do to say, with Hirsch, that meaning remains the same, while its significance changes. This is true, so far as it goes. But meaning is genre-bound, and genres are themselves in a continual state of transmutation: epic was not the same before and after Homer, or Virgil, or Spenser, or Milton. Hence recognitive interpretation—that is, re-cognition of the author's meaning—demands recovery of appropriate phases of the genre concerned. Indeed, for distant historical periods it may necessitate reconstructing the then literary model.

Determinacy of meaning takes for granted the possibility of decoding signals that belong to determinate variable systems. This is obvious in practical contexts: a meaning can never be more than potentially determinate at any given time, in that readers may not discover enough about old forms to arrive at it precisely. But it is less obvious that in theory the mutability of genres presents an apparently insuperable obstacle to complete determinacy. For the genre that binds a reader's understanding is always the latest state of it that he knows, or at best the most inclusive conception he can realize. And since he cannot unknow these states of a form, he can never wholly recover earlier meanings. Familiarity with Virgil and later epists makes it impossible quite to grasp the simplicities of Homer's epic.[12] Scholarship can mitigate but not remove this difficulty; because to explain a joke is to spoil it, to annotate an allusion to prevent the reader's ever recognizing it. We may suppose that the first mock epic was meant to elicit a response now unrecoverable unless by an eccentrically-educated tyro. And the same no doubt applies to broad effects: how did novels strike readers for whom naturalism was a rare phenomenon? Evidently generic forms are bound up with criticism in a complex way.

III. Death of Genres

Extinction will serve as the simplest instance of variation of genre. But even this change has its complications. As with biological organisms, the moment of "death" is hard to fix. Does a genre die when it

---

12 A separate problem from that presented by outmoded values, which Hirsch brilliantly treats in "Privileged Criteria in Literary Evaluation," *Problems of Literary Evaluation*, Yearbook of Comparative Criticism, Vol. II (State College, Pa., 1969), and in "Literary Evaluation as Knowledge," *Contemporary Literature*, IX (1968).

ceases to be used? Or when it is no longer regarded with interest? Or when readers become insensitive to its forms? Again, does a work's precarious survival, misinterpreted like *Gulliver's Travels*, ensure its genre's survival? Does the pastoral elegy live with *Lycidas*? Do genres "die" at all?

Such terms as "life," "death," and "extinction" imply a biological analogy. In its evolutionary form, this analogy has been attacked by René Wellek, with whose acute objections to importing specifically biological concepts many will feel inclined to agree. "French tragedies were not born with Jodelle but just were not written before him."[13] Plausible. But a weakness in Wellek's position is betrayed by the assertion that "Darwinian or Spencerian evolutionism is false when applied to literature because there are no fixed genres comparable to biological species which can serve as substrata of evolution. There is no inevitable growth and decay, no transformation of one genre into another, no actual struggle for life among genres."[14] This is true but irrelevant to the contemporary situation. Who now would wish to apply Darwinianism? Biologists no longer regard species as "fixed" or entirely determined by genetic mechanisms.[15] As for transformations of literary forms, these are obvious enough if we imagine the generic type proposed earlier. Unfortunately Wellek understands genre as a single infinite set of works, whereas it should be understood as a whole series of form-complexes occurring as elements in a series of finite subsets of works. Loosely speaking, we say that the work "belongs to" the genre or is a "member" of it. But we should no more identify individual works with what constitutes genre in them, than regard men merely as biological entities. The literary genre does not define its members, only their forms.[16]

Hence Wellek's criticism of Brunetière, that Racine's *Phèdre* "will strike us as young and fresh compared to the frigid Renaissance tragedies which, according to the scheme, represent the 'youth' of French tragedy" lacks general force: it is scarcely works that evolve, but rather their genre.[17] Nor can he persuade by invoking the author's

13 Wellek, "The Concept of Evolution in Literary History," *Concepts*, p. 44.

14 *Ibid.*, p. 51.

15 Cf. Eliseo Vivas, "Literary Classes: Some Problems," *Genre*, I (1968), 101.

16 Cf. Hirsch, *Validity*, pp. 110-11: "The only broad genre concept, then, which is by nature illegitimate is the one which pretends to be a species concept that somehow defines and equates the members it subsumes. . . . If we believe they [classifications] are constitutive rather than arbitrary and heuristic, then we have made a serious mistake and have also set up a barrier to valid interpretation."

17 Wellek, *Concepts*, p. 44. In any case, is Eohippus "young and fresh" compared to *Equus caballus*?

freedom of choice in "reaching out into the past for models or stimuli" and by claiming that "a work of art is not simply a member of a series, a link in a chain. It may stand in relation to anything in the past."[18] For only individual works reach out beyond temporal limitations, not the mutable type. Wellek is right to expose the limits of the biological analogy; but wrong to declare the analogy invalid. It would be strange if literature, life's image, contained no correlate of the evolution of biological forms. By organizing forms into complexes, a genre falls subject to such historical laws as govern all organizations in time. Like any other, it is bound to evolve.[19]

Genres, like biological species, have a relatively circumscribed existence in space and time. Individual works may elude locality and temporality: genres seldom to any extent. Though *Magister Ludi* intrigues a few British readers, the kind *Das Glasperlenspiel* belongs to finds little acceptance with us, the novel of ideas being construed here in terms of eccentricity or abortive naturalism. And cultural ethos similarly localizes other genres. The haiku is primarily Japanese; certain kinds of heroic fiction seem tolerable only to Chinese communists; and until recently France had no science fiction outside Verne. Or the geographical differentiation may be a little subtler, as between British detective story and American mystery—the latter merging easily into the thrillers of Chandler and Hammett, the former sharply distinct from the entertainments of Greene. In the seventeenth century the poem of locality begins in England rather late, whether because of national characteristics, social circumstances or a time lag in fashion.[20]

The cultural matrix limits genre as strictly in time. Sir Kenneth Clark has observed that the use of the essay—a form reflecting the liberal attitude of uncommitted interest—began and ended with Humanism.[21] So too the hymn has been in abeyance since the recession of supernatural belief. And the pastoral eclogue could not survive changes in the relation of town and country that followed urban development.

These limitations apply to genre-linked structural forms in a quite

18   *Ibid.*, p. 55.

19   To do justice to Wellek's consistency, he considers the evolutionary character of history itself problematic: see *ibid.*, p. 53 n.

20   Charles Molesworth, "Property and Virtue: The Genre of the Country-House Poem in the Seventeenth Century," *Genre*, I (1968), admirably relates the house poem genre to political and socio-historical changes, while wrongly identifying it with Puttenham's "historical poesy" instead of with encomium. But I am more concerned with local descriptive landscape poetry.

21   See Sir Kenneth Clark, *Civilization: A Personal View* (London, 1969), p. 163.

pervasive way. Thus the use of sudden surprising turns of plot in the short story took for granted a universe of belief, within which *peripeteias* would disclose mysteries and prompt at least bafflement at the "rumness of life." Kipling is a transitional case: his stories still have plots and the plots still take odd turns (as in "Without Benefit of Clergy"), but the metaphysical implication seems too explicitly realized for the device to hold much potential for future development in reserve. Or consider the sorts of allegorical images found in medieval genres. As many critics agree, "the structure of images that C. S. Lewis in *The Discarded Image* calls 'the Model' . . . provided the main organization for literature down to the Renaissance: it modulated into less projected forms after Newton's time."[22] Temporal limitations have even affected external structuring—notably numerical composition. The latter was almost completely abandoned in the early eighteenth century when cosmic proportion came to be imagined in a more impressionistically subjective way.[23] Indeed, we may say with only apparent paradox that the more formal the constituent, the more its significance depends on social context.

Genres are also limited by the intellectual capacities of readers. At least, no genre has ever been open to all social groups regardless of their level of education. Even great writers, not to speak of socialists intent on liberalizing conventions, seem to find it impossible to conceive of a universal reader. And when the education of their fit audience (few or many) ceases, the genre is in a sense finished. However, this limitation conceals a hope too. For, if a genre never was open to all men, may it not be enough that it should remain open to one or two? So long as a single scholar is fit to keep it alive, is any generic Tinkerbell quite dead?

The existence of genres is nevertheless thoroughly historical. In consequence, statements about them should always specify a chronological frame of reference. Thus a work's genre is the genre at composition, which relates to an antecedent genre, itself the cumulation of a series of earlier forms. But we are never aware of a first term of the series: we never witness the origin. Is Kipling's "With the Night Mail" science fiction? Is Verne? Lucian? This is not because of any lack of antecedents, as Wellek would have it, but rather for an opposite reason, that every work of literature (as we know it) depends for intelligibility on a prior extrinsic type. Homer's *Odyssey*, for example, is partly unintelligible

22   Northrop Frye, "Reflections in a Mirror," in Krieger, p. 136. Many, however, will disagree with Frye's continuation: ". . . but it did not lose its central place in literature."

23   See my *Triumphal Forms*, p. 122.

without an earlier genre of *nostoi* and an inherited convention of formulaic diction. Always the antecedent generic idea is subjective and cumulative, varying in response to literary and other experience, as Eliot described in *Tradition and the Individual Talent*; so that simplified synchronic analysis of genres meets with frequent pitfalls.[24] Invariable schematic classifications have often been devised, by writers as disparate as Aristotle and Scaliger, Hobbes and Frye. But all seem more or less simplistic and unconvincing.[25] Historically, it is just not the case that legends and romances constitute variants of the same genre; or that literature comprises three modes and two manners of representation yielding "neither more nor less than six sorts of poesy."[26]

This is not to rule out the possibility of a few "organic" forms determined by human rather than by cultural characteristics. The limits of short-term memory, for instance, may well have a bearing on the "breath" of the verse paragraph. But organic characteristics perhaps change more than we realize. Thus memory can be cultivated or neglected. And allegory, though it probably corresponds to a mode of thought, undeniably suffered profound changes both in popularity and in use during the late antique period, and again in the seventeenth century. Even the elementary distinction between verse and prose, which many critics believe to have a permanent psychological basis, has undergone alteration, particularly at the time when typographic culture replaced oral and cheirographic. Broadly speaking, and discounting occasional gross features of scale, proportion or diction governed by psycho-physiological laws, we may say that all generic forms are mutable.

Their death can be defined quite specifically. Pronounce a genre dead if works related to it directly are no longer widely read, so that its forms have become unintelligible without scholarly effort. Hence

24 Angus Fletcher, "Utopian History and the *Anatomy*," in Krieger, pp. 34 ff., attempts a desperate defense of Frye against charges of unhistorical schematicism.

25 Aristotle less, because some of his categories are logical (e.g. division of literature between narrative and dramatic forms) and because he takes evolution of genre into account to some extent, particularly in his description of tragedy. But he leaves to one side the question "whether tragedy is now fully developed in all its species" (*Poetics*, IV, 13) and falls back instead on the assumption that "after undergoing many changes it stopped when it had found its own natural form" (IV, 15). Scaliger introduced periodization, and was the first great exponent of the comparative method. But his famous comparison of Homer's and Virgil's epics (*Poetics* [Lyons, 1561], *lib.* V) only fumblingly begins to detect a difference between primary and secondary epic.

26 *Anatomy*, pp. 33, 36; Thomas Hobbes, "Answer to Davenant's Preface to *Gondibert*," J. E. Spingarn, ed., *Critical Essays of the Seventeenth Century*, 3 vols. (Oxford, 1908-9), II, 55. Hobbes's six sorts are: epic, tragedy, satire, comedy, pastoral, and pastoral comedy.

readership must be specified. For a genre may survive for one social group and lapse for others—like the tale of terror, which is little practiced as a literary form, but still vigorous in subliterary science fiction.

IV. Hierarchic Mobility

This brings up one of the most fundamental changes a genre can go through: change of status in the generic hierarchy. *Anatomy of Criticism* systematizes such changes in a theory of five modes, ordered by the hero's calibre—supernatural myth; romance; high mimetic (epic and tragedy); low mimetic ("most comedy and realistic fiction"); and ironic. According to Frye, "European fiction, during the last fifteen centuries, has steadily moved its centre of gravity down the list." [27] The movement turns out to be cyclical, for as the ironic mode descends from the low mimetic, though "it begins in realism and dispassionate observation . . . it moves steadily towards myth, and dim outlines of sacrificial rituals and dying gods begin to reappear in it. Our five modes evidently go around in a circle." [28]

Frye's First Essay is impressively copious and contains many interesting incidental observations; but its argument seems no more likely to stand than any other simple cyclical theory. [29] For the literary corpus is more complex than Frye's dissection suggests. Not only does he ignore many elements of generic transformation altogether; but even the historical changes he does discuss have really had a more fluctuating tendency than he suggests. In actual fact there is nothing "steady" about the movement of the hero down the modal scale and up again into myth. At the very time when the hero might plausibly be said to suffer eclipse in prose fiction, Shelley and Keats were raising his poetic status, even to the point of writing myths. [30] And Homer's epics, which ought to be "lower" on the modal scale than the romantic *Chanson de Roland* and *Passing of Arthur*, really contain more supernatural and mythological action, not less. Many will agree with Angus Fletcher when he comments (in the ironic mode?): "Another approach, perhaps more profitable, will be to see if the five modes could not occur in any order,

27 *Anatomy*, p. 34.

28 *Ibid.*, p. 42.

29 Angus Fletcher reviews the shortcomings of cyclical theories of history in Krieger, pp. 51-52.

30 A contradiction implicitly admitted by Frye: see *Anatomy*, p. 60.

without decline, ascent, or any other positive trend."[31] Frye's mistake, we suspect, lies in supposing that hero and myth are "fundamentals of an artistic process."[32] In the *Anatomy* they have to be, however, to supply the need for unchanging archetypes.

It might be more empiric to begin with changes in the dignity of genres themselves, rather than of their heroes. The status of a genre— and hence the "height" of what it communicates—depends on current evaluation of its whole conventional subject matter. (Compare generic hierarchy in the visual arts, which has been reordered to the disadvantage of religious and historical subjects and the advantage first of landscapes and still-lifes, then of abstracts.[33]) Describing the inquiry in these wide terms, however, shows what slender chance of success schematic speculation has. Indeed, one is first impressed by the abundance of paradoxes. Thus the same Christian faith that gave substance to mythic and "romantic" forms (to use Frye's term) seems also to have increased respect for "low mimetic" naturalism, as Auerbach's *Mimesis* convincingly shows.

And subject matter is only one of many factors determining dignity. Fashion plays a larger part than speculators care to allow; and so do contingencies such as the distribution and temperaments of great authors, and the environment of the practical or occasional functions of genre. Tudor sonnets circulating privately in manuscript could be relatively intimate, whereas letters in the vernacular often seem to us a bit formal. In the eighteenth century, however, letters might be more intimate even than visits: Smollett's Lady of Quality speaks of "the increasing anxiety of Lord B—, who (though I still admitted his visits) plainly perceived that I wanted to relinquish his correspondence";[34] and Richardson, used to communicating with his wife in writing while both were at home, easily turned the epistolary genre to fictional exploration of psychology. Such movements, which had widespread generic repercussions, appear not to have anything cyclic about them.

Changes in the canon and hierarchy of genres reflect the complexity of the historical process itself; so that it seems premature to attempt any comprehensive generalization. Speculative constructions may reveal patterns missed previously (including some that exist). But they are unlikely to lead to constitutive categories.

31   Krieger, p. 51.

32   Fletcher's phrase, though he uses it without disapproval: see Krieger, p. 37.

33   Max J. Friedländer, *Landscape: Portrait: Still-life* (New York, 1963), p. 11.

34   *Peregrine Pickle*, ed. James L. Clifford (London, 1964), p. 487.

V. The Phases of Generic Development

A modest but in the long term necessary preliminary is to explore the limited range of formal processes by which any individual genre can change, when numberless historical factors and authorial decisions decree that it should do so. It turns out that genre proper develops through at least three principal phases. These are organic and invariable in sequence, though development need not go beyond the first or second.

During the first phase, the genre-complex assembles, until a formal type emerges. When poets first wrote dialogues between shepherds, or singing contests, these were probably independent motifs. It was only when they occurred regularly linked with other forms, that readers could respond to them as genre-sensitive characteristics of eclogue. In phase two, a "secondary" version of genre develops: a form that the author consciously bases on the earlier primary version. He makes the latter an object of sophisticated imitation, in the Renaissance sense, varying its themes and motifs, perhaps adapting it to slightly different purposes, but retaining all its main features, including those of formal structure. The difference between primary and secondary versions stands out particularly clearly in epic, to which the terms "primitive" and "artificial" have been applied for some time. It was left to C. S. Lewis, however, to elaborate the distinction between primary epic (Homer, *Beowulf*) and secondary epic (Virgil).[35] Primary epic is heroic, festal, public in delivery and in subject, oral, formulaic; secondary epic civilized, literary, private in delivery, stylistically elevated or "sublime."

I believe that similar phases can be distinguished in other genres. Thus, the bucolics of Theocritus or his predecessors are really rural: singing matches no doubt took place in actual fact. But the shepherds in Virgil's *Eclogues* lie about a fictive landscape in literary guise. So with the novel of romantic adventure. A primary phase represented by eighteenth-century picaresque gives place to a more consciously conventional form in the nineteenth century. Stevenson's *Treasure Island* and *Kidnapped*, with much of Scott, are examples of this secondary phase; while Dumas, Marryat, Reade, Ballantyne, and Taffrail produced the subliterary equivalent.

But it is also possible to distinguish a tertiary phase of development in many genres. This occurs when an author uses a secondary form in a radically new way. The tertiary form may be burlesque, or antithesis,

35   C. S. Lewis, *A Preface to Paradise Lost* (London, 1942), Chs. iii-vii.

or symbolic modulation of the secondary. *Lycidas* is tertiary pastoral elegy because its dead shepherd not only disguises an individual but also symbolizes a *pastor*; and because it implies a criticism of the values of ordinary pastoral elegy. And *Paradise Lost* is tertiary, in that it treats Virgilian motifs antiheroically: it incorporates them within a form of larger import, which reflects Christian values, achieving heroism and satisfying divine wrath differently from any pagan epic. Stevenson's *The Dynamiter* and *Ebb-Tide* belong to a corresponding phase of the adventure story; the one as burlesque, the other as symbolic. Tertiary development seems often to constitute an interiorizing. Thus *Paradise Lost*, like *The Faerie Queene*, has little wholly exterior action, while Golding's *Pincher Martin*, which begins as a tertiary version of Taffrail's *Pincher Martin*, has none at all. Or consider the single motif of mysterious ancestry: from a primary version in medieval romances we can trace a secondary sophisticated version in eighteenth-century romance and probably also in Jane Austen's *Emma* (unless there its ironic use verges on burlesque). But George Eliot, who uses the illegitimacy of Deronda symbolically, to represent an identity search,[36] has clearly taken the motif into a tertiary phase.

The three phases are not always very distinct. They may interpenetrate chronologically and even be in doubt within a single work. Theocritus and Homer, who had each some sophistication in grasping form, may be thought to produce secondary types. And an author might exceptionally press beyond a secondary to a tertiary version in a single leap—as Virgil's *Aeneid* may sometimes have done, if his Neoplatonic allegorists are to be believed. But in any case Virgil had the shoal of secondary models reviewed by Brooks Otis[37] behind him; and my point relates to the phases' qualities and sequence only.

VI. Modal Transformation

Perhaps the sequence of phases is best described as a sequence of relations between genre, mode, and abstract formulation. At the primary stage, no equivalent mode or critical description of the genre as yet exists: following its requirements is a matter of unconscious obedience to the extrinsic type, or of imitation in the common sense. With the

36 See esp. *Daniel Deronda*, Ch. xvi.

37 *Virgil: A Study in Civilized Poetry* (Oxford, 1964), Ch. ii: "From Homer to Virgil: The Obsolescence of Epic."

secondary phase, criticism begins: the genre is labeled and its requirements are understood so abstractly that a modal form separates out. Secondary epic may therefore be defined as epic consciously in the heroic mode. During the tertiary stage, criticism may recognize variations of genre (Scaliger's comparison of Homer and Virgil; Tasso's defense of Ariosto's epic; Dryden's distinction between ancient and modern forms of drama). Now conscious modal innovations proliferate. We find not only tertiary epic, but also heroic tragedy and heroic satire: not only tertiary pastoral eclogue, but also pastoral drama, pastoral romance and burlesque pastoral. It is a phase, too, of hybrid genres, such as Sidney's heroic pastoral romance *Arcadia*.

This restatement suggests a general hypothesis: namely that genre tends to mode. The genre, limited by its rigid structural carapace, eventually exhausts its evolutionary possibilities. But the equivalent mode, flexible, versatile, and susceptible to novel commixtures, may generate a compensating multitude of new generic forms. For the mode was abstracted from an existing concrete historical genre. The latter, closely linked to specific social forms, is apt to perish with them. But the mode corresponds to a somewhat more permanent poetic attitude or stance, independent of particular contingent embodiments of it. Pastoral eclogue is dead: long live pastoral. However, a mode too may pass, if its attitude becomes inappropriate. The heroic mode may be rendered obsolete by changed attitudes to war and aggression.

A surviving modal abstraction is capable of a variety of applications, which may result in new genres distant from their original both in quality and in degree of sophistication. The gothic novel or romance (*The Old English Baron*) yielded a gothic mode that outlasted it and was applied to forms as diverse as the maritime adventure (*The Narrative of A. Gordon Pym*), the psychological novel (*Titus Groan*), the short story (Isak Dinesen) and the detective story, not to mention various science fiction genres (not wholly unpredictable, these last, in view of Mary Shelley's *Frankenstein*). The later applications show more awareness of the mode's socio-political significance. Such a motif as the piercing eye, for example, seems to have been at first an uninterpreted symbol, deeply but not consciously related to the Renaissance eye of judgment. In gothic science fiction, however, the politics are often quite conscious. So too the mode abstracted from satire proper (Juvenal, Horace) was applied to other genres to generate the satiric mock-epic (*The Rape of the Lock*), the satiric travel-book (*Gulliver's Travels*), the satiric novel (*Catch-22*) and many other forms not easy to refer to their origin.

Needless to say, the process from genre to mode is usually so gradual and continual as to escape notice. New modal applications commonly make such modest departures that we can quite properly speak of "slow, steady change on the analogy of animal growth" or at least, of animal evolution.[38] Only once in a while do bolder departures show an appearance of complete originality. This is to be expected: generic variations have to proceed from recent or familiar genres, for readers to respond to them easily. One could trace an unbroken development from Chrétien's chivalric romance, through Le Sage's picaresque inset romance, Stevenson's semi-political *Prince Otto*, Buchan's exotic adventure stories, to the modern international thriller in its several varieties: sophisticated (Fleming), naturalistic (Le Carré), symbolic (Charles Williams), and burlesque (Anthony Burgess and John Gardner). This continuity of known types is an essential condition for the new statement. Without the romance, Stevenson's anti-hero would have made no point; without Buchan's gentlemanly fisticuffs and sympathy with the enemy, Fleming's ruthless violence and Le Carré's rejection of the concept enemy would have lacked force—if indeed they had been artistically practicable. *Natura non facit saltum.*[39]

Art may take the odd leap of originality; but far less often than the disappearance of subliterary precedents or the obscurity of latent characteristics in tradition may lead us to suppose. And the *Finnegans Wake* that does depart radically from prevailing forms is likely to prove unacceptable, until subsequent more dilute imitations provide the missing extrinsic type *ex post facto*. This is not just because of difficulty, but also because of deficiency in pleasure. Much of literature's proper enjoyment depends on interweaving the pleasurably familiar with the strangely novel.

I have argued that genres may directly generate modes and hence, indirectly, new genres. They may also die (or, as Wellek would say, not be written); in which case their components disintegrate. Subsequently, works lacking in modal invention or intelligence will be strewn with the detritus of old genres—as Whitfield observes with respect to Pulci and the epic.[40] More inventive works give worn forms new applications or new meanings, by a process whose creative power is difficult to exaggerate. This difficulty has sometimes been overcome, however, by some good critics too fond of life to admit the possibility of death. Empson finds some version of pastoral in every leaf of his favorite works, and

38   The analogy rejected by Wellek, pp. 40, 44-45.

39   See *ibid.*, p. 39.

40   J. H. Whitfield, *A Short History of Italian Literature* (Harmondsworth, 1960), pp. 127-78.

Trilling applies the term "idyll" to *Emma*.[41] Better to have accepted the irreversibility of historical change, and the limitations of genres and modes. This is not to deny that an author may imitate an old master and bring a discontinued form back to life. Epic almost returns in Joyce's *Ulysses*—in a hybrid form, to be sure; but more than a modal application. You can glimpse in it ghosts of the parts of epic: silent invocation, perhaps, in Mulligan's opening oblation of a bowl of lather as he intones *introibo ad altare Dei*.[42] Scholarly resurrectionists dig up even forgotten ideas and forms: as Wellek shrewdly points out,[43] our intellectual life reaches far into the cultural past. But, just as in ordinary life we have to express our most primitive feelings in language that at least approximates to current idiom, so with literary atavism. There are limits, not only upon what we have access to, but also upon what we can assimilate and reintroduce into the cultural tradition by our own efforts. And when these succeed, the old form is not accepted without considerable modification. A genre revived is different from its first avatar, and different also from what it would be if works of its type "just were not written" for a while.

41   William Empson, *Some Versions of Pastoral* (London, 1935); Lionel Trilling, "*Emma* and the Legend of Jane Austen," *Jane Austen: "Emma,"* ed. David Lodge (London, 1968), pp. 163-65.

42   The prayer of invocation was said during the oblation, immediately after the raising of the chalice. Though the *introibo*, from the ordinary of the mass, is a comically wrong prayer to accompany the action, it adumbrates a telescoped liturgical context. Soon after, Mulligan "covered the bowl smartly" in travesty of the veiling of the oblations.

43   *Concepts*, pp. 50-51.

5

History-Writing as Answerable Style

Geoffrey H. Hartman

O quam te memorem . . .
(Virgil, *Aeneid*)

Bussoftlhee mememormee
(Joyce, *Finnegans Wake*)

I. The Style of the Historian and the Style of Art

ALL MEN desire knowledge; but not the knowledge explosion. Knowledge may always have had a "mortal taste" yet it used to contain the promise of a better position in the scale of being and a surer sense of one's true or effective identity. But what if earth becomes "an earth of ideas"? The sea "a metaphor for the multiplication of facts and sensations"? What *can* soul desire, sitting unhappily "on superstructures of explanation, poor bird, not knowing which way to fly"?[1]

The ease with which earth, sea and bird become symbolic counters is part of the problem. Their lapsed value is felt, if only in passing. Marvell's image of the soul, gliding into the boughs, waving in its plumes the "various light" while it waits to be released from earthliness, is appropriate as a counter-reminiscence: that image has a *reserve* of resonances which the mind can explore at leisure, while as a whole it evokes that very restraint of ecstasy which makes leisure possible. It does not matter, of course, that such images are, or seem to be, from nature; what matters is the quality of our association with them—the decorum of use. "It is a great Pity that People should by associating themselves with the finest things spoil them," Keats complains, "[Leigh] Hunt has damned Hampstead and Masks and Sonnets and italian tales." Hunt's fault is at once moral and aesthetic. "Instead of giving other minds credit for the same degree of perception as he himself pos-

---

1 Saul Bellow, *Mr Sammler's Planet* (New York, 1970), pp. 3-4.

sesses—he begins an explanation in such a curious manner that our taste and self-love is offended continually." [2]

Keats's sensitivity to "palpable design," to the knowing or self-assertive mind, is only as significant as his understanding of the morality of art. The figures on his Grecian Urn resist the explainer-ravisher. The poet's crescendoing questions (see stanza 1) are like the ecstasy they project onto the mute dancers: their very intensity of speculation seems to animate the urn until its mystery is in danger of being dissolved, its form broken for the sake of a message. We behold, as in a primal scene, the ravishments of truth, the identifying—and over-identifying—mind. The poem itself, however, by various, finely graded stages—part of art's ritual coldness—tempers an intellectual questing not unlike love-madness.

As the eye cannot choose but see, the soul cannot but desire truths; and art engages this lust for knowing or merging. To conceptualize art's relation to it is difficult. Aristotle's *Poetics* evolved the key notions of "recognition" and "catharsis," but even interpretations not clarified by precise concepts can do much to illumine the decorum of art by the intelligence of their despair. It is no *ultimate* objection to an interpretation that it merges partly with its object, "too much the syllables" of art itself; or lets artifacts, like Keats's urn, tease and evade our meditation.

Yet what of histories of art? While not excluded from studying the "reserve" of a work of art, the style of its resistance to ideas, they remain histories, and a function of the historical consciousness. Beyond describing the form of art they seek to link it to the quality of the artist's historical awareness. Walter Benjamin, for example, connects the disappearance of the art of storytelling to our psychological and urban restlessness:

There is nothing that commends a story to memory more effectively than that chaste compactness which precludes psychological analysis. And the more natural the process by which the storyteller forgoes psychological shading, the greater becomes the story's claim to a place in the memory of the listener, the more completely is it integrated into his own experience . . . . This process of assimilation, which takes place in depth, requires a state of relaxation becoming ever more rare. If sleep is the apogee of physical relaxation, boredom is the apogee of mental relaxation. Boredom is the dream bird that hatches the egg of experience. A rustling in the leaves drives him away. His nesting places—the activities intimately associated with boredom—are already extinct in the cities and are declining

2 Letter to B. R. Haydon, 21 March 1818, and to George Keats, 17 December 1818.

in the country as well. With this the gift of listening is lost and the community of listeners disappears . . . . It is lost because there is no more weaving and spinning to go on while they are being listened to. The more self-forgetful the listener is, the more deeply is what he listens to impressed upon his memory. When the rhythm of work has seized him, he listens to the tales in such a way that the gift of retelling then comes to him all by itself.[3]

Erich Auerbach undertakes a fuller analysis of this kind in the opening chapter of *Mimesis*, where two influential narrative styles, of the Book of Genesis and the *Odyssey*, are radically distinguished by the charm they exert on the communal listener, or conversely by the limits of their interpretability. Such an approach leads historically from the mythical way of storytelling to its difficulty in Wordsworth or Henry James—even to the difficulty of history-writing itself, which has reduced the role of fabulation in favor of psychological or sociological shading. Yet, in modern art at least, a new non-fabulous "reserve" is forged, so that Eliot remarks of James's mind that it was too fine to be violated by ideas.

Critics are right to worry about the proper relation of ideas (explanations, truths, beliefs) to art. The problem has outrun Wordsworth, Keats or James. The very word "idea" has now become problematic. It embraces things with very different status: organizing ideas or models, and truths imperatively held. It is one thing to say that certain beliefs or their symbols (pagan gods, for example) are essential to literature; another that they are true. This difference is being eroded by the historical consciousness. We live in an era of convergence where all truths, outmoded or not, seem to enjoy a "formal" value. The growth of the historical consciousness, its multiplying of disparate models all of which press their claim, amounts to a peculiarly modern burden, an overhead weighing on the individual like a new theology. To be aware of the past is to be surrounded by abstract potentialities, imperatives that cannot all be heeded, options exhausting the power of choice. One need not be a historian to suffer this state of *surnomie*. A liberation, not of men and women, but of images, has created a *theatrum mundi* in which the distance between past and present, culture and culture, truth and superstition is suspended by a quasi-divine synchronism. A living cinema surrounds us, a Plato's cave full of colored shadows.[4]

3   See "The Storyteller," in *Illuminations* (New York, 1968).

4   Cf. W. J. Ong on the "synchronic present" in *American Quarterly*, XIV (1962), 239-259, but especially Valéry's first letter on "La Crise de l'Esprit" (Paris, 1919) and its follow-up "La Politique de l'Esprit" (Paris, 1932).

If art is to retain a certain purity—that "cunning stroke," as Emerson called it, which separates out the precise symbol or the one adequate form—it must triumph over this synchronic pressure of abstract knowledge. But the crisis is not solved by bringing, once again, order out of variety and discovering new forms. There are too many forms already: they now debouch into life directly, without the special mediation of masterworks. Our hearts are sad at the culture supermarket; packaged historical reminiscences meet us everywhere; the Beatles' *Yellow Submarine* is a moving toyshop of topoi. Purity in art? It is no longer achieved by new forms but rather by new media that allow existing forms to survive the contamination of meaning—of historical or ideological accretions.

In the Renaissance the translation of Classical riches into the "new medium" of the vernacular must have been a purification of this kind, making things new and concrete at the same time. And within the vernacular itself the pastoral mode was not so much a new form as the creation of a new reserve evoking the "silence and slow time" of a fading latinity. Today we translate into the "language" of the cinema: frames speak by sheer juxtaposition (montage) or generally by the disassociation and then remixing of images and their meanings. It is far, yet not so far, from Keats's pictorialism in the "Ode on a Grecian Urn"—the way each frame in the turned object repeats a questionable shape or mysterious defilade, a mute picture dubbed by the poet—and the purification of "contaminated" images in Wallace Stevens or the scenarios of Robbe-Grillet. It is far, yet not so far, from the obsessively detailed inspections of one spot in Wordsworth's "The Thorn" to the narrative *retours* of the same, itemized scene in a *nouveau roman*. One difference, of course, is that images have now to survive explicitly sexual or vulgar attributions. But whether the "mensonge sémantique" is of a noble or vulgar kind seems less important than that structured negation by which images reject meanings they save in the end. The image is always *anathematic* in David Jones's sense, always a "Lady of silences/Torn and most whole":

La jeune femme se figera parfois, comme une statue de cire du musée Grévin, ou comme une déesse, une prostituée de convention, voire une photo érotique dans le style le plus traditionnel, le plus naif. De même pour la ville. Toute contaminée dans l'esprit de l'homme par un mélange de Pierre Loti, de Guide Bleu et de Mille-et-une-Nuits, elle passera sans cesse de la carte postale touristique au "symbolisme" affiché des chaînes et de grilles de fer, mais sans cesser pour cela d'être pleine de la rumeur vivante des bateaux, des ports et des foules.[5]

5 See David Jones, Preface to *Anathémata* (1952); T. S. Eliot, "Ash Wednesday," and Alain Robbe-Grillet, Preface to the ciné-roman *L'Immortelle*.

Can history-writing, or interpretation in touch with it, become a new medium—a supreme fiction which does not reduce being to meaning but defines a thing sharply in "the difficulty of what it is to be"? We have stressed only the moral obstacle: wrong hypotheses may "spoil the finest things" by their kind of slander. But the present situation takes us beyond questions of decorum into an ontological perplexity. The hypothesis-making mood we are in—with its variorum of perspectives or "superstructures of explanation"—threatens artifacts in a peculiar way. It endows them with a *false* reserve created by the very pressure of interpretations brought to bear. As interpretability becomes more important than historicity, and the prey is relinquished for the shadow, art objects seem to split into, on the one hand, a *gegenstand*, the artifact as indeterminable, mere ob-stance of the interpreting mind; and, on the other, a prehensile corpus of explanations incited by art's ipseity. The very openness of symbols to several, even opposed, kinds of meaning assures their impregnable reserve in the midst of explanatory assaults. This ontic stubbornness, however, is hardly sufficient to define the reserve of art, which is always a reservoir of resonances rather than a mystifying void. Modern theories attempting to distinguish between the being and meaning of art ("a poem must not mean/But be") are trapped into too empty an understanding of art's reserve. They reduce art to objects that cry, "I am dark but beautiful."

Such thoughts bear, however, on the structure of all interpretation, rather than specifically on historical kinds. To some extent this is inevitable. History, as reflected in histories, is both a series of acts and a series of intentions—acts whose intention was falsified or at least modified. A later knowledge sees they were based on myths or imperfect assumptions. History-writing, therefore, while inherently "critical" is not inherently "judgmental": it is judgmental only by the claim that human beings could act without blindness, without that which makes them finite enough to act. But this claim is not made when history is told by historians, by critics rather than gods. Men act by overlooking certain possibilities or delimiting speculation, so that history appears as an illuminating progress of errors. Though we may differ over the cause of the "blindness" which precipitates men into action or maintains them in it, central error of this kind lies in the nature of action whether or not described as "historical." Interpretation, which makes that error appear, or gives it its dignity, is always historical to this extent.

A systematic view of the problem would have to consider our greatest philosophers of existential error: Nietzsche and Heidegger. I will content myself with an eloquence of Emerson's. Emerson, seeing error of this kind as basic to the crystallization of passion or to symbol-making generally, places it under "the mystery of form":

Love and all the passions concentrate all existence around a single form. It is the habit of certain minds to give an all-excluding fulness to the object, the thought, the word, they alight upon, and to make that for the time the deputy of the world. These are the artists, the orators, the leaders of society. The power to detach, and to magnify by detaching, is the essence of rhetoric in the hands of the orator and the poet. This rhetoric, or power to fix the momentary eminency of an object . . . depends on the depth of the artist's insight of that object he contemplates. For every object has its roots in central nature, and may of course be so exhibited to us as to represent the world. . . . Presently we pass to some other object, which rounds itself into a whole, as did the first . . . . From this succession of excellent objects learn we at last the immensity of the world, the opulence of human nature . . . . [6]

Perhaps Nietzsche is, after all, the proper antidote to this astonishing optimism. Yet it is true that we constantly seek to master the accidents of life: to roll up our fortunes into a ball, to find religious, artistic or technological means of self-concentration. By such fatal centering we become conscious, then over-conscious, then flee what is desired. History is, as it were, the wake of a mobile mind falling in and out of love with things it detaches by its attachment. Its centering and decentering path leaves a chaos of forms behind. By negative transcendence it produces something as deep as a tragedy or as opulent as Emerson's view of Nature.

An updated—more realistic—Emerson would have to acknowledge a new stage, with men increasingly divided into two camps. A nihilistic period has begun in which one camp wishes to live "without reserve" —without role-models, or squandering them as a rich son his inheritance; while the other, fearing a debilitating loss of binding forms, deliberately espouses the crudest social myths. There is no "mystery of form" when forms lose their representativeness or mediating virtue: when men, distorting rather than exploring art's common-wealth, its link with an interpretable fund of roles, fall back on narrow concepts of manliness and reenact those tragedies of revenge which society was founded to control. "Greatness without models? Inconceivable. One could not be the thing itself—Reality. . . . Make peace therefore with intermediacy and representation." [7] Is it too late, or can our age, like every previous one, protect the concept of art?

6   "Art," in *Essays: First Series.*
7   Saul Bellow, *Mr Sammler's Planet,* p. 149.

II. The Reserve of Art and the Social Reserve

Art history presupposes that creation comes out of a "chaos of forms" rather than simply out of chaos or miraculously out of nothing. This chaos, with which the historical consciousness begins, has had many depictions, from the Rabbinical *Pardes* and that reservoir of perplexing images Yeats associated with the secrets of an *anima mundi*, to Dürer's *Melencolia I, The Waste Land*'s "heap of broken images" and David Jones's "anathémata." When institutionalized this chaos becomes a *thesaurus* or *museum*, and expands with the historical consciousness. Hegel's observation that the Roman pantheon relativized the gods it brought together anticipates Malraux's universal "musée imaginaire" in which the gods are pictures.

Were that museum, however, truly imaginary or "without walls," it would mean the end of art as we know it. A secular sparagmos would "carry art into the kingdom of nature, and destroy its separated and contrasted existence."[8] Our chaos of forms would move, in other words, from a beginning to an end position, one characterized by Hegel as a *revel* of forms, the sober bacchanalia of the human spirit reconciled with all its incarnations.[9] That revel might be compared to the formal dance which ends certain comedies, except that it erases rather than affirms the art-reality distinction. The reconciliation is to be real, not formal.

What lies between the "chaos" and the "revel" of forms? Conventions or institutions which are familiar, and sometimes too familiar. There exists a highly structured *reserve* of forms which claims to represent for each generation the genius of a nation, class or culture. Here are found the official commonplaces; the symbols and passwords that bind a community together or identify members to each other. It may be that the artist, at present, is tempted to pass from the chaos to the revel of forms without respecting this more structured realm. But since he cannot avoid it entirely, he violates its "reserve" by various kinds of self-exhausting parody—as in Woodstock's feast of tongues.

The image of society resulting from a century of progress in social anthropology may help to clarify these concepts. Society is built up of tribes, communities and special interests. To bind them together needs places, myths and heroes in common. The idea of a "commonplace" is more concrete here than in the History of Ideas or Topoi. There is first an official, highly organized *mythology*, a state religion, for example; but underlying it, or not quite reducible, a pervasive, unofficial *ideology*

8   Emerson, "Art."

9   See the conclusion to the *Phenomenology of Mind* (1807).

or complex of beliefs. The difference between written and oral culture connects with this division; the latter shows, in any case, that what we have called the reserve is not totally rigid but contains two systems of expression more or less conscious of each other. Sometimes, no doubt, the one will not know what the other is doing; but a strong relationship is necessary if the "higher" language is to retain its resonance and be more than superstructure.

In addition to the reserve we find an area which corresponds quite closely to the "chaos of forms." Van Gennep saw that there was a phase of aggregation rituals (*rites de passage*) in which the candidate is "betwixt and between" and which allows him a degree of self-determination in the choice of a social identity. During this *liminal* or *marginal* phase the candidate is segregated and exposed to spirit-powers directly, without forms or mediations available to men in society. He discovers in this way both his individuality and his isolation, both selfhood and the meaning of society. [10]

If we reflect that marginality is dangerous not because it is empty but because the absence of conventional social structuring allows room for an irruption of energies society has not integrated, then we see how similar this state is to the "chaos of forms" which art explores. The artist is surely the liminal or threshold person par excellence, while art provides society with a "chaos of roles" strengthening the individual's sense of unstructured community yet offering him ideal parts to try. Only the concept of liminality, moreover, as developed by Turner from Van Gennep [11] explains why art is statusless despite its civilizing role. Art is not reality; the relation of the one to the other is essentially liminal; between art and its translation into immediate relevance a threshold intervenes which cannot be crossed without destroying art's very place in society. The modern university is characterized by a similar kind of marginality, one basic to the development of man as a citizen yet an individual.

The liminal state is not restricted to puberty rites. It plays a significant role in initiations generally. Here is where the patience ("negative capability") of the candidate may be tested, where symbolic sights and acts reverse his status or question his integrity. The mature man, after all, may need more "restructuring" than the ephebe. Or his respon-

10   A. Van Gennep, *Les rites de passage* (Paris, 1907); also Mary Douglas, *Purity and Danger* (London, 1960).

11   Victor Turner, *The Ritual Process* (Chicago, 1968). Turner uses the phrase "chaos of roles" which led to my "chaos of forms." In Europe the image of what Lionel Trilling calls *the other culture,* "the idealized past of some other nation, Greece, or Rome or England" (*Beyond Culture,* pp. 112-14) strengthened the marginality of art, but from above, as it were.

sibilities may be heavier. He is therefore disoriented (disaggregated) under test-conditions imposed by the group, before being accepted in (aggregated) once more. An artist, of course, is a group of one and has little or no ritual authority. Yet art does submit us to a ritual and controlled experience of this kind. We are not compelled to participate in it, yet there are those who abide its question. It is no mean test to view what Aristotle calls a scene of pathos without being traumatized by it or distancing it into symbolic meaning—to let oneself be confronted by an ambiguity that, when it occurs in real life, splits the soul.

The ritual process leads, of course, beyond liminality. A new identity, or reidentification, should emerge. This is not so clear in art because art extends the liminal moment. There the identity quest is a formal device and always something of a deception. In fact, whereas in the primitive rite there is probably no such thing as *failing* the process of aggregation [12] (except for special cases in which "the king must die"), in art there is no such thing as fully succeeding in it. Art interests us less in the outcome of an ethical or vocational crisis than in the passion that attends, and the vision from passion. The hero, by suffering the chaos of forms, by descending into that hades, glimpses the point where "All Human Forms are Identified." [13] A Redeemed City emerges from Ancestral Chaos. Yet to bring the vision back is greater than to attain it. The return, which corresponds socially to reaggregation and psychologically to reintegration, is the moment of art itself—the opus. *Facilis descensus Averno . . . sed revocare gradum superasque evadere ad auras, hoc opus, hic labor est.*

Goethe's *Faust* is an exceptionally clear instance of the work of art conceived as a socializing *rite de passage*. It shows, at the same time, the danger of confusing art with the production of new identities or role-models. Faust moves from a spiritual acedia reflecting the burden of culture to the illusory revel of the *Walpurgisnacht* and the more sophisticated dream of a reconciliation between those mighty cultural opposites: classic and gothic, Greece and Germany. When the quest collapses and Faust adopts the pragmatic role of bridge-builder, Goethe's myriad-minded play is unmasked as a ponderous ritual *embourgeoisement*. We have entered the era of the well-made rite of passage.

But how else can we emerge from the chaos of forms? What can art create if not a reconciling social myth or an ideal personal role? Is

12 See Douglas, *Purity and Danger*, p. 116, on the "hoax aspect" of ritual dangers.

13 William Blake, *Jerusalem*, last plate (99).

art's truth merely in its obsessive consumption or negative transcendence of historical models?

We recall the contemporary situation. While primitive ritual makes room for the living by ceremonies that both propitiate and separate the dead—"the dead, if not separated from the living, bring madness on them" [14]—the growth of the historical sense makes clean, ritual separations difficult. If the dead are less dangerous when viewed as historically transcended, or sublimated, forces, they are also more insinuating. They do not fall easily into pure and impure, malevolent and beneficent, tribal and alien. The time spent in the marginal state, the submission to visions of the night, lengthen. We feel more strongly than ever that the past pollutes *and* that it saves. "Nothing human alienates me"— for the historical consciousness exotic or irrational are simply estranged potentialities of the human spirit. "All Human Forms are Identified" in Blake's redeemed city.

In these circumstances art both accepts and rejects more: it resists the spirits it calls up and absorbs conflicting traditions by a movement more eccentric than Miltonic similes. The new myth that kills the old, the new form that separates what is dead from what is living, has the value of a purification rather than of truth. The chaos of forms aspires to become a revel: in the sublimities of a Milton, Blake or Shelley there is a high laughter as well as high seriousness. There remains, of course, the shadow of the false or premature revel: promiscuous acceptance (as in the *Walpurgisnacht*) of the chaos of forms, or such fickle at-one-ments as Blake places into Beulah. The unitive vision of art is not a spiritual cannibalism or triumph of death.

Consider Goethe once more. His Faust enters the chaos of the past but rejects its abstract promises. He wants participation, mastery, universality. Yet Faust's progress in that direction gives renewed birth to sacrificial abstractions. The more universal his vision, the more blatant his disregard of parochial dignities and individual suffering. And Goethe, too, pays a price in his art for a clarity superior to that of contemporaries like Hölderlin and Blake. He stylizes the dynamic character of the vast cultural reserve embodied in his poems. The conflict of classes and tongues becomes matter for a virtuoso display. Art has now acquired its own reserve, a backlog of forms which Goethe *applies* perfectly, mixing types of verse and transcending national boundaries through a deployment of inherited topoi. This art-reserve has advantages over both the chaos of forms and the social reserve: it is better organized than the first and broader than the second. Its disad-

---

14 A Nyakusa saying, quoted in Douglas, *Purity and Danger*, p. 208. Hamlet's madness, if more than strategic, is part of his trouble with the dead—and, perhaps, with dying conventions.

vantage, however, is that charted still further by humanists like North-rop Frye it could substitute itself for the ritual process. Then art be-comes a technique and culture-grammar rather than a genuine media-tion: a wrestling with, and separating of, the dead. [15]

III. Afterthought

In the 1930's Ernst Robert Curtius began the studies that led to *European Literature and the Latin Middle Ages* (1948). For that work Goethe was the central man: through his art the great body of formal (and formative) commonplaces elaborated since Homer are said to have reached the threshold of modern German literature. Through him they were saved from becoming a dead language.

At our distance from the 1930's (which saw a parallel though less literary development in America, A. O. Lovejoy's *Great Chain of Being*, also concerned with continuity) this type of literary history seems faulty. It tends to be a courtesy book for scholars, an exercise in the urbane dif-fusion of knowledge. Histories of topical ideas, literary or philosophical, remain in the domain of *memoria technica* rather than serving the liv-ing, ancestor-haunted consciousness. Histories should tell us what made a person or a group historical: what marked them and passed into mind with the force of the Biblical injunction: "Remember, Thou shalt not forget." Or what helped them learn to forget, to remit the burden of the past. This individuating, and often delimiting cycle, dis-appears from histories of topoi. Their humanistic kind of monism sees little that is new under the sun.

Yet scholarship has its own historical context, and we easily overlook the call it answered. Faulty or not, Curtius's great commonplace book is the protest of Mnemosyne against Germania. It enlarged the memory of a nation when political pressures had reduced art to a narrow, racial-ist canon. Curtius appealed to Memory not for the sake of the past but for the sake of Romania, which he viewed as more than a country of the mind: it was a wronged spirit, a *genius loci* expelled from Ger-mania by fascism. Like Blake, therefore, but in a darker time, he en-gaged in mental fight to restore his country's genius to its memorable form.

---

15 See W. J. Bate, *The Burden of the Past and the English Poet* (Cambridge, Mass., 1970); Harold Bloom, *Yeats* (New York, 1970); and Ann Wordsworth's re-view of the latter, "Wrestling with the Dead," *The Spectator*, July 25, 1970.

6

History and Fiction as Modes of Comprehension

Louis O. Mink

I

PHILOSOPHERS have always betrayed a certain scorn for both history and romance. "I knew that the delicacy of fiction enlivens the mind," said Descartes, explaining how he had liberated himself from the errors of the schools, and "that famous deeds of history ennoble it." But in the end, he concluded, these are negligible merits, because "fiction makes us imagine a number of events as possible which are really impossible, and even the most faithful histories, if they do not alter or embroider things to make them more worth reading, almost always omit the meanest and least illustrious circumstances, so that the remainder is distorted."[1] This was Descartes's first and final word on all the tales and stories of human life, and until very recently it could have served to sum up the consensus of Western philosophy. Even when Hegel discovered that history is more philosophical than poetry, he gave no more comfort to the practitioners of historical inquiry than Aristotle had given to wise poets; for in both cases it was for relative proximity to the first principles of philosophy itself that the marks were passed out. It was the universals bodied forth rather than the vivid and particular details of the stories which bore them that commanded the attention of philosophers.

In recent years, however, there has come into being a new and still developing interest among philosophers in what is called (rather misleadingly) the logic of narration. This has not been a product of aesthetics, as one might think, and it has as yet made no connection with the sort of analysis of narrative fiction represented in such studies as Scholes and Kellogg's *The Nature of Narrative*. Rather it belongs to the analytical philosophy of history — the theory of historical knowledge, that is, rather than the speculative metaphysics of the historical process. The philosophical problems whose coastlines are being explored were discovered in the following way. Since the seven-

---

1 *Discourse on Method*, tr. Laurence J. Lafleur (New York, 1950), pp. 4-5.

teenth century, philosophy has been dominated by the problems of the cognitive status of perception on the one hand and the interpretation of natural science on the other. The great controversies of rationalism and empiricism now appear to have been complementary phases of the enterprise, extending over three centuries, to construct a comprehensive account of the relation between our direct perception of the world and our inferential knowledge of that world through the discoveries of natural science. In this epistemological enterprise there was no room for either imaginative worlds or the inaccessible world of the past. The latter, in particular, appeared significant only as something not perceptible, not as something *past*. In the riot of epistemological theories — new realism, critical realism, subjective idealism, pragmatism, objective relativism, phenomenalism, etc., etc. — in which the modern epoch of philosophy came to an end within recent memory, not one took seriously the problem of how it is possible that the past should be knowable, although each constructed a more or less embarrassed appendix which restored some sort of cognitive status to history, some possibility of meaning to "statements about the past." Meanwhile, historians were laying successful siege to the records of the past, but while they could point to notable achievements of inquiry there was no theory of historical knowledge to compare with the increasingly sophisticated philosophy of science. The "theory of knowledge" in fact was, by the implicit consensus of philosophers, the theory of *scientific* knowledge, and its very vocabulary — the language of induction and classification, of hypothesis and verification, of dependent and independent variables, general laws and probability coefficients, quantification and calculation — had its primary referents in astronomy, physics, chemistry and biology.

The clearest and most influential systematization of the view that philosophy is the logical analysis of scientific procedure has been that self-designated as logical empiricism, *né* "positivism." A major principle of logical empiricism is the so-called methodological unity of science, that is, the view that there is no formal or logical difference among the various bodies of practice and consolidated inquiry which can count as scientific. With respect to explanation and the criteria for adequate explanation, for example, there is a single although complex formal model of explanation, which consists in showing that the statement asserting the occurrence of an event or other phenomenon to be explained follows by strict formal deduction (including mathematical deduction) from one or more statements about initial conditions of the system to which the laws apply and in which the phenomenon to be explained occurs. This is also the model of prediction; one can think of, say, either the prediction or the explanation of an eclipse as a clear example in which this model is realized. Now to apply such a model of explanation to human action or social change raises grave problems; few if any explanations in psychology or social science can be shown to have this form, not least because the general laws formally required have not been empirically discovered. Nevertheless, the claim was not that the deductive or "covering-law" model of explanation can be discerned in every putative explanation but that it represents a rational demand by comparison with which most "explanations" reveal themselves as defective. The methodological preoccupations of psychology, sociology, and other social sciences in recent years have in effect resulted from the adoption of positivist prescriptions as imperatives for the organization of research. In history, however, these prescriptions have seemed least applicable and also least able to account for the fact that some historical accounts *seem* to explain and illuminate although they cannot by any Procrustean efforts be restated in such a way as to exhibit the required form. Yet the case for positivism is strong. "Do you claim to have explained why this event occurred?" it asks. "Well, then, you are claiming more than *that* it happened; you are claiming that given whatever you refer to as bringing it about or causing it to occur, it *must* have happened as it did, in fact that it could not have *not* happened. The force of explanation lies in the recognition of necessity, and necessity can be shown only by showing that the event is connected with its antecedents by a general and well-confirmed law. Until that is done, there is no explanation but only a sketch of what an explanation would be like if there were one."[2]

At this point historians have been known to say something about history being an art rather than a science. Some philosophers, however, agreeing with the positivists that the task of philosophy is to make explicit the patterns of rational inference which inform complex thinking of all sorts, but unlike the positivists willing to entertain the hypothesis that there are different patterns of rationality not reducible to a single and fundamental pattern, have taken history to be a possibly autonomous and in any case rich and logically unanalyzed mode of inquiry and knowledge. As Arthur Danto has said,

2 The classic statement is by C. G. Hempel, in "The Function of General Laws in History," *Journal of Philosophy* XXXIX (1942), later weakened to accommodate probability laws in "Deductive-Nomological vs. Statistical Explanation" (*Minnesota Studies in the Philosophy of Science*, Vol. III, ed. H. Feigl and G. Maxwell), and in "Reasons and Covering Laws in Historical Explanation," *Philosophy and History*, ed. S. Hook (New York, 1963). There are also characteristic statements in Karl Popper's *The Logic of Scientific Discovery* (London, 1959) and Ernest Nagel's *The Structure of Science* (New York, 1961).

not casually but prefatory to a detailed analysis of historical language and explanation, "The difference between history and science is not that history does and science does not employ organizing schemes which go beyond what is given. Both do. The difference has to do with the *kind* of organizing schemes employed by each. *History* tells stories."[3]

So here there is a beginning of an attempt to carry out the program originally signalled by Collingwood: that while "the chief business of seventeenth-century philosophy was to reckon with seventeenth-century natural science . . . the chief business of twentieth-century philosophy is to reckon with twentieth-century history."[4] By "history," of course, Collingwood did not mean the course of public events (as in history vs. nature) but rather the inquiry, practiced by professional historians but not limited to them, into institutional change and purposive human action (as in history vs. natural science). The change is from a preoccupation with theory to an interest in narra-tive: "narrative explanation" is no longer a contradiction in terms. But there is also a shift from the concept of explanation, defined in terms of a formal model, to the concept of understanding, perhaps indefinable but clarified by reflection on the experiences in which it has been achieved.

No one has gone further in this direction than W. B. Gallie, in his book *Philosophy and the Historical Understanding.* I shall review his argument briefly, at the expense of doing scant justice to its intrinsic interest, for the sake of calling attention to what I think to be an unusually interesting and suggestive mistake. Gallie observes, quite correctly, that no critical (that is, post-Kantian) philosopher has worked out a clear account of "what it is to follow or construct an historical narrative."[5] History, he eventually is to conclude, is "a species of the genus Story."[6] But to understand what a story is, is to know what it is to *follow* a story, that is, not merely to have done so (as everyone has) but to know what in general are the features of a story which make it followable. And this in turn is not significantly

3   Other discussions of historical narrative are by Morton White, *The Foundations of Historical Knowledge,* Ch. vi (New York 1965); A. R. Louch, "History as Narrative," *History and Theory,* VIII (1969); Maurice Mandelbaum, "A Note on History as Narra-tive," *History and Theory,* VI (1967); replies to Mandelbaum by Richard C. Ely, Rolf Gruner, and William H. Dray, *History and Theory,* VIII (1969); and W. B. Gallie, *Philosophy and the Historical Understanding* (London, 1964), which is discussed below. For the reflections of a working historian: G. R. Elton, *The Practice of History,* Ch. iii (Sydney and New York, 1967).

4   R. G. Collingwood, *An Autobiography* (Oxford, 1939), pp. 78-79.
5   *Philosophy and the Historical Understanding,* pp. 12-13.
6   *Ibid.,* p. 66.

different from following a game in progress, such as a cricket match, and understanding the features which make it followable. In following a story, as in being a spectator at a match, there must be a quickly established sense of a promised although unpredictable outcome: the county team will win, lose or draw, the separated lovers will be reunited or will not. Surprises and contingencies are the stuff of stories, as of games, yet by virtue of the promised yet open outcome we are enabled to follow a series of events across their contingent relations and to understand them as leading to an as yet unrevealed conclusion without however necessitating that conclusion. We may follow understandingly what we could not predict or infer. At the same time, following requires the enlistment of our sympathies and antipathies, the "basic directing feelings" which account for one's being pulled along by a story; in fact, "what discontinuities we are willing to accept or able to follow depends partly upon the set or orientation of our sympathy . . . and partly upon the intrinsic nature of the kind of sympathy that has been established."[7] Stories may be followed more or less completely, as a wise old hand at cricket may notice nice details which escape the spectator of average keenness, and there can be no criteria for following *completely*.[8] But the minimal conditions are the same for all. The features which enable a story to flow and us to follow, then, are the clues to the nature of historical understanding. An historical narrative does not demonstrate the necessity of events but makes them intelligible by unfolding the story which connects their significance.[9] History does not as such differ from fiction, therefore, insofar as it essentially depends on and develops our skill and subtlety in following stories. History *does* of course differ from fiction insofar as it is obligated to rest upon evidence of the occurrence in real space and time of what it describes and insofar as it must grow out of a critical assessment of the received materials of history, including the analyses and interpretations of other historians.[10] But the researches of historians, however arduous and technical, only increase the amount and precision of knowledge of facts which

7   *Ibid.*, pp. 44-47.

8   *Ibid.*, p. 33.

9   "What is contingent . . . is of course, *per se* unintelligible. But in relation to a man's life, or to a particular theme in a man's life, it can be understood as having contributed to a particular, acceptable and accepted conclusion" (p. 41). While this sums up a notion of intelligibility with which I would quite agree, it does not support what Gallie thinks it supports, namely, the "intellectual indispensability of the act of following." As I try to argue below, it is not following but *having followed* which carries the force of understanding.

10   *Ibid.*, pp. 56-64, 71.

remain contingent and discontinuous. It is by being assigned to stories that they become intelligible and increase understanding by going beyond "What?" and "When?" to "How?" and "Why?"

The difficulty in Gallie's adventurous account is not, I believe, in his emphasis on narrative but in his assumption that its essential features are revealed by a phenomenology of "following." What he has provided is a description of the naive reader, that is, the reader *who does not know how the story ends*, and who is "pulled along" by interest, sympathy, and curiosity. It is not incidental but essential to Gallie's view that contingent events are made acceptable and intelligible insofar as the story so far directs them toward a promised but open conclusion. Yet of course this is an experience which no *historian* and no moderately knowledgeable reader of historical narrative can have. Nor can a critic reading *King Lear* for the twentieth time nor any reader for the second find himself carried along by sympathetic curiosity about the fate of Lear and Cordelia. It may be that narrative historians more or less artfully construct their stories in order to lead readers through "possible routes towards the required but as yet undisclosed conclusion," but of the many historians who regard Garrett Mattingly's *The Defeat of the Spanish Armada* as the unsurpassed recent example of narrative history, I have never heard one complain that his reading of it was marred by knowing how it all came out. Among both historians and critics, on the contrary, familiarity sometimes breeds respect.

What I mean to suggest is that the difference between following a story and *having followed* a story is more than the incidental difference between present experience and past experience. Anticipation and retrospection are not simply different attitudes or vantage-points which may be taken (or must be taken) toward the same event or course of events. We know that the difference between past and future is crucial in the case of moral and affective attitudes; we do not fear something that is over and done with, nor feel regret for something not yet undertaken. My thesis is that the difference is crucial as well for cognition: at least in the case of human actions and changes, to know an event by retrospection is categorically, not incidentally, different from knowing it by prediction or anticipation. It cannot even, in any strict sense, be called the "same" event, for in the former case the descriptions under which it is known are governed by a story to which it belongs, and there is no story of the future. But to give this thesis plausibility requires a consideration of what the "logic of narration" neglects: not what the structure or generic features of narratives are, nor what it means to "follow," but what it means *to have followed* a story.

II

As we have known since Kant, one of the most difficult of all tasks is to discern and describe correctly those generic features of experience which we do not attend to and which we have no appropriate vocabulary to describe, precisely because their ubiquity leaves them unnoticed; their presence is not signaled by contrast with their absence or with competing features. It is only by the most intense conceptual effort that the structure of all experience can be distinguished from the vivid details of particular experience which commonly command our attention. It is perhaps for this reason that theories of knowledge have unaccountably neglected the significance of the simple fact that experiences come to us *seriatim* in a stream of transience and yet must be capable of being held together in a single image of the manifold of events in order for us to be aware of transience at all. It is a contingent fact of empirical psychology that the "specious present" — that duration in which we seem to be simultaneously aware of actually successive events such as the series of sounds that make up a spoken word — is of the order of between half a second and a second. But it is a necessary truth that we could not even form the concept of the specious present were we not able to hold in mind, through *this* sequence of presents, right *now*, the thought of past and future, of past futures and future pasts. Memory, imagination, and conceptualization all serve this function, whatever else they do: they are ways of grasping together in a single mental act things which are not experienced together, or even capable of being so experienced, because they are separated by time, space, or logical kind. And the ability to do this is a necessary (although not a sufficient) condition of *understanding*.

A few random examples may help to bring out the way in which the act of "grasping together" can be found in every variety of experience. For one case: in hearing the first movement of an unfamiliar Haydn symphony, one may "understand" the development in the sense that melodic motion and harmonic modulations are familiar and anticipatable. But of course this would be the case even if we had entered the hall or set down the needle in the middle of the movement. There is a different and more appropriately named kind of "understanding" when we hear and assimilate the exposition of the themes from the beginning, and then hear the development together with the retained memory of the themes. Without the ability to hold in mind the sequence already passed through, one would simply not understand, in *any* sense of "understand," musical passages such as the minuet of Beethoven's seventh symphony, in which the trio returns for a third appearance but is cut off abruptly after a few bars. Or again: Faulkner's *The Sound and the Fury* begins with the first-person impressions and recollections of the cretin Benjy. No one "understands" these pages on a first reading; no one is expected to. It is not until later in the book that these opaque pages become intelligible in retrospect; one must read the later pages with the earlier in mind, and in fact reread the earlier pages with the later in mind. But of course this is merely an especially vivid illustration of a character which every narrative has in some degree. Aristotle's observation that a play must have a beginning, a middle, and an end is not a trivially formal description but a corollary of his principle that a drama is an imitation of a *single* action, that is, that both action and mimesis must be capable of being understood as a single complex whole. It is also the sense in which Weigand said of *The Magic Mountain* that "the whole novel is present on every page."

But the phenomenon of grasping things together is not limited, as these examples might suggest, to the temporal arts. Consider logical inference, as represented in the following simple argument: All creatures are mortal; all men are creatures; all Athenian citizens are men; Socrates is an Athenian citizen; hence Socrates is mortal. Now suppose that we infer from the first two premises that all men are mortal, and then destroy our notes and forget the premises; and similarly with the premises which yield intermediate conclusions and again with these when the final conclusion has been drawn. This is analogous to the addition of a column of figures, forgetting the earlier figures with each sub-total, and also to every more complex instance of mathematical inference. In such hypothetical cases it is clear that we have lost the special quality of understanding the conclusion *as following from* the premises. We could in such a circumstance still *test* the validity of an argument, but could not *see* it. That grasping together a complex sequence of inference is possible is attested to by mathematicians, who commonly are able to see a demonstration as a whole rather than as merely a sequence of rule-governed transformations; and most probably the ascription of "elegance" to a proof acknowledges the especial neatness of its presentation in such a way as to facilitate one's seeing it as a whole.

In all of these instances, and in indefinitely many more, there thus seems to be a characteristic kind of understanding which consists in thinking together in a single act, or in a cumulative series of acts, the complicated relationships of parts which can be experienced only *seriatim*. I propose to call this act (for obvious etymological reasons) "comprehension." It is operative, I believe, at every level of consciousness, reflection and inquiry. At the lowest level, it is the grasping together of data of sensation, memory and imagination, and issues in perception and recognition of objects. At an intermediate level, it is the grasping together of a set of objects, and issues in classification and generalization. At the highest level, it is the attempt to order together our knowledge into a single system — to comprehend the world as a totality. Of course this is an unattainable goal, but it is significant as an ideal aim against which partial comprehension can be judged. To put it differently, it is unattainable because such comprehension would be divine, but significant because the human project is to take God's place. Naturally enough, attempts to describe the aim of ideal comprehension have always been put into theological terms. Boethius, explaining why human freedom does not limit God's knowledge, described God's knowledge of the world as a *totum simul*, in which the successive moments of all time are copresent in a single perception, as of a landscape of events. The omniscient scientist envisioned by LaPlace, knowing the laws of nature and the position and velocity of every particle of the universe at a single instant, could predict and retrodict the detailed character of the world at any moment of time. (So, in the classic story, when Napoleon remarked to LaPlace that he had found no mention of God in the *System of the World*, LaPlace replied, "Sire, I have had no need of that hypothesis.") And Plato, who thought divine knowledge not unattainable, regarded it as the contemplative vision of a set of essences grasped as a single intelligible system — a "comprehensive view," he calls it in discussing the education of the Rulers in Book VI of the *Republic*, "of the mutual relations and affinities which bind all the sciences together."

These different descriptions of the ideal aim of comprehension are not merely visionary. Rather they are extrapolations of several different and mutually exclusive modes of comprehension which run through our more mundane and partial understanding. There are, I suggest, three such fundamental modes, irreducible to each other or to any more general mode. I shall call these the *theoretical* mode, the *categoreal* mode, and the *configurational* mode. They are roughly associated with types of understanding characteristic of natural science, philosophy and history; but they are not by any means identical with these, and in fact their real differences expose the artificial and misleading nature of academic classifications. It is the configurational mode alone which is relevant to the concept of a story, but the issues which it may illuminate cannot be clearly stated except by contrasting it with the alternative modes.

What are the different ways in which a number of objects can be comprehended in a single mental act?

First, they may be comprehended as instances of the same generalization. This way is powerful but thin. It is powerful because the generalization refers to things as members of a class or as instances of a formula, and thereby embraces both the experienced and the unexperienced, the actual and the possible. It is thin because it refers to them only in virtue of their possession of certain common characteristics, omitting everything else in the concrete particularity of each. I discover, let us say, that a piece of paper ignites easily, and repeat the experiment with an old letter, a page from a calendar, a sheet of music, and an unpaid bill. Thus I quickly reach the generalization "Paper burns," by which I comprehend an indefinite number of similar observations. By analogous experience of needles, fenders, boathooks and washing machines, I can comprehend an equally great number of instances under the generalization, "Steel rusts." But then it occurs to me that both processes may be the result of chemical combination, and I am on the way toward explaining both combustion and rusting as instances of oxidation. And in this way I can comprehend both classes of phenomena, superficially very unlike each other, as instances of a single law. This *theoretical* mode of comprehension is also often called "hypothetico-deductive," and its ideal type is that expressed by LaPlace.

A second and quite different way of comprehending a number of objects is as examples of the same category. Thus both a painting and a geometry are examples of complex form, and Edna St. Vincent Millay's famous line, "Euclid alone hath looked on beauty bare," issues from *categoreal* comprehension in which the category of the aesthetic is linked with the category of form, and both subsume not merely works of art but all formal complexes in a scale of degrees. Categoreal comprehension superficially resembles theoretical comprehension and is often confused with it, but such confusion is virtually the defining property of philosophical obtuseness. The relation of theory to its objects is that it enables us to infer and coordinate a body of true statements about that kind of object; the relation of categories to their objects is that they determine of what kind those objects may be. Thus a set of categories is what is now often called a conceptual framework: a system of concepts functioning a priori in giving form to otherwise inchoate experience. Perhaps the simplest examples of categoreal comprehension are those cases in which a concept belonging to a developed theory — e.g., evolution, equilibrium, repression — is extended to cover a range of instances for which the theory itself has no validity in principle. Thus we come, for example, to think of the "evolution" of ideas, as a way of conceiving what counts as an idea rather than as a theory about natural variation and selection. It is categoreal comprehension, of course, which Plato — and, in fact, most systematic philosophers — envisioned as an ideal aim.

Yet a third way in which a number of things may be comprehended is as elements in a single and concrete complex of relationships. Thus a letter I burn may be understood not only as an oxidizable substance but as a link with an old friend. It may have relieved a misunderstanding, raised a question, or changed my plans at a crucial moment. As a letter, it belongs to a kind of story, a narrative of events which would be unintelligible without reference to it. But to explain this, I would not construct a theory of letters or of friendships but would, rather, show how it belongs to a particular configuration of events like a part to a jigsaw puzzle. It is in this *configurational* mode that we see together the complex of imagery in a poem, or the combination of motives, pressures, promises and principles which explain a Senator's vote, or the pattern of words, gestures and actions which constitute our understanding of the personality of a friend. As the theoretical mode corresponds to what Pascal called *l'esprit de géometrie,* so the configurational mode corresponds to what he called *l'esprit de finesse* — the ability to hold together a number of elements in just balance. The *totum simul* which Boethius regarded as God's knowledge of the world would of course be the highest degree of configurational comprehension.

Now it may seem that what I have tried to call attention to is merely an array of techniques or "approaches" from which one may select now one, now another as is appropriate to the subject-matter at hand and its particular problems. It is true that one *may* do this, and also that each mode may enter into a process of inquiry — which however must culminate in a single mode. But they cannot be combined in a single act. One reason for such a conclusion is simply the observation that notable intellectual achievements and the style of undeniably powerful minds are characterized by a kind of single-mindedness: the attempt to extend to every possible subject of interest a single one of the modes. One notes that eminently theoretical minds attempt to apply to political problems or even to personal relationships the techniques of abstraction and generalization which enable messy particularities to be stripped away from the formulary type. Configurational minds on the other hand organize whatever they know of biology into a sense of place. As ecologists, they use their theoretical knowledge to illuminate their grasp of the concrete interactions of individual plants and animals in a specific environment; for a population biologist, on the other hand, the foxglove and the hare are countable units of their species. A more general reason for concluding that the modes are incompatible is that each has ultimately the totality of human experience, or if one prefers, the "world of fact," as its subject matter. There is nothing which cannot in principle be brought within each mode, although of course it will be modified by being comprehended in one mode rather than another. Of course it would be a mistake to try to understand sub-atomic particles in the mode of configurational comprehension; but this is because sub-atomic particles are not objects of direct experience but hypothetical constructs whose very meaning is given within the mode of theoretical comprehension. Moreover, the *practice* of each mode is an object for the others; hence there can be a psychology of philosophy and a philosophy of psychology, a biography of Freud and a psychoanalysis of the biographer. Each mode tends to represent the others as special cases or imperfect approximations of itself. And those to whom a single mode has become a second nature tend to regard the others like Gulliver's Houyhnhnm master, who thought Gulliver's forelegs impractical because his forehooves were too tender to bear his weight.

One of the more convincing reasons for acknowledging the intellectual function of comprehension and distinguishing its modes, I have come to think, is that it provides a way of understanding and explaining *rationally* the disputes of the schools and the misunderstandings in which intellectual controversy abounds. One can see, in this light, that what are called "disciplines" are actually arenas in which the partisans of each mode contend for dominance, each with its own aim of understanding, identification of problems, and privileged language. Behaviorism, for example, is essentially the claim that human action and social reality can be understood only in the mode of theoretical comprehension, as against the more traditional historical and institutional schools, whose aim was to grasp configurations of organization and stages of change. Or again there are the differences among psychoanalytic critics who seek to understand a poem by psychoanalyzing the poet or the reader (seeking theoretical comprehension), the New Criticism, whose aim is to achieve configurational comprehension of the poem alone in all its internal complexity, and archetypal critics, who apply everywhere a categoreal system — which unfortunately, unlike the categoreal systems of philosophy, fails to include concepts of logic. If it is true that the three modes are incompatible as ultimate aims, we must abandon hope of achieving an eclectic or panperspectival outcome, but we might hope for an increase in intellectual charity, and be grateful for a rational defense against the imperialism of methodologies.

Everything I have said in the attempt to distinguish modes of comprehension, of course, is in the categoreal mode.

III

It is not a theory of knowledge which is at issue. Comprehension is not knowledge, nor even a condition of knowledge: we know many things as unrelated facts — Voltaire's full name, the population of Rumania in 1930, the binomial theorem, the longitude of Vancouver. On the other hand, a pseudo-scientific theory such as "hollow-earth" astronomy is as much an instance of theoretical comprehension as is astrophysics. It is by reference to standards other than comprehension that we must decide what is true and what is false. Knowledge is essentially public and may even be distributed through a community; we know collectively what no one individually could possess. But comprehension is an individual act of seeing-things-together, and only that. It can be neither an input nor an output of data-retrieval systems, nor can it be symbolically transformed for convenient reference. As the human activity by which elements of knowledge are converted into *understanding*, it is the synoptic vision without which (even though transiently and partially attained) we might forever pass in review our shards of knowledge as in some nightmare quiz show where nothing relates "fact" to "fact" except the fragmented identities of the participants and the mounting total of the score. Some physicists speculate in conversation that the physics of the future may be entirely unlike the physics of the past, since computation at electronic speeds permits the development of theories too complex for any mind to grasp as a whole. In the past, of course, the achievements of physics have been distinguished by the construction of elegant models, whether visual or just sets of equations, which were intellectually satisfying because they could be so grasped and seen to comprehend a vast range of otherwise unorganized data. So it may be that the possibility and even the desire for comprehension may disappear from some kinds of theoretical inquiry, as problem-solving and techniques of control and manipulation become dissociated from the satisfactions of understanding.

It is in the light of such a possibility that it seems not unimportant to make a just estimate of the nature and autonomy of other modes of comprehension than the theoretical mode. And it is the configurational mode which seems most often to be confused with the others or regarded, so to speak, as one of the shadows where their light has failed to reach. Implicit in the classical positivist account of explanation as it was summarized above is the theoretical principle that it is only as an instance of a law-governed type that an event or action can be truly understood. From this standpoint, a narrative may enliven sensibility (if it is fiction) or recount facts (if it is history), but it

answers no questions except, "And then what happened?" and affords
no understanding beyond such answers. In reply to this, "narrativists"
like Gallie have had a firm sense that stories produce a different and
sometimes indispensable kind of understanding. But they have, I
believe, failed to identify the genus to which narrative belongs, and
therefore have tried to find it in the sequential form of stories, in
the techniques of telling and the capacity for following, in the experience of interest, expectation, surprise, acceptability, and resolution.
But as we saw, this cannot be an illuminating account of the *historian's* understanding of his own narrative. One must set against it the
testimony of an eminent historian, in whose considered judgment
Lord Acton was an amateur, even though a prince of amateurs,
because "he was for ever expressing distress or surprise at some turn
in the story." The professional historian, Geoffrey Elton goes on to
say, must do more than just immerse himself in his period until he
hears its people speak; one must "read them, study their creations and
think about them until one knows *what they are going to say next.*"[11]
It is worth reflecting, too, on those stories which we want to hear over
and over again, and those which shape the common consciousness of
a community, whether they end with the funeral rites of Hector or
before the empty tomb.

Why do stories bear repeating? In some cases, no doubt, because of
the pleasure they give, in others because of the meaning they bear.
But in any case, if the theory of comprehension is right, because they
aim at producing and strengthening the act of understanding in which
actions and events, although represented as occurring in the order of
time, can be surveyed as it were in a single glance as bound together
in an order of significance, a representation of the *totum simul* which
we can never more than partially achieve. This outcome must seem
either a truism or a paradox: in the understanding of a narrative
the thought of temporal succession as such vanishes — or perhaps, one
might say, remains like the smile of the Cheshire Cat. It is a paradox,
of course, if like Gallie one fixes one's attention on following the
development of a story or the course of a game. But in the configurational comprehension of a story which one *has followed*, the end
is connected with the promise of the beginning as well as the beginning with the promise of the end, and the necessity of the backward
references cancels out, so to speak, the contingency of the forward
references. To comprehend temporal succession means to think of it in
both directions at once, and then time is no longer the river which

11   *The Practice of History*, p. 17; italics added.

bears us along but the river in aerial view, upstream and downstream seen in a single survey.

The thesis that time is not of the essence of narratives also loses its paradoxical air if one considers that historians commonly say (if they are asked) that they think less and less of chronology as they learn more and more of their fields. The date of an event is functionally an artificial mnemonic by which one can maintain the minimum sense of its *possible* relation to other events. The more one comes to understand the actual relations among a number of events, as expressed in the story or stories to which they all belong, the less one needs to remember dates. Before comprehension of events is achieved, one reasons *from* dates; having achieved comprehension, one understands, say, a certain action as a response to an event, and understands this directly. So one could reason *to* the conclusion that the event preceded the action, but from the standpoint of comprehension this would be trivial, except as information for someone else who did not already understand what the action was — who, that is, did not know its story. Even to describe the action correctly would mean describing it as a response and therefore *as* an element in a story. Otherwise it would not even be represented as an action (that is, as intentional and having a meaning for the agent), but as an opaque bit of behavior waiting for its story to be told.

It is implied by this account that the *techniques* by which narratives are shaped — from "Meanwhile, back at the ranch . . ." to the ironies of the fictive narrator who fails to see in his own tale a significance which author and reader share — can be regarded as, in part, instruments for facilitating the comprehension of the story as a whole. But one should ask at this point: what *are* the connections of the events arrayed in a single configuration? According to Gallie, the fundamental connection between the events of a story is their mutual orientation toward the promised end. According to Morton White's well-known account of historical narration, the fundamental connection is causal: antecedent events are presented as contributory or decisive causes of subsequent events.[12] There is also the unreflective view that the connection is simply that of temporal succession, but our whole argument has been that the significance of this connection evanesces between the activity of following a story and the act of comprehending it.

The example given above of an action in response to an event suggests an entirely different understanding of the internal organization of a comprehended story. For we do not describe the action

12 *The Foundations of Historical Knowledge,* pp. 223-25, and ch. iv.

and then add the statement that it was a response ("Next morning he sent off a telegram. I forgot to say that he had received an offer the day before for his interest in the company, and the telegram was his reply to the offer, actually . . ."). Rather we describe it correctly *as* a response ("He considered the offer overnight, and next morning accepted it by telegram . . ."). There are two points here. The first is that the correct description of the significant action is "accepting the offer," and "sending the telegram" is not a different action but part of the first. The second is that "accepting the offer" is already what might be called a story-statement. It refers to the story of which it is a part and overlaps conceptually with earlier statements about receiving the offer, and the like. "Sending a telegram" is not a story-statement. It suggests that there *is* a story to which it belongs, but it does not refer to that story and tells us nothing about what sort of earlier statements if any it may be linked to.

Not all parts of a story are about actions correctly describable only by story-statements, of course. But if we generalize from this paradigm we can say that the actions and events of a story comprehended as a whole are *connected by a network of overlapping descriptions*. And the overlap of descriptions may not be part of the story itself (as one thing after another) but only of the comprehension of it as a whole. For consider the narrative function of "discovery": we follow Oedipus on the road from Delphi to the crossroads where he is insulted by a stranger and in anger kills him. And then we follow him along the road to Thebes and across the years to his dreadful discovery. With Jocasta, we know the truth before Oedipus does, but not much before. All this occurs in following the story. But since we already know the story, we can only play at following it. In the comprehension of the story as a whole, there are no discoveries, and descriptions have no tense. For comprehension, the incident at the crossroads is *fully* describable only by a set of descriptions which jointly refer to all the rest of the story. The doomed man is a noble stranger to Oedipus, but he is also king of Thebes, the father of Oedipus, the husband of Jocasta, the predecessor of Oedipus as husband of Jocasta, the man whose house is cursed, the man who sent Oedipus to be bound and exposed as an infant, the man whose wife is a suicide, the man whose son blinds himself, and above all the man whose identity is discovered after his death by his slayer. He is alive and he is dead, and he could not be elsewhere than at the crossroads in the sunshine.

For comprehension, of course, there is a similar array of descriptions for every incident and character. The blinded Oedipus is the son of the king of Thebes, the man who brought the plague to the city, and the one who killed the stranger at the crossroads. Thus in the array of descriptions grasped together in the understanding of any incident or character, each overlaps with at least one in another array, and at least one overlaps with a description in every other array.[13] But this is only a formal account of a complex act of mind which directly apprehends its tableau of objects in their concrete particularity as well as in their manifold of relations.

IV

"Narrative," Barbara Hardy has said, "like lyric or dance, is not to be regarded as an aesthetic invention used by artists to control, manipulate and order experience, but as a primary act of mind transferred to art from life." More important than the artifices of fiction are the qualities which narrative shares with the story-telling of lived experience: "For we dream in narrative, daydream in narrative, remember, anticipate, hope, despair, believe, doubt, plan, revise, criticize, construct, gossip, learn, hate, and love by narrative."[14] It is true, I have argued, that narratives are in an important sense primary and irreducible. They are not imperfect substitutes for more sophisticated forms of explanation and understanding, nor are they the unreflective first steps along the road which leads toward the goal of scientific or philosophical knowledge. The comprehension at which narratives aim is a primary act of mind, although it is a capacity which can be indefinitely developed in range, clarity, and subtlety. But to say that the qualities of narrative are transferred to art from life seems a *hysteron proteron*. Stories are not lived but told. Life has no beginnings, middles, or ends; there are meetings, but the start of an affair belongs to the story we tell ourselves later, and there are partings, but final partings only in the story. There are hopes, plans, battles and ideas, but only in retrospective stories are hopes unfulfilled, plans miscarried, battles decisive, and ideas seminal. Only in the story is it America which Columbus discovers, and only in the story is the kingdom lost

13 Descriptions of course must belong to the narrative and not to our interpretation of it. It is not a description of Creon in *this* story that he is the man who condemns Antigone to death, nor a description of Oedipus that his downfall comes about as a result of a flaw in his nature. But we could not very well discuss the latter claim unless we already had the whole story in mind; and I even suspect that many interpretations or "readings" have very little point except as an aid to achieving or maintaining comprehension. In any case, comprehension is a necessary condition of interpretation but not vice versa.

14 Barbara Hardy, "Towards a Poetics of Fiction: An Approach Through Narrative," *Novel*, II (1968), 5.

for want of a nail. We do not dream or remember in narrative, I think, but tell stories which weave together the separate images of recollection. (One recounts a dream: "And then suddenly I was in the Piazza Navona — now how did I get *there*?") So it seems truer to say that narrative qualities are transferred from art to life. We could learn to tell stories of our lives from nursery rhymes, or from culture-myths if we had any, but it is from history and fiction that we learn how to tell and to understand *complex* stories, and how it is that stories answer questions.

7

The Reading Process:
A Phenomenological Approach

Wolfgang Iser

I

THE PHENOMENOLOGICAL THEORY of art lays full stress on the idea that, in considering a literary work, one must take into account not only the actual text but also, and in equal measure, the actions involved in responding to that text. Thus Roman Ingarden confronts the structure of the literary text with the ways in which it can be *konkretisiert* (realized).[1] The text as such offers different "schematised views"[2] through which the subject matter of the work can come to light, but the actual bringing to light is an action of *Konkretisation*. If this is so, then the literary work has two poles, which we might call the artistic and the aesthetic: the artistic refers to the text created by the author, and the aesthetic to the realization accomplished by the reader. From this polarity it follows that the literary work cannot be completely identical with the text, or with the realization of the text, but in fact must lie halfway between the two. The work is more than the text, for the text only takes on life when it is realized, and furthermore the realization is by no means independent of the individual disposition of the reader—though this in turn is acted upon by the different patterns of the text. The convergence of text and reader brings the literary work into existence, and this convergence can never be precisely pinpointed, but must always remain virtual, as it is not to be identified either with the reality of the text or with the individual disposition of the reader.

1 Cf. Roman Ingarden, *Vom Erkennen des literarischen Kunstwerks* (Tübingen, 1968), pp. 49 ff.
2 For a detailed discussion of this term see Roman Ingarden, *Das literarische Kunstwerk* (Tübingen, 1960), pp. 270 ff.

It is the virtuality of the work that gives rise to its dynamic nature, and this in turn is the precondition for the effects that the work calls forth. As the reader uses the various perspectives offered him by the text in order to relate the patterns and the "schematised views" to one another, he sets the work in motion, and this very process results ultimately in the awakening of responses within himself. Thus, reading causes the literary work to unfold its inherently dynamic character. That this is no new discovery is apparent from references made even in the early days of the novel. Laurence Sterne remarks in *Tristram Shandy*: ". . . no author, who understands the just boundaries of decorum and good-breeding, would presume to think all: The truest respect which you can pay to the reader's understanding, is to halve this matter amicably, and leave him something to imagine, in his turn, as well as yourself. For my own part, I am eternally paying him compliments of this kind, and do all that lies in my power to keep his imagination as busy as my own."[3] Sterne's conception of a literary text is that it is something like an arena in which reader and author participate in a game of the imagination. If the reader were given the whole story, and there were nothing left for him to do, then his imagination would never enter the field, the result would be the boredom which inevitably arises when everything is laid out cut and dried before us. A literary text must therefore be conceived in such a way that it will engage the reader's imagination in the task of working things out for himself, for reading is only a pleasure when it is active and creative. In this process of creativity, the text may either not go far enough, or may go too far, so we may say that boredom and overstrain form the boundaries beyond which the reader will leave the field of play.

The extent to which the "unwritten" part of a text stimulates the reader's creative participation is brought out by an observation of Virginia Woolf's in her study of *Jane Austen*: "Jane Austen is thus a mistress of much deeper emotion than appears upon the surface. She stimulates us to supply what is not there. What she offers is, apparently, a trifle, yet is composed of something that expands in the reader's mind and endows with the most enduring form of life scenes which are outwardly trivial. Always the stress is laid upon character. . . . The turns and twists of the dialogue keep us on the tenterhooks of suspense. Our attention is half upon the present moment, half upon the future. . . . Here, indeed, in this unfinished and in the main inferior story, are all the elements of Jane Austen's greatness."[4] The unwritten aspects of apparently trivial scenes, and the unspoken dialogue

3   Laurence Sterne, *Tristram Shandy* (London, 1956), II, Chap. 11, p. 79.
4   Virginia Woolf, *The Common Reader*, First Series (London, 1957), p. 174.

within the "turns and twists," not only draw the reader into the action, but also lead him to shade in the many outlines suggested by the given situations, so that these take on a reality of their own. But as the reader's imagination animates these "outlines," they in turn will influence the effect of the written part of the text. Thus begins a whole dynamic process: the written text imposes certain limits on its unwritten implications in order to prevent these from becoming too blurred and hazy, but at the same time these implications, worked out by the reader's imagination, set the given situation against a background which endows it with far greater significance than it might have seemed to possess on its own. In this way, trivial scenes suddenly take on the shape of an "enduring form of life." What constitutes this form is never named, let alone explained, in the text, although in fact it is the end product of the interaction between text and reader.

II

The question now arises as to how far such a process can be adequately described. For this purpose a phenomenological analysis recommends itself, especially since the somewhat sparse observations hitherto made of the psychology of reading tend mainly to be psychoanalytical, and so are restricted to the illustration of predetermined ideas concerning the unconscious. We shall, however, take a closer look later at some worthwhile psychological observations.

As a starting point for a phenomenological analysis we might examine the way in which sequent sentences act upon one another. This is of especial importance in literary texts in view of the fact that they do not correspond to any objective reality outside themselves. The world presented by literary texts is constructed out of what Ingarden has called *intentionale Satzkorrelate* (intentional sentence correlatives):

Sentences link up in different ways to form more complex units of meaning that reveal a very varied structure giving rise to such entities as a short story, a novel, a dialogue, a drama, a scientific theory. . . . In the final analysis, there arises a particular world, with component parts determined in this way or that, and with all the variations that may occur within these parts—all this as a purely intentional correlative of a complex of sentences. If this complex finally forms a literary work, I call the whole sum of sequent intentional sentence correlatives the "world presented" in the work.[5]

5   Ingarden, *Vom Erkennen des literarischen Kunstwerks*, p. 29.

This world, however, does not pass before the reader's eyes like a film. The sentences are "component parts" insofar as they make statements, claims, or observations, or convey information, and so establish various perspectives in the text. But they remain only "component parts"— they are not the sum total of the text itself. For the intentional correlatives disclose subtle connections which individually are less concrete than the statements, claims, and observations, even though these only take on their real meaningfulness through the interaction of their correlatives.

How is one to conceive the connection between the correlatives? It marks those points at which the reader is able to "climb aboard" the text. He has to accept certain given perspectives, but in doing so he inevitably causes them to interact. When Ingarden speaks of intentional sentence correlatives in literature, the statements made, or information conveyed in the sentence, are already in a certain sense qualified: the sentence does not consist solely of a statement—which, after all, would be absurd, as one can only make statements about things that exist—but aims at something beyond what it actually says. This is true of all sentences in literary works, and it is through the interaction of these sentences that their common aim is fulfilled. This is what gives them their own special quality in literary texts. In their capacity as statements, observations, purveyors of information, etc., they are always indications of something that is to come, the structure of which is foreshadowed by their specific content.

They set in motion a process out of which emerges the actual content of the text itself. In describing man's inner consciousness of time, Husserl once remarked: "Every originally constructive process is inspired by pre-intentions, which construct and collect the seed of what is to come, as such, and bring it to fruition." [6] For this bringing to fruition, the literary text needs the reader's imagination, which gives shape to the interaction of correlatives foreshadowed in structure by the sequence of the sentences. Husserl's observation draws our attention to a point that plays a not insignificant part in the process of reading. The individual sentences not only work together to shade in what is to come; they also form an expectation in this regard. Husserl calls this expectation "pre-intentions." As this structure is characteristic of all sentence correlatives, the interaction of these correlatives will not be a fulfillment of the expectation so much as a continual modification of it.

6 Edmund Husserl, *Zur Phänomenologie des inneren Zeitewusstseins, Gesammelte Werke* 10 (The Hague, 1966), p. 52.

For this reason, expectations are scarcely ever fulfilled in truly literary texts. If they were, then such texts would be confined to the individualization of a given expectation, and one would inevitably ask what such an intention was supposed to achieve. Strangely enough, we feel that any confirmative effect—such as we implicitly demand of expository texts, as we refer to the objects they are meant to present— is a defect in a literary text. For the more a text individualizes or confirms an expectation it has initially aroused, the more aware we become of its didactic purpose, so that at best we can only accept or reject the thesis forced upon us. More often than not, the very clarity of such texts will make us want to free ourselves from their clutches. But generally the sentence correlatives of literary texts do not develop in this rigid way, for the expectations they evoke tend to encroach on one another in such a manner that they are continually modified as one reads. One might simplify by saying that each intentional sentence correlative opens up a particular horizon, which is modified, if not completely changed, by succeeding sentences. While these expectations arouse interest in what is to come, the subsequent modification of them will also have a retrospective effect on what has already been read. This may now take on a different significance from that which it had at the moment of reading.

Whatever we have read sinks into our memory and is foreshortened. It may later be evoked again and set against a different background with the result that the reader is enabled to develop hitherto unforeseeable connections. The memory evoked, however, can never reassume its original shape, for this would mean that memory and perception were identical, which is manifestly not so. The new background brings to light new aspects of what we had committed to memory; conversely these, in turn, shed their light on the new background, thus arousing more complex anticipations. Thus, the reader, in establishing these interrelations between past, present and future, actually causes the text to reveal its potential multiplicity of connections. These connections are the product of the reader's mind working on the raw material of the text, though they are not the text itself—for this consists just of sentences, statements, information, etc.

This is why the reader often feels involved in events which, at the time of reading, seem real to him, even though in fact they are very far from his own reality. The fact that completely different readers can be differently affected by the "reality" of a particular text is ample evidence of the degree to which literary texts transform reading into a creative process that is far above mere perception of what is written.

The literary text activates our own faculties, enabling us to recreate the world it presents. The product of this creative activity is what we might call the virtual dimension of the text, which endows it with its reality. This virtual dimension is not the text itself, nor is it the imagination of the reader: it is the coming together of text and imagination.

As we have seen, the activity of reading can be characterized as a sort of kaleidoscope of perspectives, preintentions, recollections. Every sentence contains a preview of the next and forms a kind of viewfinder for what is to come; and this in turn changes the "preview" and so becomes a "viewfinder" for what has been read. This whole process represents the fulfillment of the potential, unexpressed reality of the text, but it is to be seen only as a framework for a great variety of means by which the virtual dimension may be brought into being. The process of anticipation and retrospection itself does not by any means develop in a smooth flow. Ingarden has already drawn attention to this fact, and ascribes a quite remarkable significance to it:

Once we are immersed in the flow of *Satzdenken* (sentence-thought), we are ready, after completing the thought of one sentence, to think out the "continuation," also in the form of a sentence—and that is, in the form of a sentence that connects up with the sentence we have just thought through. In this way the process of reading goes effortlessly forward. But if by chance the following sentence has no tangible connection whatever with the sentence we have just thought through, there then comes a blockage in the stream of thought. This hiatus is linked with a more or less active surprise, or with indignation. This blockage must be overcome if the reading is to flow once more.[7]

The hiatus that blocks the flow of sentences is, in Ingarden's eyes, the product of chance, and is to be regarded as a flaw; this is typical of his adherence to the classical idea of art. If one regards the sentence sequence as a continual flow, this implies that the anticipation aroused by one sentence will generally be realized by the next, and the frustration of one's expectations will arouse feelings of exasperation. And yet literary texts are full of unexpected twists and turns, and frustration of expectations. Even in the simplest story there is bound to be some kind of blockage, if only for the fact that no tale can ever be told in its entirety. Indeed, it is only through inevitable omissions that a story will gain its dynamism. Thus whenever the flow is interrupted and we are led off in unexpected directions, the opportunity is given to us to

7 Ingarden, *Vom Erkennen des literarischen Kunstwerks*, p. 32.

bring into play our own faculty for establishing connections—for filling in the gaps left by the text itself.[8]

These gaps have a different effect on the process of anticipation and retrospection, and thus on the "gestalt" of the virtual dimension, for they may be filled in different ways. For this reason, one text is potentially capable of several different realizations, and no reading can ever exhaust the full potential, for each individual reader will fill in the gaps in his own way, thereby excluding the various other possibilities; as he reads, he will make his own decision as to how the gap is to be filled. In this very act the dynamics of reading are revealed. By making his decision he implicitly acknowledges the inexhaustibility of the text; at the same time it is this very inexhaustibility that forces him to make his decision. With "traditional" texts this process was more or less unconscious, but modern texts frequently exploit it quite deliberately. They are often so fragmentary that one's attention is almost exclusively occupied with the search for connections between the fragments; the object of this is not to complicate the "spectrum" of connections, so much as to make us aware of the nature of our own capacity for providing links. In such cases, the text refers back directly to our own preconceptions—which are revealed by the act of interpretation that is a basic element of the reading process. With all literary texts, then, we may say that the reading process is selective, and the potential text is infinitely richer than any of its individual realizations. This is borne out by the fact that a second reading of a piece of literature often produces a different impression from the first. The reasons for this may lie in the reader's own change of circumstances, still, the text must be such as to allow this variation. On a second reading familiar occurrences now tend to appear in a new light and seem to be at times corrected, at times enriched.

In every text there is a potential time-sequence which the reader must inevitably realize, as it is impossible to absorb even a short text in a single moment. Thus the reading process always involves viewing the text through a perspective that is continually on the move, linking up the different phases, and so constructing what we have called the virtual dimension. This dimension, of course, varies all the time we are reading. However, when we have finished the text, and read it again, clearly our extra knowledge will result in a different time-

8 For a more detailed discussion of the function of "gaps" in literary texts see Wolfgang Iser, "Indeterminacy and the Reader's Response in Prose Fiction," *Aspects of Narrative,* English Institute Essays, ed. by J. Hillis Miller (New York, 1971), pp. 1-45.

sequence; we shall tend to establish connections by referring to our awareness of what is to come, and so certain aspects of the text will assume a significance we did not attach to them on a first reading, while others will recede into the background. It is a common enough experience for a person to say that on a second reading he noticed things he had missed when he read the book for the first time, but this is scarcely surprising in view of the fact that the second time he is looking at the text through a different perspective. The time-sequence that he realized on his first reading cannot possibly be repeated on a second reading and this unrepeatability is bound to result in modifications of his reading experience. This is not to say that the second reading is "truer" than the first—they are, quite simply, different: the reader establishes the virtual dimension of the text by realizing a new time-sequence. Thus even on repeated viewings a text allows and, indeed, induces innovative reading.

In whatever way, and under whatever circumstances, the reader may link the different phases of the text together, it will always be the process of anticipation and retrospection that leads to the formation of the virtual dimension, which in turn transforms the text into an experience for the reader. The way in which this experience comes about through a process of continual modification is closely akin to the way in which we gather experience in life. And thus the "reality" of the reading experience can illuminate basic patterns of real experience:

We have the experience of a world, not understood as a system of relations which wholly determine each event, but as an open totality the synthesis of which is inexhaustible. . . . From the moment that experience—that is, the opening on to our *de facto* world—is recognized as the beginning of knowledge, there is no longer any way of distinguishing a level of *a priori* truths and one of factual ones, what the world must necessarily be and what it actually is.[9]

The manner in which the reader experiences the text will reflect his own disposition, and in this respect the literary text acts as a kind of mirror; but at the same time, the reality which this process helps to create is one that will be *different* from his own (since, normally, we tend to be bored by texts that present us with things we already know perfectly well ourselves). Thus we have the apparently paradoxical situation in which the reader is forced to reveal aspects of himself in

9 M. Merleau-Ponty, *Phenomenology of Perception*, trans. Colin Smith (New York, 1962), pp. 219, 221.

order to experience a reality which is different from his own. The impact this reality makes on him will depend largely on the extent to which he himself actively provides the unwritten part of the text, and yet in supplying all the missing links, he must think in terms of experiences different from his own; indeed, it is only by leaving behind the familiar world of his own experience that the reader can truly participate in the adventure the literary text offers him.

III

We have seen that, during the process of reading, there is an active interweaving of anticipation and retrospection, which on a second reading may turn into a kind of advance retrospection. The impressions that arise as a result of this process will vary from individual to individual, but only within the limits imposed by the written as opposed to the unwritten text. In the same way, two people gazing at the night sky may both be looking at the same collection of stars, but one will see the image of a plough, and the other will make out a dipper. The "stars" in a literary text are fixed; the lines that join them are variable. The author of the text may, of course, exert plenty of influence on the reader's imagination—he has the whole panoply of narrative techniques at his disposal—but no author worth his salt will ever attempt to set the *whole* picture before his reader's eyes. If he does, he will very quickly lose his reader, for it is only by activating the reader's imagination that the author can hope to involve him and so realize the intentions of his text.

Gilbert Ryle, in his analysis of imagination, asks: "How can a person fancy that he sees something, without realizing that he is not seeing it?" He answers as follows:

Seeing Helvellyn (the name of a mountain) in one's mind's eye does not entail, what seeing Helvellyn and seeing snapshots of Helvellyn entail, the having of visual sensations. It does involve the thought of having a view of Helvellyn and it is therefore a more sophisticated operation than that of having a view of Helvellyn. It is one utilization among others of the knowledge of how Helvellyn should look, or, in one sense of the verb, it is thinking how it should look. The expectations which are fulfilled in the recognition at sight of Helvellyn are not indeed fulfilled in picturing it, but the picturing of it is something like a rehearsal of getting them fulfilled. So far from picturing involving the having of faint sensations, or wraiths of sensations, it involves missing just what one would be due to get, if one were seeing the mountain.[10]

If one sees the mountain, then of course one can no longer imagine it, and so the act of picturing the mountain presupposes its absence. Similarly, with a literary text we can only picture things which are not there; the written part of the text gives us the knowledge, but it is the unwritten part that gives us the opportunity to picture things; indeed without the elements of indeterminacy, the gaps in the text, we should not be able to use our imagination.[11]

The truth of this observation is borne out by the experience many people have on seeing, for instance, the film of a novel. While reading *Tom Jones*, they may never have had a clear conception of what the hero actually looks like, but on seeing the film, some may say, "That's not how I imagined him." The point here is that the reader of *Tom Jones* is able to visualize the hero virtually for himself, and so his imagination senses the vast number of possibilities; the moment these possibilities are narrowed down to one complete and immutable picture, the imagination is put out of action, and we feel we have somehow been cheated. This may perhaps be an oversimplification of the process, but it does illustrate plainly the vital richness of potential that arises out of the fact that the hero in the novel must be pictured and cannot be seen. With the novel the reader must use his imagination to synthesize the information given him, and so his perception is simultaneously richer and more private; with the film he is confined merely to physical perception, and so whatever he remembers of the world he had pictured is brutally canceled out.

IV

The "picturing" that is done by our imagination is only one of the activities through which we form the "gestalt" of a literary text. We have already discussed the process of anticipation and retrospection, and to this we must add the process of grouping together all the different aspects of a text to form the consistency that the reader will always be in search of. While expectations may be continually modified, and images continually expanded, the reader will still strive, even if unconsciously, to fit everything together in a consistent pattern. "In

10   Gilbert Ryle, *The Concept of Mind* (Harmondsworth, 1968), p. 255.
11   Cf. Iser, pp. 11 ff., 42 ff.

the reading of images, as in the hearing of speech, it is always hard to distinguish what is given to us from what we supplement in the process of projection which is triggered off by recognition . . . it is the guess of the beholder that tests the medley of forms and colours for coherent meaning, crystallizing it into shape when a consistent interpretation has been found." [12] By grouping together the written parts of the text, we enable them to interact, we observe the direction in which they are leading us, and we project onto them the consistency which we, as readers, require. This "gestalt" must inevitably be colored by our own characteristic selection process. For it is not given by the text itself; it arises from the meeting between the written text and the individual mind of the reader with its own particular history of experience, its own consciousness, its own outlook. The "gestalt" is not the true meaning of the text; at best it is a configurative meaning; ". . . comprehension is an individual act of seeing-things-together, and only that." [13] With a literary text such comprehension is inseparable from the reader's expectations, and where we have expectations, there too we have one of the most potent weapons in the writer's armory—illusion.

Whenever "consistent reading suggests itself . . . illusion takes over." [14] Illusion, says Northrop Frye, is "fixed or definable, and reality is at best understood as its negation." [15] The "gestalt" of a text normally takes on (or, rather, is given) this fixed or definable outline, as this is essential to our own understanding, but on the other hand, if reading were to consist of nothing but an uninterrupted building up of illusions, it would be a suspect, if not downright dangerous, process: instead of bringing us into contact with reality, it would wean us away from realities. Of course, there is an element of "escapism" in all literature, resulting from this very creation of illusion, but there are some texts which offer nothing but a harmonious world, purified of all contradiction and deliberately excluding anything that might disturb the illusion once established, and these are the texts that we generally do not like to classify as literary. Women's magazines and the brasher forms of detective story might be cited as examples.

However, even if an overdose of illusion may lead to triviality, this does not mean that the process of illusion-building should ideally be dispensed with altogether. On the contrary, even in texts that appear to resist the formation of illusion, thus drawing our attention to the

12   E. H. Gombrich, *Art and Illusion* (London, 1962), p. 204.
13   Louis O. Mink, "History and Fiction as Modes of Comprehension," *New Literary History*, 1 (1970), 553.
14   Gombrich, p. 278.
15   Northrop Frye, *Anatomy of Criticism* (New York, 1967), pp. 169 f.

cause of this resistance, we still need the abiding illusion that the resistance itself is the consistent pattern underlying the text. This is especially true of modern texts, in which it is the very precision of the written details which increases the proportion of indeterminacy; one detail appears to contradict another, and so simultaneously stimulates and frustrates our desire to "picture," thus continually causing our imposed "gestalt" of the text to disintegrate. Without the formation of illusions, the unfamiliar world of the text would remain unfamiliar; through the illusions, the experience offered by the text becomes accessible to us, for it is only the illusion, on its different levels of consistency, that makes the experience "readable." If we cannot find (or impose) this consistency, sooner or later we will put the text down. The process is virtually hermeneutic. The text provokes certain expectations which in turn we project onto the text in such a way that we reduce the polysemantic possibilities to a single interpretation in keeping with the expectations aroused, thus extracting an individual, configurative meaning. The polysemantic nature of the text and the illusion-making of the reader are opposed factors. If the illusion were complete, the polysemantic nature would vanish; if the polysemantic nature were all-powerful, the illusion would be totally destroyed. Both extremes are conceivable, but in the individual literary text we always find some form of balance between the two conflicting tendencies. The formation of illusions, therefore, can never be total, but it is this very incompleteness that in fact gives it its productive value.

With regard to the experience of reading, Walter Pater once observed: "For to the grave reader words too are grave; and the ornamental word, the figure, the accessory form or colour or reference, is rarely content to die to thought precisely at the right moment, but will inevitably linger awhile, stirring a long 'brainwave' behind it of perhaps quite alien associations."[16] Even while the reader is seeking a consistent pattern in the text, he is also uncovering other impulses which cannot be immediately integrated or will even resist final integration. Thus the semantic possibilities of the text will always remain far richer than any configurative meaning formed while reading. But this impression is, of course, only to be gained through reading the text. Thus the configurative meaning can be nothing but a *pars pro toto* fulfillment of the text, and yet this fulfillment gives rise to the very richness which it seeks to restrict, and indeed in some modern texts, our

16   Walter Pater, *Appreciations* (London, 1920), p. 18.

awareness of this richness takes precedence over any configurative meaning.

This fact has several consequences which, for the purpose of analysis, may be dealt with separately, though in the reading process they will all be working together. As we have seen, a consistent, configurative meaning is essential for the apprehension of an unfamiliar experience, which through the process of illusion-building we can incorporate in our own imaginative world. At the same time, this consistency conflicts with the many other possibilities of fulfillment it seeks to exclude, with the result that the configurative meaning is always accompanied by "alien associations" that do not fit in with the illusions formed. The first consequence, then, is the fact that in forming our illusions, we also produce at the same time a latent disturbance of these illusions. Strangely enough, this also applies to texts in which our expectations are actually fulfilled—though one would have thought that the fulfillment of expectations would help to complete the illusion. "Illusion wears off once the expectation is stepped up; we take it for granted and want more." [17]

The experiments in "gestalt" psychology referred to by Gombrich in *Art and Illusion* make one thing clear: ". . . though we may be intellectually aware of the fact that any given experience *must* be an illusion, we cannot, strictly speaking, watch ourselves having an illusion." [18] Now, if illusion were not a transitory state, this would mean that we could be, as it were, permanently caught up in it. And if reading were exclusively a matter of producing illusion—necessary though this is for the understanding of an unfamiliar experience—we should run the risk of falling victim to a gross deception. But it is precisely during our reading that the transitory nature of the illusion is revealed to the full.

As the formation of illusions is constantly accompanied by "alien associations" which cannot be made consistent with the illusions, the reader constantly has to lift the restrictions he places on the "meaning" of the text. Since it is he who builds the illusions, he oscillates between involvement in and observation of those illusions; he opens himself to the unfamiliar world without being imprisoned it it. Through this process the reader moves into the presence of the fictional world and so experiences the realities of the text as they happen.

In the oscillation between consistency and "alien association," between involvement in and observation of the illusion, the reader is bound to conduct his own balancing operation, and it is this that forms the aesthetic experience offered by the literary text. However,

17 Gombrich, p. 54.
18 *Ibid.*, p. 5.

if the reader were to achieve a balance, obviously he would then no longer be engaged in the process of establishing and disrupting consistency. And since it is this very process that gives rise to the balancing operation, we may say that the inherent non-achievement of balance is a prerequisite for the very dynamism of the operation. In seeking the balance we inevitably have to start out with certain expectations, the shattering of which is integral to the aesthetic experience.

Furthermore, to say merely that "our expectations are satisfied" is to be guilty of another serious ambiguity. At first sight such a statement seems to deny the obvious fact that much of our enjoyment is derived from surprises, from betrayals of our expectations. The solution to this paradox is to find some ground for a distinction between "surprise" and "frustration." Roughly, the distinction can be made in terms of the effects which the two kinds of experiences have upon us. Frustration blocks or checks activity. It necessitates new orientation for our activity, if we are to escape the *cul de sac*. Consequently, we abandon the frustrating object and return to blind impulsive activity. On the other hand, surprise merely causes a temporary cessation of the exploratory phase of the experience, and a recourse to intense contemplation and scrutiny. In the latter phase the surprising elements are seen in their connection with what has gone before, with the whole drift of the experience, and the enjoyment of these values is then extremely intense. Finally, it appears that there must always be some degree of novelty or surprise in all these values if there is to be a progressive specification of the direction of the total act . . . and any aesthetic experience tends to exhibit a continuous interplay between "deductive" and "inductive" operations.[19]

It is this interplay between "deduction" and "induction" that gives rise to the configurative meaning of the text, and not the individual expectations, surprises, or frustrations arising from the different perspectives. Since this interplay obviously does not take place in the text itself, but can only come into being through the process of reading, we may conclude that this process formulates something that is unformulated in the text, and yet represents its "intention." Thus, by reading, we uncover the unformulated part of the text, and this very indeterminacy is the force that drives us to work out a configurative meaning while at the same time giving us the necessary degree of freedom to do so.

As we work out a consistent pattern in the text, we will find our

19 B. Ritchie, "The Formal Structure of the Aesthetic Object," in *The Problems of Aesthetics*, ed. Eliseo Vivas and Murray Krieger (New York, 1965), pp. 230 f.

"interpretation" threatened, as it were, by the presence of other possibilities of "interpretation," and so there arise new areas of indeterminacy (though we may only be dimly aware of them, if at all, as we are continually making "decisions" which will exclude them). In the course of a novel, for instance, we sometimes find that characters, events, and backgrounds seem to change their significance; what really happens is that the other "possibilities" begin to emerge more strongly, so that we become more directly aware of them. Indeed, it is this very shifting of perspectives that makes us feel a novel is that much more "true-to-life." Since it is we ourselves who establish the levels of interpretation and switch from one to another as we conduct our balancing operation, we ourselves impart to the text the dynamic lifelikeness which, in turn, enables us to absorb an unfamiliar experience into our personal world.

As we read, we oscillate to a greater or lesser degree between the building and the breaking of illusions. In a process of trial and error, we organize and reorganize the various data offered us by the text. These are the given factors, the fixed points on which we base our "interpretation," trying to fit them together in the way we think the author meant them to be fitted. "For to perceive, a beholder must *create* his own experience. And his creation must include relations comparable to those which the original producer underwent. They are not the same in any literal sense. But with the perceiver, as with the artist, there must be an ordering of the elements of the whole that is in form, although not in details, the same as the process of organization the creator of the work consciously experienced. Without an act of recreation the object is not perceived as a work of art."[20]

The act of recreation is not a smooth or continuous process, but one which, in its essence, relies on *interruptions* of the flow to render it efficacious. We look forward, we look back, we decide, we change our decisions, we form expectations, we are shocked by their nonfulfillment, we question, we muse, we accept, we reject; this is the dynamic process of recreation. This process is steered by two main structural components within the text: first, a repertoire of familiar literary patterns and recurrent literary themes, together with allusions to familiar social and historical contexts; second, techniques or strategies used to set the familiar against the unfamiliar. Elements of the repertoire are continually backgrounded or foregrounded with a resultant strategic overmagnification, trivialization, or even annihilation of the allusion. This defamiliarization of what the reader thought he

20 John Dewey, *Art as Experience* (New York, 1958), p. 54.

recognized is bound to create a tension that will intensify his expectations as well as his distrust of those expectations. Similarly, we may be confronted by narrative techniques that establish links between things we find difficult to connect, so that we are forced to reconsider data we at first held to be perfectly straightforward. One need only mention the very simple trick, so often employed by novelists; whereby the author himself takes part in the narrative, thus establishing perspectives which would not have arisen out of the mere narration of the events described. Wayne Booth once called this the technique of the "unreliable narrator,"[21] to show the extent to which a literary device can counter expectations arising out of the literary text. The figure of the narrator may act in permanent opposition to the impressions we might otherwise form. The question then arises as to whether this strategy, opposing the formation of illusions, may be integrated into a consistent pattern, lying, as it were, a level deeper than our original impressions. We may find that our narrator, by opposing us, in fact turns us against him and thereby strengthens the illusion he appears to be out to destroy; alternatively, we may be so much in doubt that we begin to question all the processes that lead us to make interpretative decisions. Whatever the cause may be, we will find ourselves subjected to this same interplay of illusion-forming and illusion-breaking that makes reading essentially a recreative process.

We might take, as a simple illustration of this complex process, the incident in Joyce's *Ulysses* in which Bloom's cigar alludes to Ulysses's spear. The context (Bloom's cigar) summons up a particular element of the repertoire (Ulysses's spear); the narrative technique relates them to one another as if they were identical. How are we to "organize" these divergent elements, which, through the very fact that they are put together, separate one element so clearly from the other? What are the prospects here for a consistent pattern? We might say that it is ironic—at least that is how many renowned Joyce readers have understood it.[22] In this case, irony would be the form of organization that integrates the material. But if this is so, what is the object of the irony? Ulysses's spear, or Bloom's cigar? The uncertainty surrounding this simple question already puts a strain on the consistency we have established, and indeed begins to puncture it, especially when other problems make themselves felt as regards the remarkable conjunction

21   Cf. Wayne C. Booth, *The Rhetoric of Fiction* (Chicago, 1963), pp. 211 ff., 339 ff.

22   Richard Ellmann, "Ulysses. The Divine Nobody," in *Twelve Original Essays on Great English Novels*, ed. Charles Shapiro (Detroit 1960), p. 247, classified this particular allusion as "mock-heroic."

of spear and cigar. Various alternatives come to mind, but the variety alone is sufficient to leave one with the impression that the consistent pattern has been shattered. And even if, after all, one can still believe that irony holds the key to the mystery, this irony must be of a very strange nature; for the formulated text does not merely mean the opposite of what has been formulated. It may even mean something that cannot be formulated at all. The moment we try to impose a consistent pattern on the text, discrepancies are bound to arise. These are, as it were, the reverse side of the interpretative coin, an involuntary product of the process that creates discrepancies by trying to avoid them. And it is their very presence that draws us into the text, compelling us to conduct a creative examination not only of the text, but also of ourselves.

This entanglement of the reader is, of course, vital to any kind of text, but in the literary text we have the strange situation that the reader cannot know what his participation actually entails. We know that we share in certain experiences, but we do not know what happens to us in the course of this process. This is why, when we have been particularly impressed by a book, we feel the need to talk about it; we do not want to get away from it by talking about it—we simply want to understand more clearly what it is that we have been entangled in. We have undergone an experience, and now we want to know consciously *what* we have experienced. Perhaps this is the prime usefulness of literary criticism—it helps to make conscious those aspects of the text which would otherwise remain concealed in the subconscious; it satisfies (or helps to satisfy) our desire to talk about what we have read.

The efficacy of a literary text is brought about by the apparent evocation and subsequent negation of the familiar. What at first seemed to be an affirmation of our assumptions leads to our own rejection of them, thus tending to prepare us for a re-orientation. And it is only when we have outstripped our preconceptions and left the shelter of the familiar that we are in a position to gather new experiences. As the literary text involves the reader in the formation of illusion and the simultaneous formation of the means whereby the illusion is punctured, reading reflects the process by which we gain experience. Once the reader is entangled, his own preconceptions are continually overtaken, so that the text becomes his "present" whilst his own ideas fade into the "past"; as soon as this happens he is open to the immediate experience of the text, which was impossible so long as his preconceptions were his "present."

V

In our analysis of the reading process so far, we have observed three important aspects that form the basis of the relationship between reader and text: the process of anticipation and retrospection, the consequent unfolding of the text as a living event, and the resultant impression of lifelikeness.

Any "living event" must, to a greater or lesser degree, remain open. In reading, this obliges the reader to seek continually for consistency, because only then can he close up situations and comprehend the unfamiliar. But consistency-building is itself a living process, in which one is constantly forced to make selective decisions—and these decisions in their turn give a reality to the possibilities which they exclude, insofar as they may take effect as a latent disturbance of the consistency established. This is what causes the reader to be entangled in the text-"gestalt" that he himself has produced.

Through this entanglement the reader is bound to open himself up to the workings of the text, and so leave behind his own preconceptions. This gives him the chance to have an experience in the way George Bernard Shaw once described it: "You have learnt something. That always feels at first as if you had lost something." [23] Reading reflects the structure of experience to the extent that we must suspend the ideas and attitudes that shape our own personality before we can experience the unfamiliar world of the literary text. But during this process, something happens to us.

This "something" needs to be looked at in detail, especially as the incorporation of the unfamiliar into our own range of experience has been to a certain extent obscured by an idea very common in literary discussion: namely, that the process of absorbing the unfamiliar is labelled as the *identification* of the reader with what he reads. Often the term "identification" is used as if it were an explanation, whereas in actual fact it is nothing more than a description. What is normally meant by "identification" is the establishment of affinities between oneself and someone outside oneself—a familiar ground on which we are able to experience the unfamiliar. The author's aim, though, is to convey the experience and, above all, an attitude toward that experience. Consequently, "identification" is not an end in itself, but a stratagem by means of which the author stimulates attitudes in the reader.

This of course is not to deny that there does arise a form of partici-

23   G. B. Shaw, *Major Barbara* (London, 1964), p. 316.

pation as one reads; one is certainly drawn into the text in such a way that one has the feeling that there is no distance between oneself and the events described. This involvement is well summed up by the reaction of a critic to reading Charlotte Brontë's *Jane Eyre*: "We took up *Jane Eyre* one winter's evening, somewhat piqued at the extravagant commendations we had heard, and sternly resolved to be as critical as Croker. But as we read on we forgot both commendations and criticism, identified ourselves with Jane in all her troubles, and finally married Mr. Rochester about four in the morning."[24] The question is how and why did the critic identify himself with Jane?

In order to understand this "experience," it is well worth considering Georges Poulet's observations on the reading process. He says that books only take on their full existence in the reader.[25] It is true that they consist of ideas thought out by someone else, but in reading the reader becomes the subject that does the thinking. Thus there disappears the subject-object division that otherwise is a prerequisite for all knowledge and all observation, and the removal of this division puts reading in an apparently unique position as regards the possible absorption of new experiences. This may well be the reason why relations with the world of the literary text have so often been misinterpreted as identification. From the idea that in reading we must think the thoughts of someone else, Poulet draws the following conclusion: "Whatever I think is a part of my mental world. And yet here I am thinking a thought which manifestly belongs to another mental world, which is being thought in me just as though I did not exist. Already the notion is inconceivable and seems even more so if I reflect that, since every thought must have a subject to think it, this *thought* which is alien to me and yet in me, must also have in me a *subject* which is alien to me. . . . Whenever I read, I mentally pronounce an *I*, and yet the *I* which I pronounce is not myself."[26]

But for Poulet this idea is only part of the story. The strange subject that thinks the strange thought in the reader indicates the potential presence of the author, whose ideas can be "internalized" by the reader: "Such is the characteristic condition of every work which I summon back into existence by placing my consciousness at its disposal. I give it not only existence, but awareness of existence."[27] This would

24 William George Clark, *Fraser's*, December 1849, p. 692, quoted by Kathleen Tillotson, *Novels of the Eighteen-Forties* (Oxford, 1961), pp. 19 f.

25 Cf. Georges Poulet, "Phenomenology of Reading," *New Literary History*, 1 (1969), 54.

26 *Ibid.*, p. 56.

27 *Ibid.*, p. 59.

mean that consciousness forms the point at which author and reader converge, and at the same time it would result in the cessation of the temporary self-alienation that occurs to the reader when his consciousness brings to life the ideas formulated by the author. This process gives rise to a form of communication which, however, according to Poulet, is dependent on two conditions: the life-story of the author must be shut out of the work, and the individual disposition of the reader must be shut out of the act of reading. Only then can the thoughts of the author take place subjectively in the reader, who thinks what he is not. It follows that the work itself must be thought of as a consciousness, because only in this way is there an adequate basis for the author-reader relationship—a relationship that can only come about through the negation of the author's own life-story and the reader's own disposition. This conclusion is actually drawn by Poulet when he describes the work as the self-presentation or materialization of consciousness: "And so I ought not to hesitate to recognize that so long as it is animated by this vital inbreathing inspired by the act of reading, a work of literature becomes (at the expense of the reader whose own life it suspends) a sort of human being, that it̶ ̶ ̶d conscious of itself and constituting itself in me as the subj̶ ̶ ̶own objects." [28] Even though it is difficult to follow such a substantialist conception of the consciousness that constitutes itself in the literary work, there are, nevertheless, certain points in Poulet's argument that are worth holding onto. But they should be developed along somewhat different lines.

If reading removes the subject-object division that constitutes all perception, it follows that the reader will be "occupied" by the thoughts of the author, and these in their turn will cause the drawing of new "boundaries." Text and reader no longer confront each other as object and subject, but instead the "division" takes place within the reader himself. In thinking the thoughts of another, his own individuality temporarily recedes into the background since it is supplanted by these alien thoughts, which now become the theme on which his attention is focussed. As we read, there occurs an artificial division of our personality because we take as a theme for ourselves something that we are not. Consequently when reading we operate on different levels. For although we may be thinking the thoughts of someone else, what we are will not disappear completely—it will merely remain a more or less powerful virtual force. Thus, in reading there are these two levels— the alien "me" and the real, virtual "me"—which are never completely cut off from each other. Indeed, we can only make someone else's

28 *Ibid.*, p. 59.

thoughts into an absorbing theme for ourselves, provided the virtual background of our own personality can adapt to it. Every text we read draws a different boundary within our personality, so that the virtual background (the real "me") will take on a different form, according to the theme of the text concerned. This is inevitable, if only for the fact that the relationship between alien theme and virtual background is what makes it possible for the unfamiliar to be understood.

In this context there is a revealing remark made by D. W. Harding, arguing against the idea of identification with what is read: "What is sometimes called wish-fulfilment in novels and plays can . . . more plausibly be described as wish-formulation or the definition of desires. The cultural levels at which it works may vary widely; the process is the same. . . . It seems nearer the truth . . . to say that fictions contribute to defining the reader's or spectator's values, and perhaps stimulating his desires, rather than to suppose that they gratify desire by some mechanism of vicarious experience." [29] In the act of reading, having to think something that we have not yet experienced does not mean only being in a position to conceive or even understand it; it also means that such acts of conception are possible and successful to the degree that they lead to something being formulated in us. For someone else's thoughts can only take a form in our consciousness if, in the process, our unformulated faculty for deciphering those thoughts is brought into play—a faculty which, in the act of deciphering, also formulates itself. Now since this formulation is carried out on terms set by someone else, whose thoughts are the theme of our reading, it follows that the formulation of our faculty for deciphering cannot be along our own lines of orientation.

Herein lies the dialectical structure of reading. The need to decipher gives us the chance to formulate our own deciphering capacity—i.e., we bring to the fore an element of our being of which we are not directly conscious. The production of the meaning of literary texts—which we discussed in connection with forming the "gestalt" of the text—does not merely entail the discovery of the unformulated, which can then be taken over by the active imagination of the reader; it also entails the possibility that we may formulate ourselves and so discover what had previously seemed to elude our consciousness. These are the ways in which reading literature gives us the chance to formulate the unformulated.

29 D. W. Harding, "Psychological Processes in the Reading of Fiction," in *Aesthetics in the Modern World*, ed. Harold Osborne (London, 1968), pp. 313 f.

8

The Stylistic Approach to Literary History

Michael Riffaterre

L ITERARY history tends to interest itself in the genesis of literature, its contents, its relationship to external reality, the changes in its meaning wrought by time. Style analysis bears upon the text, which is unchanging; upon the internal relationships among words; upon forms rather than contents, upon the literary work as the start of a chain of events, rather than as an end product. The two approaches are thus complementary.

It seems further evident that literary history, ever on the verge of turning into the history of ideas, or sociology, or aesthetics, or the historical study of literary matters—should find natural safeguards in these basic assumptions of style analysis: that literature is made of texts, not intentions; that texts are made of words, not things or ideas; that the literary phenomenon can be defined as the relationship between text and reader, not the relationship between author and text.

Since this ideal complementarity has remained largely unexplored, I should like to examine three areas of literary history wherein style analysis is applicable: the assessment of literary influences, and the relation of texts to trends and genres; the successive meanings of a text for successive generations of readers; the original significance of a text.

My examples are drawn from French literature, since that is the domain I know best.

I. Filiation and Affiliation

Literary historians do pay close attention to the words themselves when they are trying to ascertain which authors a particular writer was imitating, which influences played a role in the genesis of his text, or what genre the text belongs to. They also rely upon external evidence, but they find their ultimate proof of filiation between one work and another in lexical similarities between two or among several texts, or in the identical ordering of their respective components. As proof of generic affinities they take the repeated occurrences in the text of features considered characteristic of the genre. The comparison is regarded as even more convincing if the terms compared are complex, since such complexity appears to exclude random coincidence.

These principles would be unimpeachable were we dealing with things, or were words ever independent of one another. But they are not, except in the artificial context of a dictionary. Even before being encoded within a text, words exist in our minds only in groups, in remarkably rigid associative sequences: nouns habitually go with adjectives or verbs that explicitly actualize their implicit semantic features. Entire sentences become clichés because they contain a stylistic feature that is deemed worth preserving. Finally, larger groups develop what may be called descriptive systems: [1] they are built of nouns, adjectives, ready-made sentences, clichés; stereotyped figures, arranged around a kernel word that fits a mental model of the reality represented by that word. Thus several systems of commonplaces have crystallized around the word *woman*. One of them, for example, made out of set phrases and sentences, is a list of the beauties of an ideal woman; this system has been widely used in literature—e.g. as a frame or base for feminine allegories, or as a frame or reference in love poetry. So well constructed are these systems that mention of one characteristic lexical or syntactic component is usually enough to identify the whole and can indeed be substituted for the whole.

Thanks to such groupings, even complex similarities may not prove anything. Many sources have been assigned to texts because of identical wording, when in reality these are ordinary clichés. Baudelaire specialists are convinced that an obscure poem is the source of the words, in *Hymne à la Beauté*: *Que tu viennes du ciel ou de l'Enfer, qu'importe, O Beauté*. An occasion to marvel that he would stoop so low to borrow an expression of his moral indifference. [2] In fact the phrase is found all over in the Romantics: it is a commonplace way of proclaiming that aesthetic value is independent of ethics—rather a cocky repudiation of Classicism, which held the two inseparable. The cliché may be banteringly used of a woman—angel or demon, who cares?—or, in tragic accents, of Byron's Satanism. [3] The tone does not matter: the point

---

1 On these, see my papers: "Le Poème comme représentation," *Poétique*, 4 (1970), and "Modèles de la phrase littéraire" in *Problems of Textual Analysis*, ed P. R. Léon (Montreal, 1971), pp. 133-51.

2 See Antoine Adam's critical edition of *Les Fleurs du Mal* (Paris, 1961), pp. 301-2.

3 The woman is Herodias in Heine's *Atta Troll*, cap. xix. Byron's devotee is Lamartine, *Méditations*, II, ii: "Esprit mystérieux, mortel, ange ou démon, Qui que tu sois, Byron, bon ou fatal génie, J'aime de tes concerts la sauvage harmonie."

is that the statement reflects the spirit of an epoch, that it cannot be used to demonstrate Baudelaire's borrowing habits, and that it simply confirms once again the poet's Romanticism.[4]

Similarly, the fact that the same descriptive system appears in two texts does not prove influence, nor does it prove that any such influence, if real, is of significance, because the system is only prefabricated language, so to speak. What counts is the use to which it is put. Thus, another poem of Baudelaire's, *Bohémiens en Voyage*, is interpreted by literary historians as a transposition from the visual arts, the model being an etching by Callot.[5] There are indeed many similarities of detail between the print and the poem, but these could be due simply to a parallel progression of the same system derived in both cases from the word *gypsies*. Let us assume that Callot is the proven source.[6] The fact remains that this "influence" is not relevant to literary history.

First, nothing in Baudelaire's description is so precisely oriented as to make the reader connect the poem with Callot: the connection is at best a chance encounter, the lucky find of a scholar,[7] and so an addition to the experience of the poem rather than a deduction from it. On the contrary, there are details in the poem that are not in the etching—a cricket watching the caravan, the goddess Cybele helping the travelers on their way, etc.

Second, everything in the poem, including the aberrant details, points up the superimposition of two structures. Whereas Callot uses his gypsies as an exercise in the picturesque, Baudelaire makes his description a code into which he translates something else—the theme of the Quest. The gypsies are nomads par excellence. But they are also symbols of Man's yearning for esoteric knowledge: not only because of their status as the poor man's prophets, but because nineteenth-century mythology still associates them with Egypt, as a country and as the land of the Occult. Baudelaire retains the features of the descriptive system which emphasize this symbolism: he calls them *tribu prophétique*. He shows them dreaming unattainable dreams (*chimères absentes*). Cybele *qui les aime* is significantly described in something like a Moses or Sinai

---

4 Which is proved a thousandfold. But the detail is still important: the same cliché, mistakenly believed to be Baudelaire's own coinage, is regarded by some as an indication of his Augustinian ethics: M. A. Ruff, *L'Esprit du mal et l'esthétique baudelairienne* (Paris, 1955), p. 335.

5 See M. Menemencioglu, "Le Thème des Bohémiens en Voyage dans la peinture et la poésie de Cervantès à Baudelaire," *Cahiers de l'Association des Études françaises*, XVIII (1966), 227-38.

6 Which is likely, since Baudelaire's gypsies, like Callot's, carry weapons. From what we can deduce from the various texts on the tribe, this is not a feature of the descriptive system.

7 Jean Pommier, *Dans les Chemins de Baudelaire* (Paris, 1945), p. 293.

code: for them she turns the desert green, for them she strikes a rock and water gushes forth—these gypsies become Hebrews in search of a promised Canaan. Indeed, the Canaan opened up to them in the last line is

L'empire familier des ténèbres futures

which we are free to interpret as Death or cosmic mystery.

At this point the reader is compelled to recognize in the poem a variant of the theme of the Human Caravan trudging through the desert of life towards its ultimate destiny. A theme much belabored in Romantic and post-Romantic poetry and one especially important to Baudelaire, who pours forth an endless variety of images of Life as a voyage Thither. The gypsy variant makes it a spiritual quest, and this places the poem squarely in the Orphic tradition.

These are the significant historical relationships. The similarity to Callot is limited to the lexical level. The truly meaningful likeness resides in an arrangement of the words at the higher level of syntax: the words are just "gypsy language," their ordering is regulated by the underlying structure of the caravan theme. Every stylistic stress (every point at which the systems of gypsy theme and human caravan theme coincide) is a key to the meaning, a guide for proper decoding of the poem.

Only by closely scrutinizing the structure of the poem can we arrive at a segmentation of its elements that will characterize this poem alone. Any preconceived segmentation—as by comparing words without regard to their syntax—is doomed to failure.

This is verified when we seek the significance of a text in its relationship to a genre. My example will be *Vénus Anadyomène*, a Rimbaud sonnet.[8] The deceptive title invites us to a rather nauseating spectacle: an ugly, misshapen female emerging from a bathtub of dubious cleanliness. On her fat hindquarters are engraved the words *Clara Venus*. Every term used to describe her body is calculated to unsettle the reader yet further with its unappetizing explicitness; all of which terminates fittingly with a picture of the hag's backside adorned with an anal ulcer. A sort of aesthetic climax is attained in the last line, which focuses on the ulcer.

Most exegetes have had recourse to Rimbaud's biography in their efforts to explain the poem. They seize upon the evidence we have of his homosexuality, although such evidence is foreign and exterior to the text; they find here an explosion of misogyny.[9] Other critics, while

---

8 Dated July 27, 1870. At this period Rimbaud had not yet developed the aesthetics he practiced in *Saison en Enfer* and *Illuminations*.

9 See e.g. Jacques Plessen, *Promenade et poésie* (The Hague, 1967), pp. 37, 121, 158.

not wholly excluding this personal approach, rightly concern themselves with the poem rather than the poet. They interpret it as an exercise in poetic Realism, or even Naturalism. They base their argument, of course, upon the many revolting or unpleasant details: the
assumption is that these details implicitly guarantee the fullness and
objectivity of the description, since no prudery has blurred or censored
it and no convention of aesthetic conformism has deflected the in-
discreet gaze of the observer. Another supporting argument—a specious one, though it exemplifies a common practice of pseudo-historicism
(*pseudo* because it turns contemporaneity into causality)—is that although French Naturalism was hardly dawning in 1870, when the
poem was written, the Goncourt brothers had already made some literary incursions into the realm of pathology (*Germinie Lacerteux* appeared in 1865), and François Coppée had just published his first collection of poems preoccupied with the lives of the humble, the pathos
of poverty and ugliness. In his *Les Soeurs Vatard* (1879), Huysmans
was to depict women sweatshop workers in the naturalistic vein tem-
pered with a humor unknown to Zola; Rimbaud's Venus is certainly
closer to Huysmans' girls than to the Goddess risen from the sea. Further to bolster the case for hardcore realism in the poem, a source is
alleged: Glatigny, a minor Coppée, had published a collection of poems
ten years before. Most of them were in the Parnasse manner, but quite
a few versified his experience as a vagrant, with glimpses into the special world Toulouse-Lautrec was later to make his domain. This blend
was not unlike Rimbaud's early work—which has prompted critics to
compare the two. It so happens that Glatigny describes a whore sitting
on a patron's lap, and that she is tattooed somewhat like Rimbaud's
bather. True, her tattoo is only on her arm, but then the shift down-
wards in the case of his Venus only proves Rimbaud was going one step
further in "emancipation . . . towards an unflinching realism."[10]

At most, such comparisons can account for certain elements of the
poem separately, perhaps even within their respective contexts, but they
cannot account for their function as components of the overall structure. Only such a structure can give a poem its particular meaning.
Hence it is only to such a structure that literary history may hook its
chains of causality. The sense of the poem, I believe, is a *laus Veneris*
done *a contrario*. It reads like a description of a paragon of feminine
beauty. The picture unfolds detail by detail in the stereotyped order
of female nude delineations (also the order in which the body-parts

10 Suzanne Bernard, in her critical edition of Rimbaud's *Oeuvres* (Paris, 1960),
p. 373. Glatigny's poem (*Les Vignes folles* [1860], "Les Antres malsains," ii-iii)
was unearthed by J. Gengoux, *La Pensée poétique de Rimbaud* (Paris, 1950), p. 18.

emerge from water—a scene endlessly reiterated in the visual arts). Except that here each detail is endowed with a minus sign. The grammar of the poem follows its own semantic rule: every salient trait of beauty must be stated negatively. The destructive effect of this consistent reversal is heightened by polarization; the starting point here for the creation of ugliness is not just any canon of feminine beauty, it is a hyperbolic model—to wit, Aphrodite being born. The mechanism of this inversion is a dual reading: as we decipher the text, we compare it with an implied standard which is nothing lesser than the Botticellian grace of a Goddess freshly sprung out of the sea.

Once the decor has been laid—it is also symbolically inverted word for word (instead of a rising from the sea, we have a sluggish emergence from a bathtub explicitly likened to a coffin)—the poem rolls forward as nothing more than a sequence of clichés organized on an ideal model of the body as an aesthetic archetype, each cliché being transformed into its antiphrasis. A heroine's hair must be blond and soft, fragrant and fluffy; the cliché generates the greasy stiffness of *cheveuz fortement pommadés* (similarly, in a famous phantasmagoria of Théophile Gautier's, a Goldilocks succubus is unmasked as a sorceress with a head of *raides mèches*).[11] The stereotyped white swanlike neck, sloping shoulders, svelte body and lithe waist generate, point by point, a *col gras et gris*, protruding shoulder blades, a fat back *qui rentre et ressort*. The usual erotic apotheosis—the curve of glorious buttocks (Rimbaud uses it elsewhere for a real Aphrodite)[12]—turns into its antithesis, a big broad beam, plus the sick detail confirming the polarization I have hinted at:

> . . . large croupe
> Belle hideusement d'un ulcère à l'anus.

So that none of the descriptive details has meaning, and none is compelling, except as part of the whole. It is the existence of an established, recognized model that permits a total inversion at one fell swoop—replacement of plus by minus—without the reader's being allowed to grow confused and forget the positive original. As with any structure, if you modify one component, it entails modification of the whole system.

This interrelationship of all the parts obviously makes it impossible for any explanation (historical or otherwise) of separate parts to affect our understanding of the text. Thus, even if Rimbaud must have remembered the tattooed arm of Glatigny's whore in order to think of dec-

---

11   Gautier, *Albertus* (1832), cv.

12   *Poésies*, "Soleil et Chair" (written only a few months before, April 29, 1870): "Cypris . . . cambrant les rondeurs splendides de ses reins."

orating his bather's back, that does not mean her rear end is to the other girl's arm what Naturalism is to Realism.

This detail must be read like all the others in the antiphrastic sequence, *a contrario*: the tattooed behind (no ordinary amorous tattoo, mind you, but an incongruous cliché suggestive of *celestial* Venus) is an inversion of a well-established cliché—the stigmata of election (inscription, light, imprint of the kiss of queen or goddess) that the chosen bears upon his forehead. From the grotesque medieval sculptures of two-faced demons to Rabelais' exuberances to modern (or perennial) vulgar jokes, we have ample proof that the "ass" is the symbolic homologue of the face.

If this last point is well taken, by the way, it must be the clincher. Were the unwholesome bather a naturalistic portrait, every detail being valid only with reference to a real or probable woman, then the learned writing on her rear would be a most gratuitous anomaly. Once you have a wayward detail in any portrait intended to look real, the whole *vraisemblable* falls quite to pieces. As I read it, on the contrary, *Clara Venus* is altogether natural and consistent within the allegory. Even though the allegory is upside down.

Once we adopt the structural view, we comprehend the poem as an organized whole, wherein all the parts have the same meaning—a meaning summarized in the words of the last line: *hideously beautiful*. We can now safely return to literary history and assign the poem its true place in the evolution of French poetry. We are not dealing here with Realism, but with a genre developed during the Renaissance and related to the Baroque. I am thinking of the monograph-poem celebrating some part or function of the body, discoursing upon some disease or deformity or vice. That is, the application of the *encomium* to some trivial or ugly object—like Du Bellay's *Hymne à la Surdité* (1558). In other words, a *contreblason*. Rimbaud is not attacking the modern world, as those would have it who see the sonnet as the counterpart of another poem in praise of Greek beauty. He is not in effect saying: look at what our Iron Age has done to classical forms.[13] The *contreblason* does not stand to encomiastic verse in the same relation as satire does; it is not a moral weapon or a tool of aesthetic controversy. Rimbaud's poem is not against something, it is a respondence to a given form. It is not a satire, or a take-off, not even an opposing of themes (e.g. classicism vs. modernity). It is an exercise in grammatical transformation. And perhaps *contreblason* is too narrow a term to use;

13 An interpretation skillfully argued for by W. M. Frohock, *Rimbaud's Poetic Practice* (Cambridge, Mass., 1963) pp. 52-53. There is such a motif: it was found in Coppée (see Rimbaud's *Oeuvres complètes*, Pléiade ed., p. 657), and I see it in Baudelaire's "J'aime le souvenir de ces époques nues."

perhaps it would be preferable to relate this text to Baroque poems on the theme of Topsyturvydom.

And perhaps, again, it is wrong to classify the text in relation to the past, since such classification reflects the preoccupation of literary history with cycles. It is tempting indeed to connect up the form we are analyzing with something preceding it that may be similarly analyzable, and thus to find in *Venus Anadyomène* the resurrection of a genre— some muscle-flexing by a young man who has just escaped an educational system focussed upon French literature of the past. But it will most likely profit us more to classify this *contreblason* as an omen of developments to come. The poem will then take its place alongside Lautréamont's innovations—a trend Jarry carried forward, and later the Surrealists. That is, the exploitation of the associative potentials of words. It is pure verbal creation, the arranging of words in accordance with verbal models rather than with reality. The poet draws the mirror-image of another text: just as the physicist deduces antimatter from the known properties of matter, the poet creates an anti-representation.

What we have said so far makes it clear that any historical comparison carried out word by word, or sentence by sentence, or even system by system, must be an unsophisticated method and a misleading one. Literary influence or classification can be established only by the discovery of structural parallelism. Which means that textual components should not be compared, but rather their functions.[14]

II. The History of Successive Readings

Important as it may be to find out where a novel, a poem or a play belongs in the history of literature, what trend it reflects, what genre it exemplifies, there can be no doubt that these questions remain peripheral to the problem of the very existence of the literary work. That is, to the question of whether its mechanisms work and how they work. Aesthetic or sociological definition must here yield to the test of effectiveness: no work is a work of art if it does not command the response of a public. This response may be delayed or suspended by accidents of history, but it must come some time and it must be such a response as can be explained only by the formal characteristics of the text. The response of the reader to a text is *the* causality pertinent to the explanation of literature.

The effectiveness of a text may be defined as the degree of its perceptibility by the reader: the more it attracts his attention, the better it resists his manipulations and withstands the attrition of his successive

---

14 This would effectively put an end to this kind of source studies rightly criticized by D. N. Archibald, *New Literary History*, I (1970), 442.

readings, the more of a monument it is (rather than just an ephemeral act of communication), and therefore the more literary. Now the nature of this perceptibility changes according to whether the reader is a contemporary of the text or comes to it later.

Later generations of readers have more problems to solve than the original readers had. Regrettably, this fact is often used to support the argument that the "first" meaning of the text is the standard and later readings must be inferior. This is an error, because successive interpretations of a monument are inherent in its monumentality: it was built to last and to go on eliciting responses. Later readings are as much part of the phenomenon as were the initial ones.

There is, to be sure, no dearth of *Nachleben* studies. Unfortunately, most of them are devoted to mapping variations in the popularity of the text. And they assign such variations to competition from later works, to upheavals in literary taste or sociological conditions, and above all to the evolution of aesthetics. Meanwhile the most important factor is being neglected or downgraded: that is, the evolution of language. Which is where style analysis must redress the balance.

The two types of perceptibility can be distinguished by the differences between codes. The linguistic code used by the early readers is the same, or almost the same, as that of the text. The linguistic codes used by later readers differ more and more, as time goes by, from the code of the text. The change may be drastic if the text employed a specialized code such as the conventional poetic language of French Classicism. In such cases an aesthetic revolution means a sudden linguistic break of a kind not observable in the evolution of everyday usage (let us add here that these breaks do not coincide with political changes: the French Revolution left untouched the aesthetics and poetic language of French Classicism. Nor do such breaks come simultaneously with the rise of new literary movements: French Romantics went on using much of Classical language for a long long time). Descriptive systems, clichés, and so forth, offer some resistance to change and may withstand it, but shifts in the meaning of individual words alter the meaning of such systems nonetheless, and their relationships with cultural background also change. All this comes to pass, of course, outside the literary text. For the text does not alter, and this unchanging form preserves within its structural integrity the code used by the author. A *Nachleben* study, to be relevant, must obviously focus upon the widening chasm that time has opened up between the immutable code of the text and the codes adopted by successive generations of readers. Equally obviously, style analysis can do the job by comparing two readings of the same sentence: one in the code of the context, one in the code of the later reader.

In some rare cases the analyst will conclude that the code has so evolved that the gap can no longer be closed. The text is now a dead letter. In one of his early poems—an ode on a naval battle during the Greek War of Independence—Victor Hugo tries to suggest the highly picturesque, intensely Oriental chaos in which the Turkish fleet is wallowing. He gives a long list of boat types, including *yachts* and *jonques*.[15] British pleasure boats and Chinese vessels hardly belong in the Ottoman Navy; but this incongruity is startling only to the modern French reader. For these who first read *Les Orientales*, all you needed to create the illusion of Turkish reality was a strange verbal shape. *Yacht* is completely alien to French spelling because it combines the rare initial *y* with the final consonantic cluster. *Jonque* has a sound rather unique: it does not rhyme with anything if you count the initial consonant, and if you do not, it rhymes with and resembles only six other words in the whole French lexicon—two of them obsolete and three others grammatical words not employed, stressed or connected up like fullfledged words. Today's French readers are reluctant to believe in Hugo's Turkish fleet. Their aesthetic rejects this sort of epic anyway, but that might mean only a temporary eclipse. The fact is that the poem is quite extinct, and for an evident stylistic reason. Morphologically and phonetically, *yacht* and *jonque* are as foreign as ever. But the meaning of that foreignness has changed. The French today are more familiar than they were in 1829 with other parts of the world, or rather with assorted representations of those other parts. In consequence, a word's foreignness is semantically more often oriented towards the reality the word actually stands for. In the case of *yacht* and *jonque*, the foreignness is no longer "free," it can no longer be used to conjure up just any vague exoticism.

But only in a few extreme instances does the effect of stylistic facts entirely disappear. Neologisms are very vulnerable: a new coinage will go unperceived by later readers if in the meantime it has been assimilated into common usage. Where the stylistic structure of the text rests upon such forms, it is bound to become invisible with time. It may happen that a new coinage in an ancient text is later interpreted as an archaism (whether or not it was assimilated at any point in the history of the language, but mostly if it was not). The effect remains, but with a different content (perhaps *orientation* would be the better word). Archaisms are also threatened: an archaism in a Renaissance text, for instance (let us say a word already obsolete in the sixteenth century and at that time used to a certain effect because of its obsoleteness), will be likely to blend today into its context, since the other words of that context are obsolete *for us*. Literary allusions are prone to suffer the same fate.

15 Hugo, *Les Orientales* (1829), "Navarin," lines 175 and 181.

But even where shifts in the code have destroyed a component of the stylistic structure, the text still contains the forms corresponding to that structure. Thus some effects can still be felt in most cases, either because these forms are still active, albeit in a different way, or because the context still preserves peripheral evidence of their original power.

The motifs of *basalt* and the *basaltic cave* are a good example of a form that has continued active. Both were frequent in early Romanticism, especially in French literature, although neither had any particular symbolic significance. Baudelaire still uses the basaltic cave as a simile to enhance the magic of another life remembered:

> J'ai longtemps habité sous de vastes portiques
> Que les soleils marins teignaient de mille feux,
> Et que leurs grands piliers, droits et majestueux,
> Rendaient pareils, le soir, aux grottes basaltiques. [16]

Footnotes never fail to explain that Baudelaire simply copied two of Hugo's lines, which suggests that the simile evokes nothing more per se. Such an "explanation" only pushes the problem further back, since in the earlier text the cave is already said to exemplify the motifs of poetic inspiration. [17] There are many more texts, in fact, which allude to that cave, and all of them depict it as a thing of beauty.

Literary history tells us only where the stereotype originated: it started with the Ossian fad which familiarized European readers with Fingal's cave. The underlying assumption is that the image is dead unless you recollect its origin. But experience has shown me that it still stirs the reader. This continuing effect is due to linguistic and semantic features which have survived long after the Staffa cave faded from our memories. First of all, the Staffa cave became poetic material and remained so longer than other Ossianesque paraphernalia, because, I suggest, geology had been fashionable since the eighteenth century. It enriched the literary lexicon with technical words used literally or metaphorically. Two of these, *granite* and *basalt*, proved especially successful. *Basalt* (in French, *basalte*) still holds its own, though French readers are by now inured to its technical strangeness, because it is such an exceptional word: it rhymes with only seven other words, all of them foreign borrowings. [18] Second, *grotte basaltique* survives independent of the Caledonian setting, because its descriptive system is built upon a

16 *Fleurs du Mal*, "La Vie antérieure" (1855).

17 Hugo, *Odes et Ballades*, "La Fée et la Péri" (1824). Says the fairy personifying the poetry of the Occident: "J'ai la grotte enchantée aux piliers basaltiques, Où la mer de Staffa brise un flot inégal." All editors find it necessary to explain where Staffa is and why the cave is later called Fingal's palace.

18 They are foreign, and they are perceived as such (except for *halte*).

striking semantic structure, the self-contradictory association between nature and artifice. Clichés like *architecture naturelle* correspond to the peculiar basaltic shapes; these clichés derive their impact from the all-powerful *coincidentia oppositorum*. Here the disappearance of a theme has left behind a semantic structure that remains valid despite our inability to relate it to a forgotten mythology.

Sometimes even the meaning disappears or loses its importance, and yet the literary structure survives, because the emptied words still perform a function very much in the manner of grammatical words. Nineteenth- and twentieth-century novels, for example, offer details that seem to be there only to establish a setting and add to the verisimilitude of a description. Such is *embrasure*—"window recess." The frequency of this word is out of all proportion to its descriptive value. But that recess is a stage set for a passionate exchange of confidences, it is even a trysting place, or it may be a vantage point from which the contemplative or satirical observer watches the social drama going forward in the drawing room.[19] Today these functions no longer have any connection with reality: the role of *embrasure* in the texts has survived its disappearance from architecture. Walls have grown thinner and rooms so much smaller that it is no longer possible to hold clandestine conferences in window nooks. In common parlance, actually, *embrasure* is used by hardly anyone but architects; *fenêtre* is quite enough for all practical purposes. Nevertheless *embrasure* lives on in the novel as a convention—that is where you push or pull somebody you want to have to yourself, that is where you withdraw to be by yourself. Its semantic value is all but nil, its reference to reality a thing of the past. But its constant recurrence in contexts where *embrasure* was linked to verbs that singled actors out or set them apart—this was enough to turn it into a kind of linguistic marker. In the narrative sequence, the word (or its periphrastic equivalent) is nothing but a conventional symbol of a situational transition (from several characters to one or two only, the two acting as one), or of a shift in the narrative (a functional shift of the character from actor to observer, and thus a shift from the viewpoint of insider to that of outsider, etc.). As such symbol, the word works entirely within the syntagm and is not affected by changes in the code or in the reality it is supposed to represent.

19 The only examples lexicographers were able to dig up for the entry *embrasure* are, significantly: *Dictionnaire de l'Académie* (1835), "il m'a parlé dans l'embrasure"; *Grand Dictionnaire du XIXe siècle* (1870), "causer à voix basse dans l'embrasure." Balzac uses *embrasure* in this sense very often; one example has been commented upon by Roland Barthes, *S/Z* (Paris, 1970), pp. 28-35, who does not see the stereotyped nature of the device, however. A good illustration of the sort of complex intrigue carried on in window recesses can be found in Zola, *Son Excellence Eugène Rougon* (*Romans*, Pléiade ed., II, 33, 49-51).

And finally there is the case where words have completely lost whatever meaning or functional value they had when they were encoded in the text: yet style analysis will be able to detect secondary structures they have generated within their context. These have remained immune to changes in the language. Thus, in a passage dismissing *Les Fleurs du Mal* as just a far-out bit of exaggerated Romantic hysteria, Sainte-Beuve damns Baudelaire by praising him for building at the tip of a deserted peninsula

. . . ce singulier kiosque, fait en marqueterie, d'une originalité concertée et composite, qui, depuis quelque temps, attire les regards à la pointe extrême du Kamtschatka romantique. [20]

In modern French, however, *kiosque* is only an ornate bandstand for open air concerts in public parks, or else a newsstand. Literary history could account for the discrepancy; it could point out that for the French Romantics *kiosque* symbolized bizarre Oriental architectural forms and that this function was reinforced by the absolutely unique phonetic sequence of the word, to say nothing of its spelling. At that period it was as typical and representative as *minaret* or *mosque*. Native use of this type of building as a cosy hideaway in seraglio gardens gave rise to another chain of associations: the word also came to connote refined, clandestine pleasures. Both symbolic values are exploited by Sainte-Beuve (in this particular kiosk, you smoke hashish and read E. A. Poe!). But the purely historical explanation misses the point that the image needs no resuscitation. The sentence surrounding *kiosque* still reflects the evocative power that the word alone would no longer possess. That power it still has here precisely because the word is not perceived in isolation but in its indissoluble relationship to that context. The word is only the kernel of a satellite group of adjectives (*bizarre, fort orné, fort tourmenté, mystérieux, singulier*) which literally make explicit the semantic components of the Romantic kiosk. Moreover, and more important, *Kamtschatka* (a common hyperbole for Siberia as an image of remoteness or wilderness) [21] graphemically and phonetically takes up and emphasizes the sounds that once made *kiosque* an expressive utterance. By common reversal of effects, *kiosque* now seems to be here only to reinforce *Kamtschatka* phonetically.

These clusters of concurring devices are perhaps the most frequent defenses of the language of a text against the growing estrangement of

20 Sainte-Beuve, *Nouveaux Lundis* (Paris, 1863), I, 398.
21 Speaking of E. T. A. Hoffmann, Sainte-Beuve had described his exploration of new inspirational forms in terms of Hyperborean lands (*Premiers Lundis*, Pléiade ed., I, 383).

the reader's language. And yet usually they are still ignored even by stylisticians.[22]

III. Reconstruction

Reconstructing the first, original meaning of the text used to be an attempt to restore it to its author. Reconstruction was thought successful if it came close to the author's intent. And certainly there are many literary historians who still believe this to be a fruitful undertaking. I shall not try to demonstrate anew the intentional fallacy. Since my subject is the contribution of stylistics to diachronic analysis, and since the stylistician's postulate is that the impact felt by the reader is all that counts, I shall not spend time discussing a method that disregards effects unforeseen by the writer. For the stylistician, the original meaning of a text is revealed by the reactions it elicited from its contemporary readers. We cannot hope to reconstitute the code they used, at least not well enough for our purposes, and evidence of their reactions is also fragmentary. But the code changes are mostly of a semantic nature, as was apparent in the examples discussed in section II. Our problem is that we have lost contact with the descriptive systems that the text referred to in its early life, and that we no longer know which words generated which system, or which words served as metonymic substitutes for a whole system. We read the same sentence as the first readers, but we have lost its echo. To that problem literary history provides only a partial solution: thematology. It is incomplete because *Stoffgeschichte* restores only themes and motifs, that is, descriptive or narrative sequences whose literary use is restricted by the fact that they are already stylistically marked (by their symbolism, their connection with a genre, etc.).[23]

Style analysis should contribute to thematology in the future by including all descriptive systems in these compilations arranged according to type, indicating their generic and chronological distribution.[24]

22   I myself have tried to analyze the mechanisms whereby the effect of neologisms is maintained in literary texts even after they have been assimilated into common usage (*Romanic Review*, XLIV [1953], 282-89).

23   The solution is incomplete also in that thematology summarizes themes without regard to their structures, and this should be corrected by establishing typologies on the model of Vladimir Propp's pioneering *Morphology of the Folk-Tale*.

24   A task less formidable than it appears, since it could consist of simply reordering the dictionary. We do have usable evidence in the examples compiled by lexicographers (such as the *Grand Dictionnaire du XIXe siècle*, a veritable compendium of French myths), and in Renaissance compilations of *exempla* (such as those by Ravisius Textor, Rhodiginus, etc.).

Systems should not be listed in skeletal form, but should be accompanied by their clichés, preferred sentence types, available substitutes, metonymic mechanisms, etc. In short, we should be given the structures and also the words that actualize them, and their potential for generating associative chains.

Enlarging the corpus is not enough, however. Ever since its beginnings, thematology has been justly criticized for generalizing. In the process of identifying and classifying themes, it has tended to eliminate everything distinctive and unique in the treatment of these themes. The chain of historical causality stretches from the author (and from the mythology and the language out of which he picked his themes) to the text. The explanation is thus purely genetic. It shows what raw material the text was made of, not the artifact that was made out of it. There is no way of telling what in the general theme is relevant to the text and to that text only, since the historian has had to cleanse the textual variant of all its peculiarities in order to identify the theme and then to fit it into a general category of thematic models.

The cardinal change wrought by style analysis is that this procedure is reversed. Starting from the text and faithfully retracing the reader's steps, the analyst goes back to the theme—or rather, to the descriptive system—not simply to check the particular case in hand against its composite model, but to sort out and discard all the components of the model that the text has not actualized. The structure of the system, unaffected by the fact that some of its slots remain empty, makes clear the relationship between the slots that are actually filled—and this yields up their meaning. Further, one of the slots may be filled with a word that does not belong to the system. Then that word receives a new meaning from the function that corresponds to the position the word occupies in the system—a mechanism that accounts for much of literary symbolism.

For instance, the first stanza of Baudelaire's sonnet entitled *Obsession* is a complex of three fragmentary systems: forest, cathedral, Man.

> Grands bois, vous m'effrayez comme des cathédrales;
> Vous hurlez comme l'orgue; et dans nos coeurs maudits,
> Chambres d'éternel deuil où vibrent de vieux râles,
> Répondent les échos de vos *De profundis*. [25]

Without reconstruction, the reader has only the written line to guide him. It provides him with a plain statement that he is free to agree or disagree with. His attitude and his emotive reactions will result from the chance meeting between the experience *he* has had of forests and of churches, and the experience encoded here. The likelihood is that the

25 *Les Fleurs du Mal*, LXXIX (1860).

pathos will repel him as a too obvious *parti-pris*, as too heavily pessimistic. This emotional response will in turn be rationalized into a pseudological decision: he will say Baudelaire's comparisons are gratuitous.

With the help of thematology alone, our reader will learn that there is a Romantic theme which fits in here: the forest as a church (Nature is God's temple), or in reverse form the Gothic Cathedral as a forest (sacred architecture was born of the effort to imitate the natural temple, hence its authenticity as a monument to faith). Up to a point, of course, this removes the stigma of gratuitousness. The similarity between a Gothic church and the forest is no longer questionable, it is not just one man's opinion. It refers to an accepted code. The consensus omnium is guaranteed by the place of this code within the corpus of French myths. In a word, literary history here affords the reader proof that the conventions of the text are acceptable. It informs him as to the frequency and distribution of the system(s) used in the text, as to the popularity or prestige it (they) enjoyed. The reader can now restore to these words of the text the valorization conferred upon them by membership in a system. He can understand how Baudelaire could be attracted by such a privileged code, why his choice would appeal to readers in 1860, or at least ring familiar in their ears, or even serve as marker of a certain type of poetry.

But this reconstruction remains peripheral to the text, for it enables us to understand no more than the potentials and limitations of the material Baudelaire had available. It does not tell us why he actually used that material in this specific instance. It does not tell us whether or not, or why, this use should be adjudged gratuitous. The suspicion of gratuitousness must now in fact be borne by Romanticism instead of by Baudelaire.

Style analysis, on the contrary, does address itself to the specificity of the text and to the pertinence of the theme to the text. It permits us to see that both the cathedral and forest systems are fragmentary, and that this incompleteness points up the relevancy of the theme through what has been left out. The components excluded are the very ones that would be most apt for symbolizing pantheism or animism in the positive form of the theme, or architectural authenticity in the reverse. One component retained is the music: the *organ* is a convincing, or at least acceptable, homologue to the *wind in the trees*—acceptable because the likeness is a natural one, and because the idea of that likeness has become a cliché. Just as acceptably, music generates a listener. But then, within the *cathedral* system the relation listener-music is either positive (elevation, thoughts soaring) or negative. In this context, the initial postulate (*vous m'effrayez*) entails a negative choice. Such being the case, the heart becomes the fully motivated image of a death chamber, since that is the path along which the clichés of the system lead us. For in this system the mention of church sounds (bells, organ, choir) is symmetrically balanced by mention of the crypt: the symmetry is either that of silence, as in the text of Chateaubriand's that "launched" this theme:

tandis que l'airain se balance avec fracas sur votre tête, les souterrains voûtés de la mort se taisent profondément sous vos pieds.[26]

or it is that of the echo, as in the lines of Lamartine:

Le chrétien dans ses basiliques
Réveillant l'écho souterrain
Fait gémir ses graves cantiques. [27]

This second version is the more popular, perhaps because it was reinforced by the equally lugubrious clichés of the Gothic novel, wherein dungeons echo to the roll of thunder. In both versions, the response to the plain song is given by Death. Within the frame of this descriptive structure, the image of the heart as a chamber of death is therefore not gratuitous. The logic of the cathedral image, which is further motivated by an established parallelism with the logic of the forest image, compellingly transforms the listener into a living tomb. [28]

The superimposition of the descriptive system, by eliminating certain elements and combining homologous components, has laid a sort of filter or grille of actual words on the potential lexicon of the theme: so that the overall valorization of the lexicon (its historical dimension) has been limited, focussed upon what was pertinent in context (the stylistic dimension). This sorting out is literally a dual reading, performed simultaneously on the level of the text and on the level of the theme. The resulting stresses—the poetic structure proper—occur at every point where the historical axis (mythology) and the syntactic axis (sentence) intersect.

26 *Génie du Christianisme*, III, i, Chap. viii, "Des églises gothiques."

27 Lamartine, *Harmonies*, "La Prière de Femme" (Pléiade ed., p. 1230). In another poem, Lamartine describes the Gothic cathedral, literally, as a resonance or echo chamber, built like a machine to amplify the voices of prayer (*Harmonies poétiques et religieuses*, "Hymne du Soir dans les temples," Pléiade ed., pp. 317 ff.). Cf. Baudelaire, *Les Fleurs du Mal*, "Les Phares," ll. 34-35.

28 This effect is even more compelling because the poet makes the forest noises into symbols of his own memories, and also uses images of death in painful reminiscences (in "Le Cygne," I. 50; "Spleen II," ll. 5-10, etc.).

I have tried to present my argument in pragmatic terms. I believe the examples given above speak for themselves. It seems to me they make it quite clear that the stuff literary history works with (and on)— themes, motifs, narratives, descriptions—all of it is first of all *language*. Literary history should therefore be a history of words.[29]

29 This paper applies theoretical assumptions which I developed more fully in my *Essais de stylistique structurale* (Paris, 1971). See also my paper on "L'explication des faits littéraires," in *L'Enseignement de la littérature,,* ed. S. Doubrovsky and Tzvetan Todorov (Paris, 1971), pp. 331-55, 366-97.

9

Poetry as Fiction

Barbara Herrnstein Smith

ARADOXES make intriguing titles, but I am not otherwise fond of them and intend, by the end of this article, to dissolve the one that entitles it. I mean to do this by elaborating the proposition that fictiveness is the characteristic quality of what we call "poetry" when we use the term in the broad sense bequeathed by Aristotle, i.e., to refer to the general class of verbal artworks. My primary concern will be to develop a conception of poetry that allows us to distinguish it from and relate it to both nonpoetic discourse and other artforms. The view presented here was initially, but rather incidentally, proposed elsewhere.[1] I have found the elaboration of it of continuing interest, however, especially since the grounds for those distinctions and the nature of those relationships remain, to my mind, extremely problematic in contemporary linguistic and aesthetic theory.

Before saying anything at all about poetry, I shall, in what follows, have a few things to say about language generally. Any theory of poetry inevitably, though not always explicitly, presupposes a theory of language. Thus, those who have at various times regarded poetry as inspired speech, or embellished prose, or the language of passion, or "emotive" statements, have obviously had somewhat different notions of what language is when it is *not* poetry—e.g., uninspired speech, plain prose, the language of reason, or "verifiable statements." Since, moreover, linguistic theory is now in a very volatile state, no general propositions concerning language can be offered casually or taken for granted. In any case, although I am by no means offering here anything that could be called a theory of language, the first section of this article will develop some general observations on nonpoetic or what I call "natural" discourse, particularly in those respects that are most significant in distinguishing it from poetry. The second section of the article will develop some implications of the conception of poetry as mimetic, or what I shall be calling *fictive*, discourse.

---

1 *Poetic Closure: A Study of How Poems End* (Chicago, 1968), esp. pp. 14-25.

Although the making of distinctions, definitions, and classifications will occupy a good deal of the discussion throughout, it should become clear that my ultimate interest is not in taxonomy but in poetry as an artform. I am concerned with how, on what basis, we actually do identify poetry, and how that identification directs and modifies our experience and interpretation of a literary artwork, both as distinct from a natural utterance and as related to other artforms.

I should also observe that what is presented here is actually a set of extracts from a larger study in progress, and I am conscious of the fact that many matters touched upon in what follows deserve considerably more attention than I have the space to give them.*

I

By "natural discourse," I mean here all utterances — trivial or sublime, ill-wrought or eloquent, true or false, scientific or passionate — that can be taken as someone's saying something, somewhere, sometime: i.e., as the verbal acts of real persons on particular occasions in response to particular sets of circumstances. In stressing all these particularities, I wish to emphasize that a natural utterance is an historical *event*: like any other event, it occupies a specific and unique point in time and space. A natural utterance is thus an event in the same sense as the Coronation of Elizabeth I on January 15, 1559, or the departure this morning from Albany of Allegheny Airlines Flight 617, or the falling of a certain leaf from a certain elm tree. Other events more or less resembling these in various respects may occur at other times or in other places, but the event itself—that coronation, that flight, that utterance — cannot recur, for it is historically unique.

The point requires emphasis because it reflects a fundamental distinction that may be drawn between natural utterances and certain other linguistic structures which are *not* historical events and which can be both defined and described independently of any particular instance of *occurrence*. Dictionary entries, for example, or what we refer to abstractly as "the word *fire*" or "the phrase *law and order*" are not themselves particular events; they are, rather, linguistic *forms*, or the names of certain *types* or *classes* of events. And, as such, certain observations may be made about them: for example, the morphemic or phonetic

---

* Since this article was first published, not only has the "study in progress" become even larger, but several of the points presented in this portion of it have been to some extent sharpened or otherwise qualified. Since editorial considerations did not permit substantial revisions here, these qualifications could not be indicated. They will be reflected, however, in the study itself, which will be published as *Fictive Discourse* by the University of Chicago Press.

features that define all members of the class, or the syntactic rules governing their accepted use in English sentences, or, of course, the characteristic features of the circumstances in which they *do* occur as part of utterances — in other words, their "dictionary meanings." But these linguistic forms — words, phrases, etc. — are not themselves historical events unless or until they occur as the verbal responses of particular persons on particular occasions. Obviously "the word *fire*" as a general class is a very different sort of thing from a specific utterance, "Fire!", which may warn a man that his life is in danger or send a bullet speeding toward him, very much depending on the particular circumstances in which the utterance occurs and to which it is a response.

A natural utterance not only occurs *in* a particular set of circumstances — what is often referred to as its *context* — but is also understood as being a response *to* those circumstances. In other words, the historical "context" of an utterance does not merely surround it but *occasions* it, brings it into existence. The context of an utterance, then, is best thought of not simply as its gross external or physical setting, but rather as the total set of conditions that has in fact determined its occurrence and form.[2] That total set of conditions, what makes us say something at a particular time and also shapes the linguistic structure of our utterance—the specific words we choose, our syntax, our intonation, etc.—is likely to be manifold and complex no matter how simple the utterance. Moreover, the total set of conditions that determines what we say and how we speak is by no means confined to the objects and events "spoken about," or what linguistic theorists of various persuasions refer to as "referents," "designations," "denotations," or "significations."

It is worth noting that the existence of an object or event or even, as we say, an "idea," is never a sufficient reason for responding to it verbally. In other words, the fact that something is true is never a sufficient reason for saying it. If I should be heard to say, "It's five o'clock," the reasons for my saying so would clearly include more than

---

2 Since the term *context* has been acquiring increased currency in contemporary aesthetics and linguistics, I should point out that it is not my intention here to quarrel with or qualify the sense it bears for other theorists. It might have been better to discover or devise another term altogether for what I am here defining and later elaborating, but the alternatives that presented themselves seemed just as likely to create comparable confusions, and I confess to a temperamental loathing of neologisms. It should also be noted that, in proposing that we view the context of an utterance not merely as its physical setting but as the totality of its determinants, I am not so much broadening the ordinary reference of the term as affirming the existence and significance of a particular *relation*, namely causality, between a verbal event and the universe in which it occurs. Defined in terms of that relationship, the "context" of an utterance inevitably refers to something more extensive than what the common use of the term suggests, but also something more particular.

what time of day it was just then, for at any moment it is a certain time, but I do not announce the time continuously through the day. Perhaps, on this occasion, I wished to remind someone of an appointment, or perhaps someone had just asked me for the correct time. Certainly these circumstances were as significant in occasioning my utterance as that specific one to which my words, "It's five o'clock," might seem exclusively to "refer," namely the time of day.

Given any utterable fact or state of affairs, gross or subtle, physical or psychological — the state of the weather, the color of swans, or my opinion of the war — whether or not I will actually utter it, and how I will utter it, will always depend upon other variables, i.e., attendant circumstances other than that fact or state of affairs. These variables will include, among other things, the presence of a potential listener, my relationship to him, the nature of the social occasion, the immediate verbal context (what either he or I have been saying) and, perhaps most significantly, the conventions of the linguistic community to which we both belong.

There is no reason to maintain a sharp distinction between the sort of physical and social variables just mentioned and what might otherwise be thought of as the internal, personal, mental, or psychological springs of speech. It is obvious that among the circumstances that provoke, occasion, and shape an utterance are conditions peculiar to the speaker's current state: his emotions, his feelings, his memories, expectations, beliefs, and desires. I may say "It's five o'clock" partly because I am hungry or anxious or bored, and such conditions must also be recognized as part of the context of the utterance. We should note, moreover, that the speaker's "current state" is inevitably the product of his past as well as his current experiences, including, most significantly, his past *verbal* experiences, and that part of his psychological or mental condition — and therefore part of the context of his utterance — is how he has learned to use language.

Although we may, for certain purposes, describe an utterance exclusively in terms of its linguistic form (e.g., as a certain concatenation of lexemes and/or phonemes), a natural utterance can never be adequately specified or described as an *event* except in relation to the context in which it occurred. In other words, a verbal event, like any other event, is individuated as much by its context as by its form. Thus, although we could say that two men each pulling the trigger of a gun are engaged in acts of the same *form*, it is clear that Mr. X shooting Mr. Y is not the same event as Mr. A shooting Mr. B, or as Mr. X shooting Mr. Y again fifteen minutes later. Similarly, when I say, making introductions at a party, "This is my husband," it may not be a unique event with respect to its linguistic form, but it is certainly not the same event as some other woman saying it of her husband or, indeed, as my own saying it on some other occasion, either fifteen minutes later to some other guest or even absentmindedly to the same one as before. Moreover, it is unlikely that any two natural utterances would be even *formally* identical if one extends attention to the more subtle aspects of their linguistic form. For although each utterance could be transcribed with the same symbols, such a transcription preserves only a fraction of the total physical reality constituting each utterance, a reality that would include not only a certain sequence of phonemes, but also intonational features such as pitch contours, stress, pacing, and usually facial expressions and other gestures as well. While some linguists may regard the latter aspects of the utterance with suspicion and dispute their status as linguistic features, it is nevertheless becoming increasingly evident that there is no absolute discontinuity between the part of an act or event that is called "verbal" and the totality of that act or event. In other words, a natural utterance is always continuous with the speaker's total on-going behavior and also continuous with the total world of natural events. The professional linguist's or our own ordinary description of the utterance reflects an arbitrary demarcation and abstraction from the fullness, the density, and the spatial, temporal, and causal continuity of all human action and all events in nature.

Most of us would agree that it is impossible to provide a complete and exhaustive description of a nonverbal historical event such as the Coronation of Elizabeth or the departure of Flight 617. What the historian offers will usually be a selection or abstraction of certain features of these events at a level thought adequate for the purpose at hand. It is clear, moreover, that neither an eye-witness report nor, if we had it, even a videotape, would constitute a total record of the event; and neither one, of course, would constitute the event itself. The same limits and distinctions apply to the descriptions and records of verbal events: Elizabeth's first speech to Parliament on February 4th, 1559, or my farewells this morning to my family. No description or record would be complete, neither a vocal quotation nor a tape-recording, in either of which many features of the original event would be lost. The fact, however, that verbal events can be transcribed in a standard notational system often seems to obscure for us their similarity to other events. It is true that orthography and phonetic notation allows us to record or describe natural utterances with considerable subtlety and specificity of detail through conventionalized symbols. Moreover, a transcription of this kind — i.e., a "text" of the utterance — may be an adequate description or record of it for most purposes. Nevertheless, we should not confuse a copy of that text with the verbal event itself, the historical act of a particular speaker on a particular occasion.

The relation of utterances to texts is of special interest to us here since, at least in our own culture, we typically encounter poetry as texts. The relation is extremely complex, however, with respect to both natural and poetic discourse, and, indeed, it is not always the same relation. I have just been speaking of texts that serve as records or descriptions of natural utterances, i.e., inscriptions of verbal events that occurred at some specific time, such as Elizabeth's first address to Parliament. Not all texts bear this relation to some natural utterance. Many texts — personal letters, for example — are not records or descriptions of utterances, but constitute utterances themselves, only in written rather than vocal form. It is true, of course, that there are other very significant aspects to the relation between writing and vocal speech, and they are not mutually independent or simply parallel possibilities. Nevertheless, to the extent that the writer's act of composing and inscribing is an historically specific and unique verbal event, it is analogous to the speaker's act of emitting the sounds that comprise spoken discourse. And thus we may regard the product of either act as a natural utterance.

In view of the Gutenberg revolution, the question may arise as to whether printed (or otherwise duplicated) texts can also be regarded as natural utterances, and the answer here is sometimes yes and sometimes no. A printed text may be simply one of many copies of an inscribed record of a vocal utterance that, like Elizabeth's Address, did occur at some specific time and place. In this case, the text is *not* a natural utterance, but the transcription of one. But a printed work may also be a natural utterance itself in written form, exactly like a personal letter — though the letter, of course, usually exists as only a single text. It may be initially difficult to conceive of a printed work as a natural utterance and thus, by our definition here, an historically *unique* event. We should recognize however, that no matter how many duplications of a text are subsequently produced, the writer's actual composition of the linguistic structure that constitutes that text was and remains an historically unique event. ("Unique" here does not mean *unitary*, and it is understood that the composition of the text will often consist of numerous "acts" dispersed in time, from the initial jottings to the ultimate revisions.)

To summarize these points, then: whether or not a composition was written to be printed, and no matter how long it is, or how long it took to write, and no matter how remote in time or space the writer from his ultimate audience, or how eloquent its style, or how culturally significant and otherwise estimable it is, the composition must still be regarded as a *natural utterance* so long as it may be taken as the verbal responses of an historically real person, occasioned and determined by an historically real universe. And this means that *most* of what we call "literature" in the general sense of inscribed compositions does in fact consist of natural utterances. This would include works ranging from Aristotle's *Metaphysics* and Macaulay's *History of England* to an article in a scientific journal or an editorial in this morning's *New York Times*. These are all as much natural utterances as the remarks exchanged between me and a colleague a few moments ago.

There remains, however, one other class of texts that are neither natural utterances in written form nor the transcription of natural utterances that originally occurred in vocal form, and this class consists of the texts of *fictive utterances*, including most prominently those compositions that we otherwise refer to as works of imaginative literature — poems, tales, dramas, and novels. I shall reserve comment on these texts until later, in connection with the general discussion of fictive discourse; for, as we shall see, fictive utterances bear an altogether distinctive relation to their own texts when indeed (as is not always the case) such texts exist.

But we may return now from the texts to the *contexts* of natural utterances, and thereby to the crucial question of meaning and interpretation. A natural utterance cannot be exclusively identified or described independent of its context, nor can its meaning be understood independent of that context. Indeed, what we often mean by the "meaning" of an utterance *is* its context, i.e., the set of conditions that occasioned its occurrence and determined its form. The view of meaning proposed here is not offered as an analysis of all the numerous senses in which the term has been or could be used, and certainly not as a solution to the ever-proliferating number of problems associated with it in contemporary linguistics and philosophy. Nevertheless, a causal conception of meaning — which this is — has much to recommend it, particularly here, since it permits us to appreciate better the distinctive nature of poetic discourse and of its "interpretation." Moreover, it is not so idiosyncratic as may first appear, for "meaning" in the sense of *causes* or *determinants* will often be found to accommodate or correspond to familiar usage of the term.

I must emphasize that I am speaking here of the meaning not of *words* but of *utterances*, a distinction not always grasped even by those most concerned with these problems. One may ascertain the meanings of those abstract classes called *words* by determining the conventions governing their usage in the relevant linguistic community, usually by consulting one's experience of the language or, when difficulties arise, either a dictionary—or an analytic philosopher. Dictionaries and philosophers are of only limited help, however, in ascertaining the meaning of particular verbal events. When we speak ordinarily of the meaning of a particular utterance—i.e., what someone has said—we are usually concerned not with the definitions of the words that compose it or even, in a restricted sense, with what it "refers" to, but rather with *why it occurred*: the situation and motives that produced it, the set of conditions, "external" and "internal," physical and psychological, that caused the speaker to utter that statement at that time in that form—in other words, what we are calling here its *context*.

For example, definitions and referents are not what interest John when he asks, "What do you mean?", in response to his friend's remark, "You know, I think Bill is a fool." Pointing to Bill and offering an analysis of the "concept" of folly will probably not answer his question. Knowing this, his friend is more likely to describe certain circumstances, observations he has made, impressions he has had (and perhaps also his motives for articulating them at that moment), and so forth, until John says, "Oh, well, now I understand what you mean," meaning that he has located to his own satisfaction the reasons for or *causes of* his friend's remark. The qualification here, "to his own satisfaction," is an important one, for it is most unlikely that John would in fact have identified *all* the determinants involved.

We rarely "understand completely" one another's utterances, nor do we need or seek to do so. Criteria for the adequate understanding of an utterance vary widely, depending on the nature of the utterance and the primary purposes and interests of the speaker and listener. And although sometimes — for example, in a psychoanalyst's office — one may probe for increasingly subtle and obscure determinants, both speaker and listener are usually satisfied with considerably less than a total identification of *all* of them. It is usually not necessary, and of course it is usually not possible, for the listener to ascertain all the conditions that make up the context of an utterance. It is not necessary because many of them will be trivial and irrelevant to his concerns. And it is not possible either because the speaker's original context is remote in time or space, or because many of the springs of speech are not apparent from the immediate context or, as we say, are private or internal to the speaker. The listener or audience, therefore, is always obliged to "interpret" what is said or written. That is, to the extent that the listener *has* an interest in those unavailable determinants, he must hypothesize, imagine, or *infer* them.

When we read the inscribed utterance of a friend, such as a letter from him, we may be more aware of interpreting as such than when we listen to him speak, but we do so in both instances and by the same process: partly through inferences based on what we know of him personally, but mostly through inferences based on all our own prior experiences, especially our prior experiences with language. And, when he alludes either in speech or writing to matters of which we have no specific knowledge—e.g., a third person whom we have never met, a place we have never visited — we supply our ignorance by an imaginative projection of what we do know generally. It is important to emphasize, however, that these projections are attempts to infer or approximate *actual* circumstances, and thus are subject to correction should our knowledge become more specific. ("Oh, *you're* Charlie's brother. From what he said, I pictured you as much older.")

What makes a letter particularly interesting as an utterance is the fact that, since it lacks the supplementary information usually conveyed to the listener by intonation and gestures as well as by shared physical contexts (we cannot point to things in letters), this sort of information will commonly be supplied by the writer in other ways: by explicit allusions ("As I write this, I am sitting by my study window—you know, the one that looks out over the back garden, etc.") by graphic substitutes for intonation (e.g., underlining, punctuation, spacing), and by more subtle modifications of the language itself (e.g., in diction, syntax, turns of phrasing, and metaphor). Our syntax in letters, because it carries a greater burden of information than in conversational speech, not only *can* be but *must* be more controlled. To be sure, since we are often more or less conscious of the generic relation of our letters to "literature," we will employ forms such as archaisms and metaphoric imagery that would seem pretentious or otherwise inappropriate in conversational speech. This, however, does not altogether account for the fact that some of us become, in our letters, rather uncharacteristically eloquent and "literary"; for, as we shall see, there are other reasons why the linguistic features of letters often bear an interesting resemblance to those commonly associated with poetic discourse.

II

Poems are not natural utterances, not historically unique verbal acts or events; indeed a poem is not an event at all, and cannot be said ever to have "occurred" in the usual sense. When we read the text of a poem or hear it read aloud, our response to it as a linguistic structure is governed by quite special conventions, and it is the understanding that these conventions are operating that distinguishes the poem as a verbal artwork from natural discourse. The operation of these conventions is most readily apparent in dramatic poetry, i.e., plays, where it is understood that the acts and events performed upon the stage are not *happening* but are being *represented* as happening. When we see a production of *Hamlet*, we do not watch a queen drinking poison, but the enactment of such an event, which may be said to "occur" only in being thus enacted. But among the acts and events represented upon the stage are also verbal ones. As the actor who portrays Claudius leans forward and extends his arm in a gesture of horror and abortive warning, thus representing a man leaning forward and extending his arm, etc., that actor also utters the words, "Gertrude, do not drink," thus representing a man uttering those words. We are not aware here of any radical discontinuity between the enactment of a physical action and the enactment of an utterance — and of course an utterance *is* a physical action, though it has other characteristics that sometimes obscure that fact.

Most of us would be quite willing to grant the existence of what could be called *mimetic discourse* — i.e., the fictive representation of speech — at least in dramatic poetry. What I would like to suggest, however, is that *all* poetry may be so regarded, that we could conceive of as mimetic discourse not only the representation of speech in drama, but also lyrics, epics, tales, and novels. Indeed, I wish to propose that this, the fictive representation of discourse, is precisely what defines that class of verbal compositions we have so much trouble naming and distinguishing, i.e., "imaginative literature" or "poetry in the broad sense."

The conception of poetry as mimetic is, of course, quite ancient, and modern theorists do continue to assert that literature is a representational art. It is by no means clear, however, what or what kind of thing it is that the poem "imitates" or represents. One common notion seems to be that poetry, apparently on the analogy of painting, somehow represents "images in words." Or, in view of the existence of numerous image-less poems and passages in novels, that it represents ideas or feelings, either the author's or those of his characters. Or, in view of how restrictive even this formulation is, it is sometimes suggested that literary works, especially narrative fictions, represent imagined events or even worlds — *in*, it will solemnly be added, *the medium of language*. I will not attempt here to indicate all the problems entailed by such suggestions,[3] for I wish only to point out that they all ignore what might be thought most apparent, namely that what poems do represent "in the medium of language" is *language*, or more accurately, speech, human utterance, discourse. The definition proposed here attempts to close in on poetry from two directions: one, as it may be distinguished from

3   I have considered the matter elsewhere: see "The New Imagism," *Midway* (Winter, 1969), pp. 27-44.

other mimetic artforms, and two, as it may be distinguished from other verbal compositions. As a mimetic artform, what a poem distinctively and characteristically represents is not images, ideas, feelings, characters, scenes, or worlds, but *discourse.* Poetry does, like drama, represent actions and events, but exclusively verbal ones. And, as a verbal composition, a poem is distinctively and characteristically not a natural utterance, but the *representation* of one.

A poem represents discourse in the same sense as a play, in its totality, represents human actions and events, or a painting represents visual objects. When we speak of the objects represented in or by a painting, it is understood that they need not correspond to any particular objects, but rather to an identifiable class of them. A painting can depict a landscape that exists as a visual object only in the depiction itself. Thus, when we speak of *mimesis* or representation in an artwork, we recognize that it does not constitute the imitation or reproduction of existing objects or events, but rather the fabrication of fictive objects and events of which there are existing or possible instances or types — whether they be rural landscapes, star-crossed lovers, or laments for dead friends. In other words, to say that an artist has represented a certain object or event is to say that he has constructed a fictive member of an identifiable class of natural (real) objects or events.

Part of what has obscured the relation of poetic *mimesis* to pictorial and other kinds of artistic representation are traditional notions that identify the various artforms in terms of their characteristic *media.* Thus, sound is said to be the medium of music, pigment the medium of painting, and of course words or language the medium of poetry. The corollary formula—X (artwork) represents Y (object of imitation) in Z (medium)—has created more problems than it has illuminated, most conspicuously, perhaps, in regard to music, where art theorists, under the presumed obligation to locate the object that music imitates, have come up with an amazing assortment of chimeras, from shapes of feeling to states of being. It is another problem, however, that concerns us here. The plastic materials that are presumably the media of the visual arts — pigment, stone, metal, and so forth — do not have an expressive function independent of the artworks into which they are fashioned. These materials, moreover, do not in themselves resemble the objects and scenes that they represent. A block of marble is a very different thing from a human figure. The corresponding medium of poetry, however, *language,* is not a "raw" material, but itself a symbolic system with expressive functions independent of its use in artworks. For this reason, it has been difficult to conceive of language as both the medium of an artwork and also what is represented by it.

The difficulty here, however, is really the traditional concept of the art medium itself, particularly its implicit dualism of form and matter. This dualism — i.e., the notion of the art medium as formless matter — not only creates problems with regard to poetry (for language is obviously not formless matter), but it also obscures the nature of other artforms. We could just as readily and, I think, more fruitfully, think of the medium of the visual arts not as pigment and stone but as the visually perceived properties of matter or, indeed, as the elements and dynamics of visual perception itself. And, if we must have a corresponding "medium" for poetry, we would do better to locate it not simply in words or language conceived abstractly, but in the whole dynamic complex of verbal behavior and verbal experience.

But if we are content to do without the traditional notion of the art medium altogether, we may be better able to appreciate the essential nature of poetic representation and its relation to artistic *mimesis* generally. As I suggested above, we may conceive of an artwork not as the imitation, in some different "matter," of the "form" of particular objects or events already existing in nature, but as the creation of a fictive member of a certain class of natural objects or events. Thus, paintings are fictive instances of what, in nature, are visually perceived objects. Musical compositions are fictive instances of acoustically perceived events, in other words *designed* sounds as distinguished from sounds simply occurring in nature. And poems are fictive utterances. The kinds of natural events represented in poetry are, of course, quite special: utterances are themselves human constructions, and in that sense "artificial." This should not, however, obscure the sense in which they are nevertheless *natural events*, like the flight of birds, the falling of leaves, and all the particular actions of individual men moving about in, and being moved about by, the natural universe.

We can, I think, readily conceive of a-man-walking as a natural event and should be able to conceive of a-man-talking as such; for, as I have already suggested, there is no real discontinuity between verbal and non-verbal actions. A painting can represent, through a visual configuration of line and color, a man walking or a child sleeping, because such events are ordinarily perceived primarily as visual events. And although a visual artist can also represent a man talking (one may think, for example, of some of Daumier's prints of lawyers in animated conversation), he cannot represent pictorially the utterance itself, for speech is not perceived as a visual event—except of course, when it is in written form, a matter to which I will return later. But for now let us pursue the example of Daumier a bit further. As a visual artist, he was of course extraordinarily sensitive to the expressive and otherwise interesting qualities of the *appearances* of his fellow creatures: the way they stood and grouped themselves together, the "expressions" on their faces, the gestures of their hands, and so forth. Had he also been, as some people are, extraordinarily sensitive to the expressive and otherwise interesting qualities of the *speech* of his fellow creatures, he might have sought to represent that too. But how could he do so? The answer I am suggesting here is that he could fashion a fictive representation of speech, i.e., a poem — something, perhaps, like Browning's "The Bishop Orders His Tomb", which I think we might recognize as a verbal counterpart of a satiric Daumier print: *ut pictura poesis.*

The relation of "dramatic monologues" to dramatic poetry proper is, of course, readily appreciated, and we can see how either could be regarded as mimetic discourse. My claim here, however, is more general, for what is central to the concept of the poem as a fictive utterance is not that the speaker is a "character" distinct from the poet, or that the audience purportedly addressed, the emotions expressed, and the events alluded to are fictional, but that *the speaking, addressing, expressing and alluding are themselves fictive verbal acts.* To be sure, a fictive utterance will often resemble a possible natural utterance very closely, for the distinction is not primarily one of linguistic form. Moreover, although certain formal features — verse, most notably — often do mark and indeed identify for the reader the fictiveness of an utterance, the presence of such features are not themselves the crux of the distinction. The distinction lies, rather, in a set of conventions shared by poet and reader, according to which certain identifiable linguistic structures are *taken* to be not the verbal acts they resemble, but representations of such acts. By this convention, Keats's ode "To Autumn" and Shakespeare's sonnets are precisely as fictive as "The Bishop Orders His Tomb" or Tennyson's "Ulysses." All of these poems are understood not as the inscriptions of utterances actually uttered by men who spoke poetically, but rather as linguistic structures composed by men whom we call poets because they compose such structures. The statements in a poem may, of course, resemble quite closely statements that the poet might have truly and truthfully uttered as an historical creature in the historical world. Nevertheless, insofar as they are offered and recognized as statements in a poem, they are fictive. To the objection, "But I know Wordsworth meant what he says in that poem," we must reply, "You mean he *would have* meant them if he *had* said them, but he is not saying them." As I shall explain later, we may choose to regard the composition not as a poem but as an historical utterance, but then the conventions by virtue of which its fictiveness is understood and has its appropriate effects are no longer in operation.

Another matter should, however, be clarified at this point. I have said that novels and tales, as well as lyrics, epics, and dramatic poems are also fictive representations of discourse. The fictiveness of prose fiction is, of course, commonly acknowledged, but it is more radical than is sometimes supposed. For not only are the characters and events narrated in a novel fictional, and not only is the narrator whose voice relates the events fictional, but most significantly, so also is the entire structure of discourse through which the narration is presented. Indeed, as we all know, many novels such as *War and Peace* allude to quite real persons and events, a consideration that has created theoretical problems for many literary theorists. The essential fictiveness of novels, however, as of all literary artworks, is not to be discovered in the unreality of the characters, objects, and events alluded to, but in the unreality of the *alludings* themselves. In other words, in a novel or tale, it is the *act* of reporting events, the *act* of describing persons and referring to places, that is fictive. The novel *represents* the verbal action of a man reporting, describing, and referring.

Consider the following two passages:

(a) "He was a gentleman of good family in Buckinghamshire, and born to a fair fortune, and of a most civil and affable deportment. In his entrance into the world, he indulged himself all the license in sports and exercises and company which was used by men of the most jolly conversation; afterwards he retired to a more reserved and melancholy society."

(b) "He had been a member of the Court of Justice, and died at the age of forty-five. His father had been an official who, after serving in various ministries and departments in Petersburg, had made the sort of career which brings men to positions from which by reason of long service they cannot be dismissed."

The first is from the description of John Hampden in Clarendon's *History of the Rebellion*; the second is from Tolstoi's "Death of Ivan Ilyitch." (In both, we might note, allusions are made to real places, Buckinghamshire and Petersburg.) I am suggesting here that the relation between the two passages is that the second is a representation of the kind of thing the first really is, namely a biography. "The Death of Ivan Ilyitch" is not the biography of a fictional character, but rather a fictive biography. The fiction attaches no more to the narrated facts of Ilyitch's life than to the fact of someone's narrating them. Tolstoi is, if you like, pretending to be *writing* a biography while actually *fabricating* one.

If we consider literature from the point of view I am developing here, it becomes evident that the various genres of literary art — for example, tales, classical odes, and lyrics — can often be distinguished from each other according to what types of natural discourse they represent: here, respectively, anecdotal reports of past events, public speeches, and more or less private or personal utterance.[4] Poetry itself, as distinct now from novels and stories, traditionally represents various kinds of *spoken* discourse. Certain types of discourse, however, are themselves typically textual inscriptions; i.e., they exist characteristically in written and often in printed form — for example, chronicles, journals, letters, memoirs, and biographies. And certain genres of literary art, roughly what we refer to as "prose fiction," characteristically represent such varieties of *inscribed* discourse. Novels, for example, a distinctively post-Gutenberg genre, have typically been representations of chronicles, journals, letters, memoirs, and biographies. This aspect of prose fiction has some interesting implications for the nature of novels as *texts*, but they will be better appreciated after we have given some attention to literary texts generally.

A poem — i.e., a fictive utterance — consists entirely of a linguistic structure, unlike a natural utterance, which consists of a linguistic event occurring in an historical context. In a non-literate culture, e.g., among Northwest Indian tribes, the linguistic structure that would be identified as *that* song or story is preserved and duplicated, if at all, only in being remembered and recited. But in a literate culture, the identity of the poem may be preserved and reproduced through a standard notational system, i.e., in a written text. The text of a poem, however, bears a quite special relation to the utterance of which it is presumably an inscribed counterpart. For it is neither a transcription of an utterance that actually occurred at some specific prior time, like Elizabeth's first speech to Parliament, nor is it a natural utterance in written form, like a personal letter. It is, rather, like the score of a musical composition or the script of a play, i.e., formal specifications for the physical production of certain events. The text of the poem tells us, in other words, how to produce the verbal act it represents. This is evident enough for a playscript, which directs the performer's *verbal* actions along with other more obviously physical actions: e.g., "enter," "exit," "is stabbed," "falls," *says* "I am dead, Horatio; wretched Queen, adieu." But this is true of any poetic text, i.e. of any verbal artwork that represents spoken rather than written discourse. The text of a novel must be regarded somewhat differently, as I will explain below. But, allowing for this exception, the text of any poem is to be interpreted, in the first instance, as, in effect, a score or stage directions for the performance of a purely verbal act that exists only in being thus performed. A poem is never spoken, not even by the poet himself. It is always re-cited; for whatever its relation to words the poet could have spoken, it has, as a

4 "Private or personal utterance" may be extended to include not only overt but interior speech. The representation of the latter, particularly in romantic and modern lyrics, is discussed in *Poetic Closure*, pp. 139-50.

poem, no initial historical occurrence. What the poet composes as a
text is not a verbal act but rather a linguistic structure that becomes,
through being read or recited, the *representation* of a verbal act.

As I pointed out above, works of prose fiction are characteristically
representations not of spoken but of inscribed utterances, and for this
reason the texts of novels are, interestingly enough, closer to pictures
than to musical scores. What the text of Richardson's *Clarissa* represents is not the speech of certain characters but a collection of their
letters; what *David Copperfield* represents is not the spoken remini-
scenses of a man, but his autobiography. Each novel itself, i.e., the
marks printed on its pages and, if you like, the pages themselves, plus
covers and binding, is a depiction of — a fictive instance of — a kind of
book. Indeed, in view of its three-dimensionality, the copy of the novel
we hold in our hands could be conceived of as a sculpture, where the
sculptor has not satisfied himself in representing the gross physical and
visual qualities of a book, but has sought to represent the very text of
one. But, rather than complicate matters, we may at least agree that
what the text of a novel represents is, precisely, a *text*.

In what follows, I shall be speaking again of poetry in the narrower
sense, i.e., as representations of spoken discourse, usually in verse. Some
of the points I shall be making would require a somewhat different or
additional formulation with respect to novels or representations of
written discourse, but I will not have the space here to develop them.

Although a poem, unlike a natural utterance, consists entirely of a
linguistic structure, we obviously do not respond to poems as pure forms
or merely as organizations of sound, any more than we respond to plays
as purely formal structures of movement or to traditional paintings as
pure configurations of line and color. For each of these is understood
to be a *representational* artform, and the spectator readily infers a
meaning or context—though a fictional one — for the objects, actions,
and events represented. The curtain rises on *Hamlet*, and we
see a human figure blowing his fingers and stamping his feet on a
dimly lit stage. Before a word is uttered, we have already inferred at
least a cold night as the context for his speech. We read or hear recited
a sonnet by Shakespeare: "To me, fair friend, you never can be old
...," and no matter how little we know about William Shakespeare of
Stratford and the various earls with whom he may have been intimate,
we immediately begin to create for those words a plausible and
appropriate context: at the minimum, a speaker addressing some
other person whom he regards as fair and, in some sense, as his
friend. All our experiences with language and the contexts in which
men speak not only enable us to make this inference but really *oblige*
us to make it.

Throughout our lives as verbal creatures, we have learned to respond to linguistic structures in a certain way: namely to interpret their meanings, i.e., to infer their contexts from their forms. The effects of poetry as a representational artform depend upon the strength of our habitual tendency to infer contexts from verbal structures. We should note that Milton, in *Paradise Lost*, does not create Eve or Eden; what he creates, rather, are statements about "Eve" and "Eden" that lead the *reader* to create a woman and a place — in order, as it were, to provide referents for those statements. Other representational artforms depend for their effects upon comparable tendencies in the spectator: illusionist painting, for example, depends upon fundamental habits of visual perception to transform a configuration of lines and colors on a flat surface into the appearance of a three-dimensional scene or object. It is only because of perceptual conditioning produced by our experiences in the natural visual world that we *can* see, as a cow grazing in the distance, what is actually only a few brushstrokes of color on the upper part of a canvas. This process of interpretive filling-in or perceptual inference is very similar to the process by which we infer, from a few lines in a poem, a rich context of motives, feelings, and situations. "To me, fair friend, you never can be old . . . ." Nine small words that summon up for us a man, his consciousness of the pathos of mutability, and his impulse to deny its hold upon his friend.

Thus, although a poem is a fictive utterance without a real and particular historical context, its characteristic effect is to create its own context or, more accurately, to invite and enable the reader to create a plausible context for it. And what we mean when we speak of *interpreting* a poem is, in large measure, precisely this process of inference, conjecture, and indeed creation of contexts.[5] But these contexts — i.e., "meanings" — that we half create and half perceive can be no *more* than "plausible," for the poem is a *fictive* utterance and its contexts can be neither discovered nor verified in nature or history. As we saw earlier, when we interpret a *natural* utterance, we seek to ascertain its real historical determinants, the context that did in fact occasion its occurrence and form. However complex and elusive that context, it is nevertheless historically determinate and particular. The context of a fictive utterance, however, is *historically indeterminate*. This is not to

5 I should emphasize that I am not specifically referring here to those formally and publicly articulated "interpretations" of poetry that we associate with academic or professional criticism, but rather to the informal and often enough private activities of the reader as such, or what we might otherwise speak of as his response to or experience of the poem. Of course much formal criticism is an extension of these informal activities, but the very fact that professional critics are offering public statements entails other concerns and responsibilities, and I am not presuming here either to limit or to account for them. See, however, fn. 7 and p. 186, below.

say that we must regard the poem as an anonymous gift dropped from the Empyrean or ignore the fact that it was composed by a real man at a particular time and place. It is to say, rather, that we must distinguish between the poet's act of composing the poem and the verbal act that the poem represents, just as we would distinguish William Shakespeare's act in composing *Hamlet* and the acts of the Prince of Denmark represented in the play. Shakespeare composed the play, let us say, in 1603, but in what year did Hamlet kill Claudius? In one sense, he kills Claudius every time the play is performed, whether in 1603 or 1970; but in another sense the slaying of Claudius is an act that never did, never will, and never can occur *in the historical world*. It can only be represented as occurring. The composition of the play, then, was an historically determinate event, but the events represented in the play are historically indeterminate. This means, among other things, that when we ask why Hamlet abuses Ophelia in the nunnery-scene, we do not expect to find the answer in any historical particulars of the life of William Shakespeare or of the circumstances that occasioned his composition of the play. Knowledge of these particulars and circumstances may, of course, help us account for why Shakespeare wrote a play in which a character named Hamlet abuses a character named Ophelia, but that is an altogether different question. To understand *why Hamlet abuses Ophelia*, the reader must infer from, on the one hand, the linguistic structure of the play and, on the other hand, everything he knows about the world of men and the relation of their acts to their situations and motives, a plausible set of motives and situations for *that* act.

Similarly for a sonnet by Shakespeare, say 87, which begins: "Farewell, thou art too dear for my possessing,/And like enough thou knowst thy estimate . . . ." To interpret it as a poem, to understand why the speaker is saying "farewell" in such bitter tones to someone upon whom he thought to have some claims of love, the reader will not require any particulars concerning Shakespeare's private life: the identity and moral character of whatever young men he knew at the time, the specific incidents of personal betrayal from which he may have suffered, or his opinion of himself as a lover. What the reader does require is the capacity to conceive of the *kind* of situation that *might* lead a man to feel thus and speak thus, and the reader can develop that capacity only out of his own experiences with men, their situations, their feelings, and especially their language.

The interpretation of a poem as an *historical* utterance may serve the special purposes of the literary historian or biographer, but it is likely to appear shallow, reductive, or "literal-minded" precisely to the degree that it restricts the context of the poem to historical particulars and suggests that the meanings of the poem are to be located exclusively in an historically determinate context. For example, a recent editor of Shakespeare's *Sonnets* prefixes the following note to Sonnet 107 as part of his running commentary on what was happening in Shakespeare's personal life at the very moment he was writing the poems: "Shakespeare had just escaped from the danger of his Company's involvement with the Essex rebellion and . . . the Queen, furious with Pembroke for fathering Mary Fitton's child and refusing to marry her, had sent Pembroke to jail . . . ."[6] Then comes the sonnet:

> Not mine own fears, nor the prophetic soul
> Of the wide world dreaming on things to come,
> Can yet the lease of my true love control,
> Supposed as forfeit to a confined doom. . . .

Forfeit, indeed, to a confined doom, if interpreted as this editor suggests. But for the reader who regards the sonnet as a poem, this sort of interpretation is absurd not only because its foundations in history are, in fact, quite dubious, but because the invocation of particulars of this kind — even if they were accurate — have no greater claim to constituting the "real" meaning of the poem than an interpretation that infers from it and provides for it an appropriately rich, subtle, and coherent context of human feelings, quite independent of Pembroke, Mary Fitton, particular jails and particular rebellions.

I pointed out earlier that personal letters often exhibit characteristics that we associate with poetic discourse, a "literariness" that is produced, for example, by unusually well-controlled syntax, precision of diction, elaborateness or specificity of descriptions, imagery, allusion, and metaphor. Since a letter will be read in a context both temporally and spatially remote from that in which it was composed, the writer must provide exclusively *through* its linguistic structure the sort of supplementary information that is otherwise, in a spoken utterance, provided by the physical context shared by speaker and listener and also by the speaker's intonation and gestures. The letterwriter, in other words, must exploit all the expressive possibilities of language itself to enable his reader to infer and reconstruct properly the meanings and context of his original utterance.

The poet is obviously operating under the same limitations, but even more so. He must convey to his readers not only a context remote from them in space and time, but one that never existed in history or nature, and consists entirely of what the reader will be enabled to construct (rather than reconstruct) from the verbal form of the poem. More-

6 *The Sonnets, Songs, and Poems of Shakespeare*, ed. Oscar James Campbell (New York and Toronto, 1964), p. 136.

over, the poet must suggest, through the possibilities of language alone, not only a plausible and interesting context that has no independent reality, but also the experiences, attitudes, and feelings — and, indeed, the identity — of a speaker who has no other existence and of whom the reader has no other knowledge. Finally, especially since the text of the poem will function as the script for its future performance (and by reciters other than the poet), it must specify or direct its own vocal realization, including its pacing and other intonational features.

The poet will, therefore, in the verbal structure he composes, be straining to the limit all the expressive resources of language. And, beyond that limit, he will sometimes devise new ones. But what are sometimes spoken of as "poetic devices" (and we may include here rhythm or meter) are really the potentially expressive features of *natural* discourse. Tropes and figures, distortions of idiomatic syntax, departures from idiomatic diction, imagery and allusion—all these are certainly not restricted to poetic discourse; nor can they be taken as the distinctive characteristics of poetic language. They are not what defines poetry but are, rather, entailed by what does define it, namely its fictiveness.

Because a poem does not reflect but *create* the context in which its meanings are located, its linguistic structure must carry an extraordinary burden. Poetic language seems — and indeed *is* — richer, more "suggestive," "connotative," and "evocative" than natural language precisely because and to the extent that it requires the reader to cooperate in the creation of its meanings. In our efforts to interpret the poem, to construct the context of human situations and motives it demands in order that its meanings be realized, we will draw upon all our experiences of the world and words of men. Indeed, the activity of interpreting poetry often becomes the occasion for our recognition and acknowledgement of otherwise inaccessible feelings and, in a sense, our own otherwise unknowable knowledge. The richer and more extensive our experiences and feelings — or as we say, "the more we *bring to* the poem"—the more significance it can have for us, which is why, of course, subsequent readings of a poem "reveal" more meanings. The language of a poem seems characteristically "concentrated" because it allows for such an extraordinary and continuous expansiveness of meaning, not confined to its own finite and particular determinants, but drawing on all we know that we can relate to it. The language of the poem continues to mean as long as we have meanings to provide for it. Its meanings are exhausted only at the limits of the reader's own experience and imagination.

But now I should address myself to the suspicion that the view of interpretation developed here leads one directly into the camp of the subjectivists: those who, scorning the revelations of literary history and scholarship, would maintain that all and any meanings of a poem are essentially "personal" and equally valid. This is not, however, the case. In speaking of the contexts created or projected by the reader, I have repeatedly used the term *plausible*; and although I have seemed to be saying, "If the meaning fits, wear it," I have also implied that the meaning must fit. This fitness and plausibility relate to very significant constraints on interpretation that are themselves among the conventions of fictive discourse. Though these constraints differ in many respects from those involved in our interpretations of natural discourse, they are nevertheless substantial; and although there are inevitably grounds for argument in determining them for individual poems, they are nevertheless relatively objective.

The poet, in composing the poem, will have made certain assumptions regarding his audience, specifically that they are members of a shared linguistic and cultural community, and thus able and willing to abide by relevant linguistic, cultural, and indeed literary conventions. To the degree that our interpretations of a poem are ignorant of those assumptions or violate these conventions, *we are not that poem's audience*, and whatever use we may be making of it, we are not responding to it as what it is.

Although a poem is a representation of discourse, we can understand it, infer meanings for it, only through our prior experiences with the sort of thing it does represent, namely natural utterances in historical contexts. The poet assumes, therefore, that his reader has a knowledge of the language represented by the poem and the linguistic conventions that govern the relation of an utterance to its meanings in that language. However, as we all know, linguistic convention can hardly be separated from cultural convention. The reader who encounters the word "God" in a poem by a seventeenth-century Englishman is not free to interpret it as the deity of the Muslims or Hopi Indians, any more than he is free to interpret a painting of the coronation of Elizabeth as the crowning of the Queen of Siam. Furthermore, the poet will assume that his readers are capable of identifying his composition as one of a kind — a *genre* — of artwork, and therefore of interpreting it in relation to those generic and artistic conventions that operated for him in composing it. Thus the reader who is quite unfamiliar with the forms and traditional functions of the masque, and mistakes *Comus* for the script of an ordinary theatrical comedy, will obviously be interpreting it improperly. We should note here that the poet's assumptions are not to be confused with his intentions. Whereas the latter — his intentions — are specific, personal, and can only be surmised or hypothesized, the former

— his assumptions—are general, communal, and can be reasonably determined or at least sought.[7]

A final observation should be made here regarding the view of interpretation I have been developing. To recognize a poem as mimetic rather than natural discourse, as a verbal artwork rather than an event in nature, is to acknowledge it as the product of a human design in accord with certain valued effects. I have not discussed here the very crucial question of the distinction between the effects or functions of fictive and natural discourse because it is a question that involves substantial problems in linguistic as well as poetic theory, and could not be dealt with briefly. We should, however, at least acknowledge the fact that part of the effect of a poem, as distinct from a natural utterance, derives from the reader's awareness of the poet standing, as it were, behind the poem as its creator and artificer. This awareness is also commonly reflected in our interpretations, for among the meanings we seek for and infer from a poem are those that, in Aristotelian terms, might be called its *final* causes: i.e., the motives or intentions, the governing design, of the poet as an artist, distinct from either a natural speaker or the fictive speaker of a poem. Thus, we can interpret Hamlet's abuse of Ophelia both in terms of a plausible set of human motives projected for Hamlet *and* in terms of a plausible set of artistic motives projected for Shakespeare;

7   The linguistic, cultural, and generic constraints on interpretation alluded to here are, of course, what much professional criticism (or "philology" in the broad sense) is directed toward establishing. And to the extent that it is engaged in determining the existence and nature of such assumptions and conventions on the basis of historical and publicly accessible data, criticism is a cognitively respectable enterprise issuing in objectively verifiable and indeed cumulative knowledge (granting the probabilistic nature of "verifiability" in regard to historical facts and the inevitable grounds for uncertainty and controversy regarding their relevance to individual poems). It would be well, however, to recognize the distinction between this enterprise, which is more or less continuous with that of the cultural historian, and the aspect of professional criticism mentioned in fn. 5, i.e., the public articulation and elaboration of the critic's experience as the audience of an artwork. Both are commonly spoken of as "interpretation" and, of course, both frequently appear in conjunction, but claims that may be made for the one cannot be made for the other, and their functions and value are distinctively different. The meanings of a work that a philological "interpretation" seeks to establish are those that the poem bears in relation to the historical universe in which it was composed, and are themselves historical and determinate; but the meanings that the poem has by virtue of its characteristics as a fictive utterance are historically indeterminate and thus cannot be the object of objective or cumulative knowledge, though we may for various reasons find their "interpretation" by individual readers interesting and valuable. It might be added that each of these types of interpretation may, in turn, be distinguished from those interpretations briefly alluded to below as the reader's (and, when publicly elaborated, the critic's) hypotheses and inferences concerning the poet's governing artistic design. The meanings of "interpretation" are no less multiple than the meanings of "meaning."

and the same sort of double interpretation could be offered for any poem.

This double aspect of interpretation reflects a more fundamental doubleness in the nature of poetry, indeed the duplicity of art itself. As we view the canvas, the myriad spots of paint assume the guise of natural objects in the visual world, but we are nevertheless always half-conscious of them as spots of paint. As we watch the play, the stage recedes and the personal identities of the actors yield to those of the fictions whom they portray, but when, at the final curtain, we clap our hands, it is not Hamlet whom we are applauding, but the performers and the playwright himself. The illusions of art are never *de*lusions. The artwork interests, impresses, and moves us both as the thing represented and as the *representing* itself: as the actions and passions of Prince Hamlet and as the achievement of William Shakespeare, as the speech of men—and as the poet's fictions.

10

The Limits of Literature

Henryk Markiewicz

INTEREST in the specific characteristics of literature dates from the beginnings of theoretical reflections on this subject; this interest has grown in recent times with the efforts to establish the limits and content of literary studies. To determine specific characteristics of literature and to relate them to other verbal works would make it possible to distinguish literary from nonliterary works. Such a procedure would designate the field of literary inquiry as well as the characteristics of literary works. The approach to the subject, however, has been based either on a premise which erroneously identifies the specific with the essential characteristics of literature (while the concepts merely overlap in their scopes), or on a methodologically controversial thesis which claims that only "adequate" judgments (those which refer always and only to their subjects) have scientific value.

Without claiming historical or bibliographical completeness, we may distinguish a few trends in theoretical studies of the distinguishing characteristics of literature. The first trend sees the peculiarity of a literary work in the fact that it is a work of art, or the object of an aesthetic experience. For example, Gustav Lanson wrote:

The mark of a work of art is the artistic intent and effect, is the beauty and the charm of form. . . . Literature consists of all those works whose content and impression can be fully revealed only through an aesthetic analysis of their form. It therefore follows that of the great number of printed texts only those belong to us in a special way which, as a result of their form, can stimulate the imagination, the sensibility, and the aesthetic sensitivity of the reader.[1]

Such a view deals not with all literary works, but only with those that have aesthetic value. Therefore it raises immediately the questions, what is a work of art, and what is an aesthetic experience? Aesthetics has no satisfactory answer to either of these questions.[2]

1 G. Lanson, "La méthode de l'histoire litteraire," in *De la méthode dans les Sciences* (Paris, 1911).
2 Cf. W. Tatarkiewicz, *Skupienie i marzenie (Concentration and Reverie)* (Krakow, 1951), pp. 61–70.

Identical questions arise when attempts are made to define a literary work as a work of verbal art. Some theoreticians attempt to define literature "objectively" by reducing the distinctiveness of literature to the distinctiveness of its language. Imagery, or figurativeness (*Bildlichkeit*), is most frequently mentioned as the particular characteristic of literary language. The concept of imagery itself need not necessarily be part of the linguistic sphere. Certain theoreticians separate the image as a representation existing in the mind of the author or the reader from its linguistic carrier. It ought to be pointed out, though, that the image thus understood can be the subject of literary studies only in so far as it is determined by linguistic means.

The concept of "figurativeness" has been popular in aesthetics and in literary studies since the time of Hegel, and the Hegelian sources are responsible for Bielinskij's and Taine's views in this matter. Though frequently questioned,[3] the concept has not lost its scientific timeliness; scholars of such diverse orientations as the Marxist theoreticians of literature, on the one hand, and Ingarden or Kayser, on the other, are emphasizing it today.

As pointed out by Hegel,[4] two distinct phenomena are usually termed "figurativeness": one is the capability of linguistic forms in a literary work to evoke in the reader frequent, distinct, and qualitatively rich representations (*eigentliche Verbildlichung*), and the other is the figurative (metaphorical or metonymical) use of words (*uneigentliche Verbildlichung*), which, we might add, creates a sort of fictional situation. The first phenomenon need not necessarily occur in a literary work (one could enumerate a number of excellent lyrical works which do not fulfill this condition), while the second one, the figurative aspect, cannot and need not always be imaginatively realized by the reader: sometimes it is unimaginable; other times—when attempts are made at imagining—it becomes an aesthetic horror, which suggests that it is intended only for conceptual and emotional perception.

Even less satisfying is the treatment of the language of literature as a variant of emotive language. This view is related to romantic theories which, starting from the lyric as a standard for poetic work, emphasize the expressive element in poetry; among our contemporaries the view was represented primarily by I. A. Richards in his early writings. According to Richards, emotive language communicates the attitudes, emotions, and beliefs of the speaker, but not information about objective

3   Among others, by T. Meyer in *Das Stilgesetz der Poesie* (Leipzig, 1901), and by Russian formalists.
4   G. W. F. Hegel, *Aesthetik* (Berlin, 1955), pp. 905-06.

reality; the distinguishing factor of poetic language, as opposed to colloquial language, is the high degree of purposeful organization[5] or the simultaneous satisfaction of contradictory impulses, which brings about a state of psychic equilibrium but inhibits the tendency to act.[6] Yet such definitions deal not with the language of literature, but only with its expressive functions and its effects on the audience. After all, Richards himself agrees that apart from poetry of the greatest worth, the "synesthetic" poetry of inclusion, there exists also the poetry of a given emotion, mood, or attitude.[7] His is most clearly not a descriptive, but a normative, definition of poetry.

The conception of Cleanth Brooks, which is similar to views expressed by Richards, raises the same doubts. According to Brooks, the language of poetry, which is governed by the principle of "paradox" or "irony" (understood as the coexistence within a work of opposed statements and points of view), is purposely "compact," ambiguous, marked by multiple association, the meaning of words being determined mainly by the pressure of their context.[8] Such a proposition is itself nothing but an ingenious paradox, since the meaning of a metaphor depends primarily on the general linguistic meaning of its components and can be understood and judged only in relation to them; it should also be apparent that dependence on context occurs in every utterance, especially in colloquial speech. The counterargument, that in poetry, and only in poetry, the context is different in every case, is answered by invoking the role of poetic convention.[9]

The above reservations seem obvious, yet ambiguity and the contextual character of poetic semantics are among the most popular and lasting theses of contemporary theory in the United States. The Russian formalist school has voiced other propositions. The most daring of its theoreticians, Roman Jakobson, in various of his older works defined poetry as "language in its aesthetic function," as "organized violence against colloquial everyday language," and finally as "vyskazy-

5 E.g., R. Wellek and A. Warren, *Theory of Literature* (New York, 1948), p. 14.

6 This concept refers to Coleridge's famous statement about the power of poetry which is expressed in "the balance or reconciliation of opposite or discordant qualities."

7 I. A. Richards, *Principles of Literary Criticism*, 14th ed. (London, 1955), pp. 249-50.

8 C. Brooks, "Irony as Principle of Structure," in *Literary Opinion in America*, ed. M. D. Zabel (New York, 1951), pp. 729-41.

9 Cf. R. S. Crane, "The Critical Monism of Cleanth Brooks," in *Critics and Criticism* (Chicago, 1952), pp. 100 ff.; W. Sutton, "The Contextual Dilemma or Fallacy," *Journal of Aesthetics and Art Criticism*, No. 2 (1958); M. Krieger, in *The New Apologists for Poetry* (Minneapolis, 1956), pp. 198 ff., made an attempt at a partial defense of Brooks.

vanije s ustanovkoj na vyraženije."[10] The formula is a difficult one to translate. Its sense can perhaps best be interpreted as: "an utterance focused on the way it is expressed." In his most recent paper, "Poetics in Light of Linguistics," Jakobson has modernized the terminology, adjusting it to contemporary information theory. He now identifies the poetic function as the "focus on the message for its own sake."

Any attempt to reduce the sphere of poetic function to poetry or to confine poetry to poetic function would be a delusive oversimplification. Poetic function is not the sole function of verbal art but only its dominant, determining function, whereas in all other verbal activities it acts as a subsidiary, accessory constituent. This function, by promoting the palpability of signs, deepens the fundamental dichotomy of signs and objects.[11]

The linguistic criterion of the poetic function of language is marked by a special use of *selection* and *combination*, the two basic modes of arranging verbal behavior. In poetry, the principle of equivalent terms, a matter of *selection*, becomes the constitutive device o *combination*. As Jakobson expresses it, "the poetic function projects the principle of equivalence from the axis of selection into the axis of combination." An explanation of these highly metaphoric formulas can be found in Jakobson's work, but, simply put, they state that the poetic function is manifested when an utterance is ordered additionally in a way which cannot be justified by the usual requirements of linguistic communication.[12]

Despite the attractive exposition, especially of the exemplification, this theory, too, is questionable. First of all, we do not know how to interpret the statement that equivalence is the constitutive factor of the poetic sequence. In principle the constitutive factor is the contiguity; the attempt to achieve equivalence or similarity must be con-

10 R. Jakobson, *Novejšaja russkaja poezija* (Prague, 1921), p. 10. A similar statement was made earlier by L. P. Jakubinski in "O zvukax poetičeskogo jazyka," in *Poetika* (Petrograd, 1919), p. 17. In it he distinguished between "the system of the practical language, in which linguistic representations have no independent value and are only a means of communication," and a system of poetic language in which "the practical goal becomes less important and linguistic systems gain independent value."

11 R. Jakobson, "Closing statement: Linguistics and Poetics," *Pamietnik Literacki*, 1960, No. 2, 439. (English text in *Style in Language*, ed. T. A. Sebeok [New York, and London, 1960], p. 356.)

12 In later parts of his work Jakobson, following W. Empson, considers ambiguity to be an inseparable element of poetry ("Poetics in Light of Linguistics," p. 461). E. Stankiewicz, "Linguistics and the Study of Poetic Language," *Style in Language*, ed. T. A. Sebeok (New York and London, 1960); S. R. Levin, *Linguistic Structures in Poetry* (The Hague); and J. Lotman, *Struktura xudožestvennogo teksta* (Moscow, 1970), are among those who refer to Jakobson's views.

fined within the range determined by the requirements of contiguity.[13] In a conflict between the requirements of contiguity and those of equivalence, contiguity is as a rule a more important factor; examples of the contrary are usually evaluated negatively, as in cases where meaning is sacrificed to rhyme. Regardless of this, we do not know what objective indicators allow us to conclude that the poetic function dominates others.

Another difficulty is even more serious: Jakobson, as well as the above-named American theoreticians, has spoken about the "language of poetry," not about "the language of literature." English linguistic custom does not consider fiction—narrative prose—to be poetry. Therefore either the above characteristics refer only to poetry as part of literature, and in that case they might be valid, but they do not answer our question, or they offer a false answer leading to a definition so narrow that it excludes the greater part of literary prose. Žyrmunskij warned the Russian formalists against this:

While lyric verse is the art of the word, a novel by L. Tolstoy, not restricted in its linguistic composition, uses the word not as an element with an artistic function, but as an artistically indifferent stratum or series of signs which are, as is the case in colloquial speech, subordinated to communication, and which introduce us to thematic elements independent of the word. Such a literary work cannot be termed the art of the word, certainly not in the same sense in which a lyric poem deserves the designation.[14]

Perhaps Žyrmunskij goes a bit too far; it is nevertheless this particular problem that causes such difficulty for the theoreticians of literature.[15] L. Beriger once stated that a literary work written in prose is, in its linguistic aspect, a deviation from the essence of poetry. It is possible to follow his example and answer the whole problem by saying "the worse for reality," yet such an answer seems anachronistic.[16]

Difficulties with narrative or dramatic prose are conveniently solved by the theory which points to the fictional element as the main discriminant of literature. In its more extreme statements this view sees a total autonomy of the world represented in a literary work. Both

13 Jakobson himself seems to admit as much when he continues: "similarity is built over contiguity" ("Poetics in Light of Linguistics," p. 460).

14 W. Žyrmunskij, *K voprosu o "formalnom metode,"* (1923). Polish translation, "W sprawie metody formalnej," *Życie Literackie,* 3-4 (1947), 75.

15 M. Krieger (*The New Apologists for Poetry,* pp. 72-73) admits it.

16 L. Beriger, "Poesie und Prosa," *Deutsche Vierteljahrsschrift für Literaturwissenschaft und Geistesgeschichte* (1943), pp. 132 ff.

theories have an old tradition behind them.[17] Even in antiquity mimesis, seen as the creation of an illusion only simulating reality, was considered to be characteristic of poetry. Generally, though, the concept of fictionality was not used to negate the ties between the represented world and objective reality. Only in the eighteenth century was the tendency in this direction intensified; a poetic work came to be treated as a self-contained and self-sufficient whole, isolated from and independent of objective reality, subject only to the rules of inner consistency and cohesion. The beginnings of this concept can already be seen in some statements by Lessing and Goethe.[18] Its importance in contemporary thought is due to Richards' analysis of pseudostatements and Ingarden's work on quasi-judgments in literature. While Richards influenced the Anglo-Saxon critics, Ingarden has a following in Germany, mainly through the writings of Günther Müller and Wolfgang Kayser. His influence can also be seen in the views of René Wellek. In Poland an analogous role was played by Manfred Kridl's book *Introduction to Studies of a Literary Work* (1936), which strongly emphasized the importance of fiction as a characteristic of literature.

Here too certain difficulties occurred. A contradiction was apparent between the extreme view of the fictionality of the represented world and those views which ascribed to literature a cognitive function in relation to objective reality. American critics, unconsciously following Croce, spoke of an intuitive knowledge of individual objects;[19] German critics spoke of an insight into the sphere of the "essence of things." Most important, though, the occurrence of quasi-judgments and the idea of fictionality proved debatable in the area of lyric poetry,[20] and even more so in didactic, reflective, and descriptive poetry, and in numerous forms of nonfictional prose, such as essays, memoirs, letters, reporting, etc. Fictionality as the determinant of literature is unacceptable especially to those involved in the study of older (pre-romantic) and contemporary literature.

None of these difficulties are accidental, nor do they result solely from the common error of formulating either too broad or too narrow definitions. The cause is much deeper because difficulties are inescapable as long as the aim is to find one specific difference of literariness applicable to all works. The reason is not, as is usually thought, the

17 Here and in the later part I have used material from W. Tatarkiewicz, *Aesthetics in Antiquity* and *Aesthetics in the Middle Ages* (Wroclaw, 1960).
18 Cf. M. H. Abrams, *The Mirror and the Lamp* (New York, 1958), pp. 278 ff.
19 Cf. M. Krieger, pp. 140-55.
20 The difference between lyric poetry, as a statement about reality, and other "fictional" genres was discussed by K. Hamburger, *Die Logik der Dichtung* (Stuttgart, 1957), pp. 144-208.

existence of shared features between literature and nonliterature, but the heterogeneous character of linguistic works now accepted as literary. Let us begin by recalling the known fact that the term "literature," in the sense that interests us here, is rather recent. Until the middle of the eighteenth century only the term "poetry" was known, yet since it first appeared, the scope of its application has been controversial. The sophist Gorgias accepted as a formal criterion the idea that poetry was "every speech in meter." A contrary view was expressed by Aristotle. To him the characteristics of poetry were: first, mimesis, understood most probably as imitative fiction, and second, the use of rhythm, language, and harmony. He demanded a second term for art which "imitates by means of language alone, and that either in prose or verse" (without a musical accompaniment), perhaps also for those works which had no mimetic character, since in them the poet "speaks in his own person." And he protested against the use of the term "poetry" when "a treatise on medicine or material science is brought out in verse," when their authors were named poets "as if it were not the imitation that makes the poet, but the verse that entitles them all indiscriminately to the name." [21]

Contained in these intricate and hypothetically reconstructed Aristotelian arguments are the premises of all later controversies concerning the borderline between poetry and nonpoetry. During the Hellenic period the situation was to become even more complex as a result of greater proximity and mutual influence between poetry and oratorical art. In the Middle Ages they became further and more permanently interwoven: poetics became subordinated to rhetoric (Dante defined poetry as "fictio rhetorica in musica posita"); at the same time the border between the area of reality and the area of fiction in literature disappeared. *Res fictae* and *res gestae* were considered equally subjects of poetry.

During the Renaissance the differences between poetry and oratory were theoretically clear, though their functions were seen as related. Consequently, they were considered a common subject for the study of "litterae humaniores," later of "belles lettres," and finally, in the middle of the eighteenth century, of "literature." The term itself had undergone various transformations of meaning which, for lack of space, cannot be reconstructed here. [22] To take Poland as an example: in 1786 F. N. Golanski entitled his textbook *On Oratory and Poetry*, but

21 Aristotle, "Poetics," in *Criticism: The Foundations of Modern Literary Judgment*, ed. M. Schorer, J. Miles, G. McKenzie (New York, 1948), pp. 199-200.
22 They are presented by R. Escarpit, "Histoire de l'Histoire de la Littérature," in "Histoire des Littératures," *Encyclopédie de la Pléiade* (Paris, 1958), III, 1737-44.

as early as 1816 Jan Śniadecki proposed to follow the French example and to consider as literature the study which examines "the works of poetry and oratorical art accessible to general understanding, such as plays, exemplar poetry of various kinds, and in prose everything that has eloquence for general understanding or can serve as a model of good writing."[23] As a result of such works like Mme. de Staël's *De la Littérature* (1800), the term "literature" soon came to be understood not as referring to the study of poetry and oratory, but to the poetry and oratory itself, or rather to all literary genres derived from ancient oratorical art. In practice this included all *humaniores*, with the exception of text books, compendiums, etc. The tendency was aided by the romantic theory of "universal poetry" which negated the existence of rigid genre norms and of distinct borders between poetry and other creative fields.

Only in the nineteenth century—with the gradual disappearance of the art of oratory and with the development of aestheticism in literature and criticism, of tendencies towards "dissimilation" and "purity" of the various cultural forms, and of a trend toward the scientific approach in the humanities, which increased their distance from literary prose—did the field of literature begin to narrow by excluding the border genres. The various criteria employed were discussed in the introduction to this essay. At the same time attempts were made to distinguish within the field of literature either a group of particularly valuable works, which could be viewed as "poetry" (B. Croce), or a still narrower range of works or fragments of "pure poetry" defined variously, though usually in a vague opposition to intellectual or utilitarian elements (G. Moore, H. Brémond). The sharp opposition of "poetry" and the "art of prose" in Sartre's essay on literature had a similar meaning.

Recently, though, we are again observing a blurring of distinctions between, on the one hand, poetry and artistic prose, and on the other between literature and philosophy, science, reporting or journalism. The importance of fictionality as a determinant of literariness has been greatly diminished. The Soviet "literature of fact," the reporting by Kisch, and Gide's journals were already significant examples of the trend.

So the close affinities between poetry and eloquence lead to the inclusion of both under the term "literature," and finally to the illusion that there indeed exists a homogeneous class of literary objects. In a sense it is an example of the process which, in connection with

23 J. Śniadecki, *Selected Scientific Works* (Warsaw, 1954), pp. 97-98.

the concept of an aesthetic experience, was so well described by Wladyslav Tatarkiewicz:

The name of an object may be used loosely and applied to other objects partially similar to it. For example, the name X, proper for objects with the characteristics of a and b, is frequently applied to object A, because it has the characteristic of a, as well as to object B, because it has the characteristic of b. Thus we have a common name for A and B, though they can have no characteristics in common. In such a case there is the name X, but a class of objects X does not exist. This way of proceeding, proper for colloquial speech, but also encountered in those sciences which have not achieved a higher degree of conceptual precision, resembles the game of dominoes, where a single domino is added to the previous one on the basis of partial similarity. A sequence of dominoes is composed in which the neighboring pieces are similar, but the further ones may have nothing in common.[24]

We see, therefore, that even after eliminating definitions which are clearly false or merely normative, none of the qualities of literature is generally valid. The reason is the heterogeneous character of literature itself. Verbal works are today considered part of literature when the represented world is fictional (even if only partially), when, in relation to the requirements of ordinary linguistic communication, a "superimposed ordering" is observed, and finally in virtue of figurativeness (indirect figurativeness has as well the characteristics of fiction).

For those who have a formalist orientation and develop general theoretical statements using works with a plot as their starting point, fictionality is the strongest signal of "literariness." To those with a "cognitive" orientation, direct figurativeness is the essential signal. When lyric poetry is the starting point, "superimposed ordering," such as the rhythm of an utterance or indirect figurativeness, takes on that same function.

Let us test these generalizations on the example of two sentences: "Burglary usually occurs at night" and "The Kowalskis' apartment on Zlota Street was burglarized yesterday." Such sentences, while they can be included in a literary work, have no literary characteristics. But if we say "With the fall of dusk Arsène Lupin broke into the Dupont's apartment," and we know that Lupin is a fictional character, the sentence becomes, in our view, "literary." We can achieve the same result by introducing into the text superimposed order, rhyme for example, without any fictional element: "Night is falling, the thief is crawling," or finally direct or metaphoric figurativeness: "Amidst

24 W. Tatarkiewicz, *Skupienie i marzenie (Concentration and Reverie)*, p. 68.

total silence he heard" (or metaphorically: "the silence was exploded by") "the sound of loud knocking on the door."

Literary beyond dispute are those literary genres in which, as if according to Dante's definition, all three characteristics of "literariness" occur simultaneously (e.g., an epic poem). If even one characteristic is absent, their "literariness" is questioned (as in a didactic poem or novel). Jakobson speaks of the prose forms of the art of the word as being a "transition" stage between the strictly poetic and strictly cognitive language.[25] From a contemporary perspective it seems odd that in the sixteenth and seventeenth centuries it was frequently questioned whether lyrics are part of poetry because of the absence of the fictional imitative element.[26] When a given work has only one of these characteristics, it is treated as a "borderline phenomenon," e.g., a film story (only fictionality), a rhymed political or advertising slogan (only "superimposed ordering"), reporting (only figurativeness).

Finally, a question poses itself: is it indeed possible to find a common denominator for the three characteristics of "literariness" which would justify an objective relationship between works described as literary, and indirectly justify also a relative unity of the subject matter of literary studies? The following is a highly imperfect answer to this question: the hallmark of "literariness" is that a work fulfills the basic linguistic functions—the informative, emotive, and appellative—differently from colloquial or scientific utterances, employing the elements of fictionality (thus with diminished assertiveness and increased plurisignation), or "superimposed ordering," or, finally, heightened figurativeness. Only in extreme cases can the basic functions be absent; as a rule such a work will represent that border of literature beyond which lies the sphere of senseless sound formations.

(Translated by Uliana Gabara)

25   R. Jakobson, "Poetics in Light of Linguistics," p. 467.
26   Cf. I. Behrens, *Die Lehre von der Einteilung der Dichtkunst* (Halle/Saale, 1940).

Ut Pictura Noesis?
Criticism in Literary Studies and Art History

Svetlana and Paul Alpers

ART HISTORY is one of the most prestigious fields in the humanities. On the two fronts on which it operates most powerfully—the study of style and the study of iconography—it has had great influence on other humanistic disciplines. We owe to Wölfflin our ideas about period style and to Mâle, Panofsky, Wind and others our knowledge of iconography, as both a cultural fact and a method of interpretation. Ever since Burckhardt, our consciousness and understanding of cultural history have been intimately connected with art history and enhanced by those who study it. Because of their debt to art historians for methods of interpretation and principles of historical ordering, literary scholars have had little occasion to notice the almost complete absence from art historical writings of the kind of critical considerations which are normal, not to say basic, in the academic study of literature. There are various reasons for this. Students of literature (at least in America) seem puzzled by the visual arts and uncertain of how to deal with them, and thus have been simply grateful for the breadth of coverage and extraordinary learning characteristic of the best art historians. On the other hand—and rather contradictorily— it often seems to be assumed that a slide or photograph introduced into a literary analysis or exposition has a real presence to which it is unnecessary to add any words of explanation or interpretation. The work of art, unlike a literary text, seems self-explanatory. Whatever his use of or relation to the visual arts, the student of literature is rarely aware of the problems of writing art criticism or of the weakness of art history as a critical discipline. Indeed, professors of English, many of whom think of themselves as literary critics, may be surprised to learn that no self-respecting art historian would call himself a critic. In the field of art history, art critics are journalists, and what students of literature call criticism is patronizingly referred to as art appreciation.

Though it seems to us important to call attention to the differing status of critical writing in the study of art and literature today, our aim is less to belabor this fact than to investigate its reasons. Is it simply an historical phenomenon related to the development of each discipline? To what extent is it due to certain differences inherent in the phenomena being studied? Drawing analogies between painting and poetry has a long and august tradition in the West, but the relationships have commonly been argued for specific programmatic purposes, often an attempt in the theoretical realm to argue the worth of painting in the face of the acknowledged pre-eminence of poetry.[1] However, with the example of twentieth century literary criticism before us, it seems worthwhile to look at the problem once more, to see whether there is any likeness between the ways we attend to and speak about literature and art. The issue of what is peculiar or intrinsic to the visual arts has been very much alive in the discussion of *avant-garde* painting since the middle of the last century. From Zola's defence of realism to Michael Fried's defense of "modernist" painting,[2] the argument has been that finally art is dispensing with irrelevancies (be it the evocation of a tear and a smile, or representation altogether) and getting down to its essential concerns. A somewhat analogous development of self-consciousness about the intrinsic nature of language and the literary text, particularly in France, has brought us to the point where it is the distinctions, not the similarities, between the arts of which we are made particularly aware. At the moment, perhaps the only unifying approach being offered is through the cumbersome and unsatisfactory machinery of structuralist analysis— a philosophy one might think was invented specifically to deal with the situation of the arts at present. For this reason, too, it seems the right moment to ask whether kinds of similarities do or at least did exist between the arts that would perhaps make criticism in the traditional sense possible.

If "criticism" as "criticism" exists, there should be some similarities between the way we teach and write about works of art and the way we teach and write about works of literature. But at first glance, the differences are more striking than the similarities. The literary critic— heir to Eliot and Richards, Empson and Leavis—attempts to convey matters of sensibility, attitude, expression. Even without accepting the full implications of Coleridge's organicism, he assumes that form and content are inseparable, and that they work together to produce individual meanings, attitudes, and revelations of reality. The New

1 See Rensselaer W. Lee, " 'Ut Pictura Poesis': The Humanistic Theory of Painting," *Art Bulletin,* 22 (1940), 197-269; paperback reprint (Norton), 1967.
2 Michael Fried, *Three American Painters,* the catalogue (with a long introductory essay) of an exhibition of Kenneth Noland, Jules Olitski, and Frank Stella at the Fogg Art Museum, Cambridge, in 1965.

FIG. 1   Rubens, *The Kermess*, Paris, Louvre

FIG. 2 Rembrandt, *The Supper at Emmaus*, Paris, Louvre

FIG. 3   van Eyck, *The Arnolfini Portrait*, London, National Gallery

FIG. 4   Titian, *Pesaro Madonna*, Venice, Santa Maria dei Frari

Critics at their most "formalist" do not attend to form alone: they are formalist in that they seek to make sensibility, expression, and the like objective properties of the work itself. The methodology of the art historian, on the other hand, is based on a clear separation between style and iconography, form and content. The poles of this methodology can be roughly represented by the dual influence of Wölfflin's *Principles of Art History* and Panofsky's iconographic studies. A quotation from Wölfflin dramatizes this split in unforgettable terms:

The imitative content, the subject matter, may be as different in itself as possible [between works of different periods], the decisive point remains that the conception in each case is based on a different visual schema—a schema which, however, is far more deeply rooted than in mere questions of the progress of imitation. It conditions the architectural work as well as the work of representative art, and a Roman baroque façade has the same visual denominator as a landscape by Van Goyen.[3]

The assertion of stylistic identity between seventeenth century works as different as a church façade and a landscape painting goes to an extreme which few art historians would accept. Nevertheless, it reveals a habit of mind the effect of which can be seen, for example, in the fact that of the numerous studies in recent years on the subject and meanings of the paintings of Poussin, not one considers how the "classical" figure style and compositional format affect the meanings of the works. Rather the very interest in certain kinds of meanings is seen as characteristic of a classical style of painting, and the matter is left at that. This separation of form and content in art is possible because each is seen as a function of an historical situation. The art historian tends to look at an individual work in order to discover the elements it has in common with other works. He has little sense of the integrity of the individual work, which the literary critic takes as axiomatic and which is the basis of his axiomatic refusal to separate form and content. As a field, art history is appropriately named, and its practitioners are indeed art historians.

There are many practical reasons why the study of art is primarily historical in its concerns. Its own history as a field has involved rejecting what might be called the nineteenth century's Grand Tour attitude toward the pleasures of the arts. Berenson's lists of *Italian Pictures of the Renaissance* (1932), for example, brought order in the attribution and dating of a mass of works that were indiscriminately appreciated or simply not looked at. The very nature of the materials with which art historians work demands, at least initially, a much more

3 Heinrich Wölfflin, *Principles of Art History*, trans. M. D. Hottinger (New York, n.d.), p. 13; originally published in 1915.

archaeological approach than does the study of literary texts. Most works of art are unsigned and undated, and their history and condition are often uncertain. Copies and even fakes must be sorted out from "original" works which themselves often present evidence of more than one hand. With so much attention necessary to objective properties, is it any wonder that critical concerns are slighted? But this is not the whole story. For in a quite positive (indeed, positivistic) sense, the discipline still subscribes to a Rankean notion of building up an historical account from objectively ascertained facts. At the same time, its overall historical task is enormous. Art history sets out to encompass the entire history of world art. Not only do art historians take all architecture, sculpture, and painting as their province; the scope of the field extends to the so-called minor arts and artifacts, such as furniture, devotional objects, book bindings, and in some cases even scabbards and stirrups. Making some order of all this is a pressing problem. It is interesting and characteristic of the field that one of the first major efforts at making order was the work of the keeper of textiles at the Austrian Museum for Applied Arts. Beginning with re-peated motifs in the history of textiles, Alois Riegl (d. 1905) went on to separate studies of late Roman arts and crafts, Dutch group portraits, and Baroque art, in terms of what he determined to be their essential compositional and formal elements. He saw these, in turn, as revealing something essential about the way a particular culture perceives the world. Riegl's assumption that styles are generalizations or abstractions that we arrive at by defining the common denominator of all the works of one period, and his determination to get rid of any evaluative statements (whether distinguishing between periods or kinds of works) would still seem valid to many art historians today. As a recent commentator says, "Because of Riegl, art historians have been able to esteem a gem-studded fibula as highly as a cathedral and can use both to shed light on the 'dark ages.' "[4] As in so many matters these days, like political right and left, *les extrèmes se touchent*: the conservative field of art history joins with the structuralist *avant-garde* in rejecting distinctions between the arts and traditional hierarchies of evaluation.[5]

4 W. Eugene Kleinbauer, *Modern Perspectives in Western Art History* (New York, 1971), p. 125.

5 Admittedly, most art historians, as the previous quotation demonstrates, hope to employ this kind of analysis in the interests of cultural history. But cf. Sheldon Nodelman, "Structural Analysis in Art and Anthropology," in *Structuralism*, ed. Jacques Ehrmann (New York, 1970), pp. 79-93. Nodelman cites Riegl as being the first to attempt a structural analysis of works of art, although significantly he cau-tions that his "analytic strategy . . . still depended in a sense on the external ap-pearance of the work of art, thus still on the subjective 'impression' " (p. 87).

The difference between critical and historical assumptions and biases can be seen most clearly and importantly in the differing ways in which art historians and students of literature think of style. To an art historian, style is a radically historical concept. As Meyer Schapiro says, in the best known article on the subject, "Common to all these approaches [archaeological, art historical, cultural historical, and critical] are the assumptions that every style is peculiar to a period of culture and that, in a given culture or epoch of culture, there is only one style or a limited range of styles." The concern with style is based on the true perception that "works in the style of one time could not have been produced in another."[6] Style conceived of at this level of analytical and historical generality transcends considerations of individual works and individual artists. The impulse that led Vasari, the first historian of art, to talk of the first, second and third ages of Italian painting, is the same that has led art historians of this age to speak of the Renaissance, Mannerist, Baroque, and finally even proto-, early, and high Baroque styles. Following Vasari's example, art historians generally treat major artists as the makers of style (Raphael the maker of the High Renaissance, Rubens the maker of Baroque) and the minor ones as those who follow in their stylistic footsteps. How to deal with a great master whose idiosyncratic style does not fit into the general scheme (e.g. Bruegel or Rembrandt) or how to handle the particular achievement of the style-makers remain problems for art historians today, even as they were for Vasari in the sixteenth century. In his skillful study of Mannerism, part of a series on "Style and Civilization," John Shearman largely omits the art of Pontormo—perhaps the greatest of the painters commonly considered mannerists—presumably because his paintings do not sufficiently exemplify the general stylistic traits of the time.[7]

In literary studies, on the other hand, considerations of style are characteristically critical: the main purpose of analysis is to interpret individual works and authors. This is true, for example, of Leo Spitzer's work in stylistics, though it has great methodological ambitions. It is characteristic of English studies that perhaps the most significant postwar work on Renaissance prose style is a book devoted to a single author[8]—Jonas A. Barish's *Ben Jonson and the Language of Prose*

6 Meyer Schapiro, "Style," in *Aesthetics Today*, ed. Morris Philipson (New York, 1961), p. 82; originally in *Anthropology Today*, ed. A. L. Kroeber (Chicago, 1953).
7 John Shearman, *Mannerism* (Penguin Books, 1967). The only work by Pontormo illustrated in this book is a tapestry he designed.
8 Cambridge, Mass., 1960. By the same token, the most important recent study, Joan Webber's *The Eloquent "I"* (Madison, Wis., 1970), proceeds author by author, work by work.

Comedy. It is not that Spitzer and Barish eschew general concepts and historical categories; on the contrary, "baroque" is an important term for both of them. But each views period style not as a separable and self-sufficient phenomenon, but as an instrument of expression or a set of rhetorical possibilities. Hence there is no contradiction in their treating style as an integral aspect of individual works—a manifestation of the essential life of the work or an author's imagination. Barish neatly summarizes the way a critic focuses on the individual:

The narrowing circles of convention bring us closer and closer to the individual writer, and to conscious linguistic artistry. The gulf between Hopi and English exists on a deep, unconscious level, as does that between one Indo-European language and another until bridged (if at all) by study. Conscious purpose plays some part in the historical transformations of a single language, but here too no doubt the determining factor is still the imponderable calculus of thousands of instances of unreflecting usage. When we reach literary categories such as Croll's "baroque," we are dealing with a convention that is at the same time a collective style, since its practitioners have chosen more or less deliberately to adhere to one set of conventional practices rather than another. When we move from the collective style to the individual artist, we reach the province of style *tout court*, where the writer stamps the shared style with the imprint of his own temperament.[9]

All of this suggests that art history has much to learn from literary criticism, and we indeed think this to be the case.[10] Nevertheless, art history seeks a level of generality that can profitably challenge students of literature. Although terms like "mannerist" and "baroque," when used as they are in art history, are realities only by courtesy of the fallacy of misplaced concreteness, it is still the case that, as Schapiro says, "works in the style of one time could not have been produced in another." The abuse of terminology—which, Lord knows, is not confined to one field or one time—is no reason not to pursue valid syntheses and generalizations, and the endeavors of literary historians and art historians should no more be separated from each other than were the respective arts themselves in most periods of Western culture. However, both art history and literary history are in stages of transition and redefinition—as the existence of this journal witnesses—and the cooperative pursuit of historical generalizations is more a future prospect than a present reality. At the moment, the most impressive instance of the high level of generalization that art history fosters is analytic

9 Barish, pp. 43-44.
10 See Svetlana Alpers' review of Kenneth Clark, *Rembrandt and the Italian Renaissance, Art Bulletin,* 52 (1970), 326-29.

rather than historical—E. H. Gombrich's *Art and Illusion* (1960).
Gombrich's work is important and stimulating, because he illuminates
problems common to all the arts—the nature of realism, the role of convention, problems of ordering, the participatory role of reader, viewer,
and listener. But it is important to recognize that the power and insight
of *Art and Illusion* are not due to any attempt to deal with all the arts,
but to the fact that Gombrich deals specifically with painting and with
problems unusually prominent in it. The basis of the book, as the title
succinctly puts it, is the dual recognition of Western artists' concern
for and success in imitating nature and of style as the means by which
they do this. Although it has been traditional since Aristotle to speak
of all the arts as imitative, imitation has a uniquely concrete presence
in the visual arts. Similarly, the manner or style in which a painting
is executed—which includes everything from the formal organization
and the character of the figures to the brush strokes and the handling
of pigments—has an undeniably tangible presence not found in a text.
The physical presence of the visual arts explains why art historians
can treat style and imitated content as objective realities, and Gombrich's ideas must be seen, at least in the first instance, as his challenging
the way his fellow art historians have interpreted these two aspects
of an art work. He turns attention away from the *observation* of
nature—the term usually used to praise imitation in painting—to "the
systematic modification and refinement of traditions"[11] by which the
effect of observing nature is achieved. Similarly, and with rather more
animus, he rejects the habit of treating style as a mode of perception
(Wölfflin) or a mode of expression (in the sense of its expressing the
spirit of an age) to argue for style as the means of representation itself.
To contrast his basic argument with that of Schapiro, it is not that
"works in the style of one time could not have been produced in
another," but that since art can never be identical with reality, there is
style present in every work. This very attention to style as a fundamental, constitutive reality enables him to interpret Schapiro's point
in a new way. Gombrich, whose antagonism to Hegel is notorious,
demystifies art history by viewing creative development and historical
change in a realistic way—as the exercise of artistic choice, and not
as the result of mysterious historical forces.

In a well known study of the field of art history, James S. Ackerman
remarks that criticism "is concerned with the problem of defining the

---

11 E. H. Gombrich, "Light, Form, and Texture in Fifteenth-Century Painting,"
reprinted in Kleinbauer, *Perspectives*, p. 283; originally in *Journal of the Royal
Society of Arts*, 112 (1964), 826-49.

unique qualities of single works of art." [12] But this general formula conceals an interesting disparity between works in literature and the visual arts. Our usual comparisons are between artists—Rubens and Spenser, Shakespeare and Rembrandt, Milton and Poussin—and in comparing artists we are implicitly comparing aspects common to all (or most of) their works. But if we compare works, we find there is no single work of Rubens or Rembrandt or Poussin that can usefully be compared to *The Faerie Queene* or *Hamlet* or *Paradise Lost*. There is, in other words, a certain imbalance between "a work" of art and "a work" of literature. Of course we can find pairs of "equal weight" beyond the obvious comparisons of single paintings with single lyric poems—the Sistine ceiling and *Paradise Lost*, Rembrandt's Biblical etchings and a collection of religious lyrics like Herbert's *The Temple*. But it seems more important to remember how often the imbalance can exist than to claim it as a rule which must stand the proof of all exceptions. It is certainly of great practical importance to the critic who seeks to give an account of an individual work. Rubens' rendering of a low life celebration in his *Kermess* (Fig. 1) could be usefully compared, one would think, to *Bartholomew Fair*, a roughly contemporary work which seems to provide a perfect literary analogue to its teeming world. But *Bartholomew Fair*, with its range of characters and modes of life and its artistic self-reflection (as in the puppet show), encompasses much more than this one painting does. To find a comparable variety and complexity in Rubens, we must link the *Kermess* to other works which share with it certain features of style and subject matter— the so-called *Peasant Dance* in the Prado and the Vienna *Worship of Venus*, with its very similar swirling figures of nymphs and satyrs, and Rubens' (presumably) copy of a lost work by Bruegel, depicting quarrelling card-players. But these paintings do not constitute "a work" by Rubens, and interpreting them as a group is a different act from interpreting an individual work. Similarly, the student of *Orlando Furioso* who looks to the visual arts would have to seek out not one

12   James S. Ackerman and Rhys Carpenter, *Art and Archaeology* (Englewood Cliffs, N. J., 1963), p. 140. This volume is one of a series devoted to "Humanistic Scholarship in America." Ackerman makes many of the points we do about the field of art history. In our view, he underestimates the extent to which art history as a discipline is, by its nature, antagonistic to criticism. He also underestimates the problems of writing good art criticism—partly because he assumes techniques of literary criticism can be directly transferred to writing about art, and partly because he does not recognize that the nature and function of criticism are still at issue in literary studies.

    This might be the place to remark that the critical writings of Clive Bell, Roger Fry, and Herbert Read have worn considerably less well, in our opinion, than the best literary criticism contemporary with them. Hence we have not considered them in this essay.

work with which to compare the poem, but rather the complete works of individual painters and/or whole genres of painting. Here again, the imbalance we have described emerges as a problem of interpretation. Huge as it is, *Orlando Furioso* is one work, and to seek out the ordering of and relations between its parts is very different from doing the same thing with, say, the paintings of Veronese.

Another way of seeing the imbalance between individual works of art and of literature is to compare the characteristic ways in which they are described and interpreted. In literary studies, books devoted to single works are a matter of course. They are not in art history, and the rare example will have the proportions of Julius Held's fine study of Rembrandt's *Aristotle Contemplating the Bust of Homer*.[13] This long article exhaustively treats the provenance of the work, the traditions of presenting Aristotle, his relationship to Homer and Alexander (whose portrait he wears on a gold chain around his neck), the iconographic type of the painting (portrait with a bust), the depiction of the melancholy sage, the history of the chain of honor. Held devotes only the concluding pages of each section to the painting itself. As he himself says, his study "brings into focus a variety of themes and traditions conjoined in one of the most richly structured works of the master."[14] Similarly, an art historian's treatment of Rubens' *Kermess* would seek to explain the scene by an account of those elements which are traditional in the depicting of such peasant festivals. The setting (by an inn, with a church tower just visible on the horizon) and the actions (dancing, love-making, eating, fighting, vomiting, and bagpipe-playing) and the types (short, squat figures, with some ragged beggars in the middle) can be traced back to Bruegel and in some cases to even earlier German woodcuts. As for the meaning of the work, the art historian would ask, what is the relationship of this work to the didactic meanings which are basic to the tradition? Such a study would also take into account a well known drawing in which Rubens crowds together into a single study many of the figures for the painting. Here the questions are how the painting

13 Julius S. Held, *Rembrandt's Aristotle and Other Studies* (Princeton, 1969), pp. 3–44. Like Held's study, Edgar Wind's books on Bellini's *Feast of the Gods* (Cambridge, Mass., 1948) and Giorgione's *Tempest* (Oxford, 1969) are essentially articles in conception and length.

The current paperback series entitled "Norton Critical Studies in Art History" has the admirable purpose of devoting separate volumes to gathering together "all the necessary material for the comprehensive study of a work of art." But in each volume, the section entitled "criticism" or "critical essays" is selected from art historical studies, past and present. In spite of the series title, the critical gap is not filled, but revealed.

14 Held, p. 41.

makes use of these materials, reassembles the figures, alters the perspective viewpoint. Since the subject is unique in Rubens' oeuvre and the work is undated, an attempt would be made to place it stylistically in relation to his other works: in what other works does he depict similar figures and landscape or employ similar techniques? Compare this prospective treatment with Eugene Waith's introduction to *Bartholomew Fair* in the Yale Ben Jonson.[15] With the briefest of references to Jonson's previous plays and to the Smithfield Fair, he turns to the play itself and discusses the comic oppositions, the kinds of human behavior central to the play, the verbal means by which these are presented and exposed, and Jonson's extraordinary achievement in preserving a comic tone and in making us feel the presence of his own voice. Waith assumes the play can be satisfactorily described and interpreted without an extensive account of the traditions out of which it comes. Unlike our hypothetical introduction to the *Kermess*, his description and interpretation assume that a commentator's central concern is the nature and workings of the particular play. What the art historian finds in tradition and the artist's style at a certain stage of his development, the critic finds in the work itself.

But could it not be argued that the different treatment of individual works is due to intrinsic differences between art and literature? The traditional saying that poetry is a speaking picture and painting a mute poesy is perhaps more witty than truthful. The implicit interchangeability of the arts may be less important than the fact that literature is verbal and painting, sculpture, and architecture are mute. Combine this difference with the fact that we apprehend written works in time and the visual arts in space, and we have what might be considered a sufficient explanation of the art historian's practice: there is simply not much one can say about an individual work, taken by itself. Art works, being non-temporal, are not susceptible of internal development, and their parts are not susceptible of extensive verbal interpretation. This may sound condescending or implausibly reductive, but in fact some formidable individuals and schools of thought regard the visual arts in precisely this way.

Rudolf Arnheim, who bases his analysis on the Gestalt principle that perception is concerned with the grasping of significant form, argues that it is precisely formal, mute pictorial art, rather than language, that is in direct touch with the basic way in which we perceive the world.[16] The formal ordering of a work of art is seen not as a version or model of our perception of the world, but as a rendering of the thing itself.

15 (New Haven, 1963), pp. 1-22.
16 Rudolf Arnheim, *Visual Thinking* (Berkeley and Los Angeles, 1969).

Although few today would take issue with the assertion that perception and thinking are related (i.e. the senses are no longer considered to be a separate system), the notion that thought takes the form of abstract images is surely problematic. When Arnheim supports his point by claiming that a drawing of two meeting triangles or two interlocking trapezoids gets at the core of what he calls the abstract theme of the good marriage,[17] one wonders if Rubens would not have countered with Mars and Venus and argued that there was nothing abstract about a good marriage at that. Arnheim would probably answer that it is the geometry of a painting which explains the underlying thought: in other words, the pattern made by a Mars and Venus is in fact the carrier of the central theme. Thus, in Rembrandt's *Supper at Emmaus* (Fig. 2) he claims that the relationship of Christ's head to two tri-angular configurations denotes the humility of the Son of God: "It presents the underlying thought in a highly abstract geometry, without which the realistically told story might have remained a mere anecdote."[18] We would reply that it is because we recognize this figure as Christ and the scene as the Supper at Emmaus that we know that the work is more than a mere anecdote. Whatever the triangles might tell us of Christ's humility (something which his role in this particular incident reveals quite independently), the underlying, or better the central thought of the work has to do with the recognition of Christ and the paradox that the simple companion is discovered to be the Son of God. The unelevated rendering of Christ combined as it is with the light reflecting off the tablecloth and filling the monumental arch over His head is the main artistic expression of this paradox.

The danger (or the delight) in reducing works of art to their formal basis is related to the arguments offered recently by structuralism, which celebrates what has been termed the separation of the signifier from what is signified. While Arnheim defines and elevates all pictorial images as the basic components of human perception and thought, a structuralist argument sees them as similar to Lévi-Strauss's myths, and specifically prizes recent developments in art for coming closer and closer to the truth contained in mythic structure:

In a sense avant-garde art is the process of unlearning all conscious forms of adult perceptual knowledge. . . . If one were to relate semiotic systems to Piaget's genetic epistemology, it could be said that sign systems seem to evolve in complexity and abstractness directly in proportion to their social usefulness. Art has accomplished the reverse; in losing semiotic complexity it has lost its cohesiveness. Yet ironically avant-garde art has

17 Arnheim, pp. 120-29.
18 Arnheim, p. 270.

achieved this by regressing from a secondary, abstract form of spatial organization (pictorial illusionism) toward a much broader and more fundamental basis (the three structures found in all mathematical and operational thinking). Thus it appears that not only are conscious mythologies sign systems which have lost their powers of signification, but in the case of art this loss is biologically systematic, recapitulating the stages toward a child's earliest means of perception.[19]

Such an explanation appears to answer to the peculiar critical problem presented by contemporary non-representational art even more obviously than it does the problems of contemporary literature. Critics sympathetic to this position frequently argue that it is only since the nineteenth century that art has specifically dealt with the problems intrinsic to the medium. It is a curious fact that these attempts to articulate the peculiar nature of the pictorial arts do it at the expense of, and largely in antagonism to, common assumptions about the nature of language. In this connection, we should recall that Lévi-Strauss himself puts music, like myth, ahead of literature, because it is the language that transcends the level of "articulated language" and is unique in being "at once intelligible and untranslatable."[20]

While these writers praise the inarticulateness of painting, there is at least one writer today who frankly sees this as a limitation which painting is hard put to overcome. Far from seeing pictorial art as having access to special, non-verbal truths, Gombrich sees it as continually attempting to overcome its limitations as a medium. As he argued some years ago, images are not the equivalent of verbal statements: for example, "the image unaided (because of the absence of such formators as definite and indefinite articles) is unable to signify the distinction between the universal and the particular."[21] In a series of studies which have followed *Art and Illusion*, Gombrich has pursued individual problems such as how expression or movement (rather than illusion itself) "get into" works of art. There is no writer today who has posed so acutely the problem of the peculiar nature of the pictorial image. How is it possible for a mute and still object to communicate meanings or represent narrative events? Gombrich

19 Jack Burnham, *The Structure of Art* (New York, 1971), p. 31.

20 Claude Lévi-Strauss, "Overture to *le Cru et le cuit*," in *Structuralism*, ed. Ehrmann, p. 55.

21 E. H. Gombrich, review of Charles Morris, *Signs, Language and Behavior*, *Art Bulletin*, 31 (1949), 72. Cf. Gombrich's recent statement: "The means of visual art cannot match the statement function of language. Art can present and juxtapose images, even relatively unambiguous images, but it cannot specify their relationship," "The Evidence of Images," in *Interpretation: Theory and Practice*, ed. Charles S. Singleton (Baltimore, 1969), p. 97.

answers this question by appealing to what he calls the "beholder's share"—both knowledge (of artistic conventions, gestures, stories and so on) and the capacity to interpret visual signals. In general, Gombrich argues that art activates the projective capacity of the beholder in order to make up or compensate for the limitations of the medium, which he sees as having the same aim, but as lacking the means, of verbal narratives. He thus places himself in opposition to the non-representational tendencies in contemporary art, which far from offering us basic truths of human perception are, to his mind, insufficiently interpretable by the viewer.

All these writers assume a sharp dichotomy between language and pictorial images. But are we really to say that the verbal and the pictorial are *not* different? Perhaps the difficulty lies in accepting this dichotomy as fundamental. For example, why should the light emanating from Rembrandt's Christ or the figure of Christ Himself be any less visual or intrinsic to the painting than the triangles Arnheim delineates? Presumably because they have specific meanings and these meanings are referential—pointing to phenomena and their connections in the real world or in history. It is referential meaning that both a traditional humanist like Gombrich and an antagonist like Burnham attribute to language and deny to the visual arts. Gombrich has to maintain a quite pure notion of the pictorial in order to make "the beholder's share" extrinsic to the work; his reasons are perhaps less necessary to this very fruitful concept than they are to his general moral effort to demystify art and promote common humanity.

In the scope of this essay, we can scarcely do more ourselves than make reference to the daunting problem of "reference." But we can at least make the practical point that a Biblical painting seems no more opaque, no less referential than the verse read as the text for a sermon; or that allusions to myths in poems are no more self-contained or self-explanatory than paintings of those myths; or that proper names (Minerva, Diana, John the Baptist) are no more significant or referential than the iconographic attributes that identify these characters in paintings. Indeed, our brief survey of this problem suggests that the important differences are not between the arts, but between cultural epochs. Painting, in the Renaissance, is just as significant, "meaning-ful," as poetry. Literature, in our time, is just as involved in self-questioning and just as hostile to referential meaning and extractable content as the visual arts are. These cultural changes raise important questions about the nature and possibility of criticism, but the problems they involve are not due to permanent and intrinsic differences between the arts.

However, the problem of criticism itself is another area in which the muteness of art has been powerfully invoked. In *Prints and Visual Communication* (which probably seems less eccentric today than it did to Ackerman a decade ago),[22] William Ivins argues that since language, as opposed to visual images, is by nature "not nicely calculated to convey either precise meanings or any definite idea of the character, personality, or quality of anything," so-called descriptions of works of art tend to be "merely accounts of subjective feelings or emotions that an object has given rise to in a beholder."[23] The suspicion of the subjectivity of criticism is of course common in literary studies, but there at least the work, like the commentary, consists of words. What gives Ivins his complete confidence is the notion that the work of art is a purely physical object. The undeniable physicality of a work of art is what gives art historians in general their confidence in objective attributes and encourages their insistence that critical interpretation is a quite separate and purely subjective activity.

One way to defend criticism against these objections is simply to up-end them, as Northrop Frye does:

There is another reason why criticism has to exist. Criticism can talk, and all the arts are dumb. In painting, sculpture, or music, it is easy enough to see that the art shows forth, but cannot *say* anything. And, whatever it sounds like to call the poet inarticulate or speechless, there is a most important sense in which poems are as silent as statues. Poetry is a *disinterested* use of words: it does not address a reader directly. When it does so, we usually feel that the poet has some distrust in the capacity of readers and critics to interpret his meaning without assistance, and has therefore dropped into the sub-poetic level of metrical talk ("verse" or "doggerel") which anybody can learn to produce. It is not only tradition that impels a poet to invoke a Muse and protest that his utterance is involuntary. Nor is it strained wit that causes Mr. MacLeish, in his famous *Ars Poetica*, to apply the words "mute," "dumb," and "wordless" to a poem. . . . The axiom of criticism must be, not that the poet does not know what he is talking about, but that he cannot talk about what he knows. To defend the right of criticism to exist at all, therefore, is to assume that criticism is a structure of thought and knowledge existing in its own right, with some measure of independence from the art it deals with.[24]

This seems to us a mistaken answer to skeptical views of criticism. Frye entirely, indeed too eagerly, accepts Ivins' way of describing the art

22   Ackerman, *Art and Archaeology*, p. 191. Ivins' book was published in 1953; the recent reprint (Cambridge, Mass., 1968) has attracted some interest.
23   Ivins, p. 57.
24   *Anatomy of Criticism* (Princeton, 1957), pp. 4-5.

object, and differs only in his view of the critic's discourse. Whereas
Ivins is willing to say that "the only wonder about the system [lan-
guage] is that men are able to get along with it as well as they do,"[25]
Frye trusts the power of language to express and communicate the
meaning of works of art. By the same token, he turns a skeptical view
of the critic into a heroic one, and suggests a dependency of art on
the critic that looks a great deal less certain today than when he first
wrote these words, twenty years ago.[26] Frye's position here is all or
nothing: if his views cannot be sustained, there seems to be no defence
of criticism. We would like to suggest—we will not say "a more
modest"—but a more pragmatic and less absolute view of the critic,
and we think the proper starting point is to question the view of the
art object that Frye shares with his hypothetical antagonist.

It seems to us that no work of art is so completely an object as Frye
says it is—so completely mute, in the sense that it implies no relation(s)
to a perceiver. Even in the visual arts, the problem is trickier than it
first appears.[27] Art historical method is predicated on the assumption
that it deals with physical objects whose material, size, shape, and date
can be discovered and set down. A painted panel can thus be treated
much as a snuffbox or a scabbard is. But as soon as what we can at
least call the decoration of the panel is described, quite different elements enter in. Let us look at part of an entry from a recent catalogue
of the National Gallery in London, as a capsule version of art historical
method at work (Fig. 3):

The Marriage of Giovanni (?) Arnolfini

and Giovanna Cenami (?)

They stand side by side in a bedroom, her right hand in his left; he
raises his right hand as for an oath. On a chairback by the bed, a
statuette of S. Margaret; one candle burns in the chandelier. The room
is reflected in a mirror on the back wall; the two figures are seen from
behind, and between them are two very small figures in a doorway, one
of these presumably Jan van Eyck himself. The frame of the mirror is orna-
mented with designs illustrating the Passion; beginning at the bottom and
going left, the Agony, the Capture, Christ before Pilate, the Flagellation,
Christ carrying the Cross, the Crucifixion, the Deposition, the Entomb-

25 Ivins, p. 57.

26 The "Polemical Introduction" of *Anatomy of Criticism* first appeared, with the
Arnoldian title "The Function of Criticism at the Present Time," in *University of Toronto
Quarterly*, 19 (1949-50), 1-16.

27 For an introduction to philosophical excogitation on this problem—which is
one of the *topoi* of aesthetics—see Richard Wollheim, *Art and Its Objects* (New
York, 1971).

ment, Christ in Hell and the Resurrection. Signed: *Johannes de eyck fuit hic.* | .1434.

Oak, painted surface, 32¼ x 23½ (0.818 x 0.597).

Excellent condition; small local damages. Many alterations in varying stages of completion, especially to Arnolfini himself; his raised right hand was intended in a different position, two fingers of his left hand have been drawn in to come forward over her right hand, there are probably three positions for each of his legs, etc. Among other changes, it may be noted that the mirror-frame was once intended to be octagonal.

The picture is not to be considered as a work of pure portraiture. An elaborate account of the subject and its symbols is given by Panofsky. Although no priest is present, he maintains that a marriage is really being performed; the statuette of S. Margaret and the single candle are symbols proper to a nuptial chamber. Panofsky interprets the peculiar inscription as "Jan van Eyck was here (as a witness to the marriage)."[28]

As the tone implies, this entry is intended to be purely descriptive and objective, but is it? In order to understand what is represented, it seems we must have in mind things external to the painting itself, such as the identity of St. Margaret and the events of the Passion. The quasi-factual assertion (note the passive verb), "The picture is not to be considered as a work of pure portraiture," depends on Panofsky's powerful iconographic reading.[29] Moreover, only in the light of Panofsky's interpretation can certain details be described as they are here—the right hand raised "as for an oath," the reflected figure in the doorway "presumably" van Eyck himself. To challenge the assumption of objectivity is not necessarily to tip the balance towards subjectivity. We would argue rather that these are artificial poles in dealing with the actual enterprise of understanding a work of art. Van Eyck assumed that a viewer would know certain Christian symbols and further that he would understand the pictorial and iconographic conventions by which a work of art could represent one thing (a portrait of two people) and conceal another meaning: Panofsky called this "disguised symbolism." Interpretation by the viewer is assumed—indeed, we would say "intended"—by the work.

It seems an obvious fact that works of art, with rare exceptions, are made by artists to be viewed, or better, with viewer(s) in mind. Even today's so-called earth art—where the work is assimilated to the natural setting (a hole in the desert, furrows in a field) and the artist is present

28 Martin Davies, *Early Netherlandish School,* 2nd ed. rev. (London, 1955), p. 38.

29 Erwin Panofsky, "Jan van Eyck's Arnolfini Portrait," *Burlington Magazine,* 64 (1934), 117 ff.

in the verbal account of the making of the work (the digging of the hole, the making of the furrows) and the viewer sees it through the photographs which record the work—can be understood as simultaneously testing and testifying to the fact that artist and viewer are inevitable factors in a work of art.[30] Of course art historians realize that works are made to be looked at. But it is characteristic that this fact is most often taken into account in those instances in which the viewer's relationship can be treated as an external fact about an art object. Several recent studies discuss the architectural setting for which works were originally designed and the resultant angle of the viewer's vision. A fine study of Titian's famous *Pesaro Madonna* (Fig. 4)—a work noted for its innovative asymmetrical composition (the Virgin is to the right, rather than at the center of her adorers)—argues that it is the oblique angle of the viewer's approach (coming down the nave he sees it to the left, above an altar against the wall) rather than "artistic adventurousness alone" that dictated the compositional innovation.[31] This seems to be a happy instance in which an aesthetic problem can be completely resolved (even made to disappear!) by appealing to the concrete physical fact of the viewer's line of vision.

In the case of the *Pesaro Madonna*, a particular stylistic feature has been explained in terms of the physical circumstances of the work. In other cases, the style might be explained in other terms—the function of the work, the thought or attitudes of the time, the vagaries and progress of the history of style itself. The most common appeal is to the last, the history of style. These diverse types of explanation are linked by a common assumption—that the style of a work can be objectively explained. We argued earlier that to an art historian style is essentially an historical phenomenon. It is precisely because he assumes that period styles and stages of stylistic development, whether cultural or individual, are objective realities that the art historian is able to treat the style of an individual painting as an objectively describable attribute of a work.

No one would want to criticize objectivity, but it can lead to a rather high-handed way of reading both artist and viewer out of the work of art. Let us grant that the *Pesaro Madonna* is a work designed to be seen from the side by the approaching viewer, that it graces a family altar, and that it fits into Titian's stylistic development of the years 1519-26. Some aesthetic questions still remain. Surely this is not the first Italian

30   Readers interested in earth art can consult the following issues and pages of *Artforum*: vol. 8, no. 2 (Oct., 1969), 34-38; vol. 8, no. 4 (Dec., 1969) 32-39; vol. 9, no. 1 (Sept., 1970), 48-49.

31   David Rosand, "Titian in the Frari," *Art Bulletin*, 53 (1970), 206.

altarpiece to be approached from the side. Why then was it Titian who saw this as a problem and devised the asymmetrical design as a solution? Further, as Rosand's study points out, the altarpiece, once reached, was in fact worshipped *en face*. It is thus obvious that Titian intentionally created an asymmetrical front view of a scene of the Madonna and Saints, as previous artists had not.[32] In doing so he gives unusual prominence to Pesaro's patron saint Peter, whose position and movements coordinate the parts of the painting. This is also part of the viewer's experience of the work.

If we close this discussion of the part played by the viewer with a reference to Gombrich, it is not because he would entirely agree with what has just been said. But it is Gombrich who has paid the most serious attention to the viewer and the part that he plays in the under-standing of a work of art. He describes a collaboration, as it were, between the artist and the viewer which is a basic assumption of criticism. However, Gombrich sees this situation not as the condition of all art, but as being necessitated by the limitations of the pictorial arts. It seems to us that intentions and conditions which can be so reliably fulfilled are scarcely to be regarded as regrettable limitations.

The inherent relation between work and perceiver and the corre-sponding relation between artist and work are much more fully recognized in literary studies—so much so that it is unnecessary to develop the remarks that follow from concrete analysis like that of the *Pesaro Madonna*. Readers of this journal know what practical criti-cism is; they have seen the quarrel between criticism and scholarship end in mutual reconciliation; they do not share the art historian's more old-fashioned and naive notions of objectivity. Nevertheless, it is salutary to remember that not so long ago literary critics, as well as scholars, assumed that they treated works as objects. Though pri-marily identified with the New Critics, this notion was by no means confined to them. In the passage quoted earlier, Frye not only espouses this view, but shares other New Critical assumptions associated with it—notably the dichotomy between meaning and being and the equa-tion of the poet's addressing the reader with the assertion of flat and simple meanings. As our discussion of Van Eyck's and Titian's paint-ings may already have suggested, we think that the critic not only can but must violate the two great dogmas of the New Criticism, the pro-hibitions against the Intentional Fallacy and the Affective Fallacy.

---

32 The work remains asymmetrical in spite of the fact that a measure of sym-metry is introduced by the placing of the patrons to the left and right in the foreground. Rosand persuasively argues that the large columns, which counteract the asymmetry, were later additions.

The promulgation of these fallacies was of course directly connected
with the desire to treat the poem, in Wimsatt and Beardsley's words, as
"an object of specifically critical judgment."[33] It is startling to return
to their essays and see how flatly they mean this. They call the following proposition "axiomatic" (note that they invoke the notorious last
line of the MacLeish poem cited by Frye):

Judging a poem is like judging a pudding or a machine. One demands
that it work. It is only because an artifact works that we infer the intention of an artificer. "A poem should not mean but be." A poem can *be*
only through its *meaning*—since its medium is words—yet it *is*, simply *is*,
in the sense that we have no excuse for inquiring what part is intended or
meant. Poetry is a feat of style by which a complex of meaning is handled
all at once. Poetry succeeds because all or most of what is said or implied
is relevant; what is irrelevant has been excluded, like lumps from pudding
and "bugs" from machinery.[34]

As Stanley Cavell has recently argued, the fallacy of the intentional
fallacy is due to this mistaken view of a poem. If a poem is viewed
as a real physical object, then its human intention will be seen as a
prior cause, external to it.[35] But it is truer to say that intention is
intrinsic to language, poems, and indeed all human gesture: they
inherently call for understanding. One need not be committed to
Cavell's Wittgensteinian views to acknowledge the force of his objections to the intentional fallacy. Its weaknesses are due not simply to
Wimsatt and Beardsley's dubious ontology, but to their very partial
view of the whole problem. Their main target is the attempt to account
for poems by the poet's documented or imagined biographical circum-

33 W. K. Wimsatt, Jr, *The Verbal Icon* (New York, 1958), p. 21.
34 *Verbal Icon,* p. 4. "The Intentional Fallacy" was first published in 1946.
35 Stanley Cavell, *Must We Mean What We Say?* (New York, 1969), pp. 225-
28. Cf. the first of Wimsatt and Beardsley's axiomatic propositions: "A poem does
not come into existence by accident. The words of a poem, as Professor Stoll has
remarked, come out of a head, not out of a hat. Yet to insist on the designing in-
tellect as a *cause* of a poem is not to grant the design or intention as a *standard* by
which the critic is to judge the worth of the poet's performance" (*Verbal Icon,*
p. 4). Cavell would reply that a critic seeks not to apply standards, but to ask
questions: "Nothing could be commoner among critics of art than to ask *why*
the thing is as it is, and characteristically to put this question, for example, in the
form 'Why does Shakespeare follow the murder of Duncan with a scene which
begins with the sound of knocking?' " (p. 182).
    As our discussion of the Titian altarpiece suggests, art historians generally are
most comfortable when intention can be identified with the peculiar demands of a
commission and the development of personal and period style. Conversely, it is not
only because of the nature of Rembrandt's work, but probably also because we
know so little about the occasion for any of his works that he has been the subject
of so much critical discussion.

stances. No doubt this was a bad tradition, but attacking it does not sufficiently "attack" the normal problem of intention, what one has in mind in asking (as Cavell puts it) "Why this?" of some aspect of a work of art. Wimsatt and Beardsley do not attempt to deal with the obvious relation between writer (or utterer) and writing (or speech), and their argument has therefore been subjected to criticism not from one philosophical point of view but from several.[36]

By the same token, Wimsatt and Beardsley's attack on attending to the reader gives a prejudicial, indeed trivial view of the problem. They set up as their opponents such straw men as "young persons interested in poetry, the introspective amateurs and soul-cultivators"[37] and (not to discriminate on the grounds of age) such pontificating old fogies as William Lyon Phelps and J. Donald Adams. Hence their view that emotion in poetry is "contemplated as a pattern of knowledge" has, in its context, an unduly narrow and complacent meaning:

The emotions correlative to the objects of poetry become a part of the matter dealt with—not communicated to the reader like an infection or disease, not inflicted mechanically like a bullet or knife wound, not administered like a poison, not simply expressed as by expletives or grimaces or rhythms, but presented in their objects and contemplated as a pattern of knowledge.[38]

"Such prohibitions bind not." It is no wonder that critics less suspicious of their feelings have been paying attention to the way works appeal to a reader. There has been some good theoretical writing on this problem, but equally important is the body of practical criticism and scholarship that assumes that paying attention to the rhetorical dimensions of literary works is simply to acknowledge an obvious fact about them.[39] It is worth recalling what has often been remarked, that

36 Paul de Man, *Blindness and Insight* (New York, 1971), pp. 20-35; E. D. Hirsch, *Validity in Interpretation* (New Haven, 1967); William Empson, "Still the Strange Necessity," *Sewanee Review*, 63 (1955), 475-77; Leslie Fiedler, "Archetype and Signature," *Sewanee Review*, 60 (1952), 253-73.

37 *Verbal Icon*, p. 29.

38 *Verbal Icon*, p. 38.

39 For a theoretical argument particularly focused on the fiction that a poem is an object, see Stanley Fish, "Literature in the Reader: Affective Stylistics," *New Literary History*, 2 (1970), 123-62. Among books of practical criticism, we have in mind not only those consciously concerned with the reader (like Fish's *Surprised by Sin* [1967] or Paul J. Alpers, *The Poetry of "The Faerie Queene"* [1967]), but also, perhaps more significant, those which take the importance of reader or audience for granted. These latter include such distinguished (and different) studies as C. L. Barber, *Shakespeare's Festive Comedy* (1959); Robert Garis, *The Dickens Theatre* (1965); Barbara Herrnstein Smith, *Poetic Closure* (1968); Helen Hennessy Vendler, *On Extended Wings* (1969).

the New Criticism was a decidedly American phenomenon. The great English critics of this century—men as diverse in other respects as Richards, Lewis, Empson, and Leavis—never doubted that writing is a human act and implies an audience or reader.

It will be clear that along with rejecting the view of art works as objects, we reject the notion that their interpreter—whether a New Critic or art historian—should emulate the scientist. But what should a critic be? We are tempted to answer Eliot's words and say simply that he should be very intelligent. But what does than mean, aside from its being a caution against seeking salvation in rules and methods? In our present context, it means staying in touch with the realities of human utterances and artifacts. (These of course include historical realities: one of the casualties of the New Criticism was its perpetuating the assumption that scholarship and criticism are separable and antithetical.) The critic's writing should work along—literally, collaborate—with the intentions, both large and small, of art works—not as if the critic were a uniquely authoritative expounder, but in a way that manifests an ability to take on the role of either artist or perceiver and treat them as aspects of the same phenomenon, as the human dimensions implicit in a text or painting or whatever else. If we feel inhibitions about "taking on the role of the artist," we might remind ourselves how natural this seems in some studies that are examples not only of critical insight but of its fruitful union with scholarship—Rosemond Tuve's *Allegorical Imagery*, Geoffrey Hartman's *Wordsworth's Poetry*, James Ackerman's *The Architecture of Michelangelo*.

To speak of "the human dimensions implicit" in a work opens up a host of problems just when we should be coming to a conclusion. In what sense and in what ways are intention, comprehension, historical reality, social situation and purpose, human use implicit or implicated—literally, enfolded—in works of art? These are the great questions for all critics, whose main task, as we know, is to ex-plicate. We hope at least to have shed some light on these topics by suggesting ways in which they are common to the arts. However, we do not think that comparative studies are the only or even the best way to address these questions. As we said earlier, in discussing Gombrich's *Art and Illusion*, very fruitful general ideas can result from powerful insight into one of the arts. Indeed, it seems to us that art criticism and literary criticism are the same activity only in the most general—though therefore in the most important—ways. The specific nature of the criticism depends on the specific nature of the art work. Attempts to compare the arts characteristically come to grief in forced equations between specific features. Something is badly wrong when a man as intelligent and knowledgeable as Mario Praz compares the cupola, as the crowning feature of a church, with the couplets that conclude the *ottava rima* stanza and the Shakespearean sonnet.[40] In order to make such comparisons, fixed likenesses must be assumed in such elusive and problematic phenomena as form, structure, and harmony. Surely the game is not worth the candle. The arts differ profoundly in their conditions and "languages" (also in their developments and national histories, but those need not concern us here.) For example, one cannot find in painting anything analogous to tone of voice in poetry. This is not simply because tone of voice is a verbal phenomenon, but also because it implies the presence of a speaker, and no aspect of a painting so decisively suggests the presence of a "painter" (note we do not even have a word for the visual analogue of "speaker.") By the same token, nothing in literary works—not even the much vaunted point of view— has the power of some modes of sculpture or painting to establish a concrete relation between perceiver and work. To take another example, the importance of style in the study of art is due not solely to the need for historical order, but also to the fact that style is an immediately perceived aspect of works which are physical objects and which can be taken in at a glance. Finally, to return to the question with which we began, there seem some real differences between what "a work" is in literature and in the fine arts. These differences are due not simply to the difference between extension in space and in time, but also to the normal conditions of production and consumption in the various arts.

We do not want to say that the moral is "Good fences make good neighbors." It seems clear that the various academic disciplines and departments have become altogether too fenced off from each other. But on the other hand, we should not take the commune as a model for solving the problems created by specialization. In the community of humane studies, students of art and literature will necessarily do different things. They can learn from each other by taking each other's work as they take the arts themselves—on their own terms.

---

40 Mario Praz, *Mnemosyne: The Parallel Between Literature and the Visual Arts* (Princeton, 1970), pp. 86-89.

12

Notes for an Anatomy of Modern Autobiography

Francis R. Hart

FOR whatever reasons, autobiography has become a flourishing and sophisticated art, and literary critic and theorist alike pay it increasing attention. The new sophistication of the artist has modified older expectancies and methods; and predictably, the New Critical apologists divide into traditionalists, who seek to regularize what they take to be a "genre" with a hereditary essence — "true autobiography," Gusdorf's *"autobiographie proprement dite,"* and relativists such as Alfred Kazin, who begin with what looks peculiarly new and postulate that "autobiography, like other literary forms, is what a gifted writer makes of it."[1]

Both sides are continually preoccupied with a question which, while inescapable, is in part a pseudo-problem: the relation in autobiographical writing of the fictive and the historical, "design" and "truth," *Dichtung und Wahrheit.* But two other questions also persist. The evaluative question of formal consistency and integrity provokes theorists to specific judgments that are conventional and premature. Moreover, analytic surveys of the question of autobiographical intention become rigid and exclusive, identifying "autobiography proper" with a single "form" or intention, and excluding works that differ in formal perspective, dramatic focus, or rhetorical end. The questions are neither improper nor irrelevant. But if their answers are not to be narrow or premature, they had best be considered first in light of the wide plurality of mimetic and formal value of which autobiography has proved capable. Following is a brief contribution to such an anatomy, focused on the three preoccupations I have singled out: the mimetic question of the interplay of history and fiction, the formal question of the tension between purposive form and experimental development, and the generic question of intention, of the autobiographer's fluctuating idea of his purpose and of the reader he would

---

1 Kazin, "Autobiography as Narrative," *Michigan Quarterly Review*, III (1964), 210-16, page 211; Georges Gusdorf, "Conditions et limites de l'autobiographie," in *Formen der Selbstdarstellung*, ed. Reichenkron and Haase (Berlin, 1956), 105-23.

reach. The present state of such questions may be seen in the valuable pioneering works of Shumaker, Kazin, Spender, Gusdorf, Pascal, Sayre, Morris, and Mandel.[2] Noticing their problems, I shall offer my own less prescriptive approach to truth, form, and intention in modern autobiography. The formulation will proceed into a considerable body of possible — and controversial — applications. On the equally controversial assumption that modern autobiography began two centuries ago, I shall limit these applications to Rousseau and his successors.

On the first question, Rousseau sounds the keynote.[3] He will display *to his kind* "a portrait in every way true to nature" (17) by relating "in simple detail all that has happened to me, all that I have done, all that I have felt," and, says Stephen Spender, "of course Rousseau does not tell the truth. There is a lie concealed within his very method" (70). Truth is a definitive but elusive autobiographical intention. John Morris is right: "autobiography is . . . a species of history — a narrative of events occurring in time" (10). But, notes the Bergsonian Gusdorf, "l'historien de soi-même" inevitably commits "le péché original de l'autobiographie . . . revenant en visite dans son propre passé, il postule l'unité et l'identité de son être, il croit pouvoir confondre ce qu'il fut avec ce qu'il est devenu" (116-17). And so Renan was right, too, when he reflected on Goethe's title (*Vérité et poesie* for him), "Ce qu'on dit de soi est toujours poesie." Seeking to be history, autobiography must be fictive. The pages given to demonstrating this truism might be better spent exploring it.

Gusdorf and Kazin both contradict themselves on it. Gusdorf observes that in autobiography we are given "le témoignage d'un homme sur lui même . . . à la recherche de sa plus intime fidelité," that the search itself is (like the mirror in a Dutch interior) a dimension of the life imaged; and then he pronounces surprisingly that it matters little if the picture (the mirror!) is full of errors, omissions, lies: "fiction or imposture, the value of art is real"! Kazin observes

2 W. Shumaker, *English Autiography: Its Emergence, Materials, and Form* (Berkeley, 1954); S. Spender, "Confessions and Autobiography," *The Making of a Poem* (London, 1955), pp. 63-72; also, *World Within World* (pub. 1951; cited below), the Introduction; R. Pascal, *Design and Truth in Autiobography* (Cambridge, Mass., 1960); Gusdorf and Kazin (1956 and 1964), above; R. F. Sayre, *The Examined Self: Franklin, Adams, James* (Princeton, 1964); J. N. Morris, *Versions of the Self* (New York, 1966); B. J. Mandel, "The Autobiographer's Art," *Journal of Aesthetics and Art Criticism*, XXVII (1968), 215-26. Among the few older works many suggestive insights are still to be gleaned from A. M. Clark's *Autobiography: Its Genesis and Phases* (Edinburgh, 1935).

3 *Confessions*, trans. J. M. Cohen (Baltimore, 1953).

that Hemingway, Nabokov, Dahlberg, and others like them are auto-biographers who *simply use the appearance* of fact to produce enjoyable narrative, "designed, even when the author does not say so, to make a fable of his life, to tell a story, to create a pattern of incident, to make a dramatic point." Yet, he acknowledges, the creative writer "turns to autobiography out of some creative longing that fiction has not satisfied," and finds there "some particular closeness and intensity of effect" that he values, some "felt relation to the life data themselves" (211-12). Autobiography, then, whatever the reader's response, must be a profoundly different activity. But perhaps the contradictions — or paradoxes — of Gusdorf and Kazin are truer than the categorical insistence of Shumaker that the autobiographer invariably "wishes to be understood as writing of himself and as setting down . . . nothing that is not literally and factually true" (105), or the shifting rigidity of Mandel (220): "the autobiographer . . . may never falsify his facts for a fictional purpose without giving up his claim to the name of autobiographer"; he strives "to sound as truthful as possible"; he gives what he "wishes to be taken as true about his life" (220). The truism that in autobiography history and fiction are intentionally distinct proves too slippery to hold.

Nevertheless, such theorists are on the right track. The autobiographer knows there are differences and struggles with them. Edwin Muir wistfully speaks of the freedom of fiction: "I could follow these images freely if I were writing an autobiographical novel. As it is, I have to stick to the facts and try to fit them in where they fit in."[4] Spender wonders in retrospect "whether I would have done better to write my autobiography as a novel," without "the immediacy of the writer who says: 'the hero is I,'" and then replies to his own doubts. He could not give "the truth about himself within the decent and conspiratorial convention of contemporary fiction"; that would be offering both reader and writer "avenues of escape from the glaring light of consciousness of him who says: 'I am I'" and would therefore defeat his confessional purpose.[5] Nabokov, for whom the tracing of images into intricate harmonies is what autobiography does, nevertheless (like Goethe and other artist-autobiographers) deliberately writes to repossess the realities of his past from the sterile fictive world to which he has sacrificed them. "The man in me revolts against the fictionist" is both a theme and a motive of *Speak, Memory*[6] (as of many autobiographies). The historicity of the recreation is impera-

4 *An Autobiography* (New York, 1954), p. 174.
5 *World Within World* (Berkeley, 1966), p. 310.
6 *Speak, Memory*, the revised edition (New York, 1966).

tive, *even though* the autobiographer knows the terrible elusiveness of that historicity. "I have changed nothing to my knowledge," says Yeats, "and yet it must be that I have changed many things without my knowledge."[7]

But when George Moore insists that *Hail and Farewell* (and O'Casey from the outset implies that *Mirror in My House*) is an autobiographical *novel*, or when Dahlberg remarks "I have come to that time in my life when it is absolutely important to compose a good memoir,"[8] or when Hemingway prefaces *A Memorable Feast,* "If the reader prefers, this book may be regarded as fiction. But there is always the chance that such a book of fiction may throw some light on what has been written as fact"[9] — when these are the signals, then the signals are distinctively (and no doubt deliberately) ambiguous. Mailer, for example, scrupulously and subtly disjoins such signals into the structural principle of *Armies of the Night.*

There is, as Norman Holland observes,[10] nothing in an autobiographical passage itself to distinguish history from fiction. Response is determined strictly by the expectation the reader brings, and the autobiographer who supplies ambiguous signals establishes his work (for whatever reason) on a basis of ambiguous expectancy. The reader is of course free to respond, however unmistakable the mimetic or historical signals, as if the autobiography had the fictive autonomy of narrative invention, and "understand" it accordingly. But in understanding fiction one seeks an imaginative grasp of another's meaning; in understanding personal history one seeks an imaginative comprehension of another's historic identity. "Meaning" and "identity" are not the same kind of reality and do not make the same demands. One has no obligation to a fantasy. Holland quotes Sidney — "For the poet, he nothing affirmeth, and therefore nothing lieth" — and interprets the continuation to mean that when we look only for fiction our imaginations are liberated to carry on our own "profitable invention." There is — or should be — no such freedom, no such total imaginative access or response, for either writer or reader, in the historiographical transaction that is autobiography. For both, as Pascal puts it, "there is a cone of darkness at the centre" (184); "unreliability" is an inescapable condition, not a rhetorical option; truth, like form and intention, is a problematic goal to be sought in various ways; "one of

7 *The Autobiography of W. B. Yeats* (New York, 1967), "Preface."
8 *Because I Was Flesh: the Autobiography of Edward Dahlberg* (New York, 1967), p. 4.
9 *A Memorable Feast* (New York, 1965), Preface.
10 *The Dynamics of Literary Response* (New York, 1968), pp. 67ff.

the joys of reading autobiographies," says Pascal, is watching "a wrestling with truth" (75). The reader who treats the conditional effort as mere fantasy or free creation, or who uses the published vulnerability of another historic person as mere signals from one fantasy world to another, is repudiating the basic human implication that is the inescapable condition of his access to the autobiographical situation.

Critics such as Gusdorf and Pascal recognize this. But the recognition has not yet had much effect on considerations of autobiographical form and intention. Neither can be thought of as having the autonomy or rhetorical accountability of form and intention in a purposive fiction; each may or may not reach a final state of articulation, for each must be experimental, dynamic. Yet even the best theoretic discussions of autobiography seem committed to forms that are "unified" and "appropriate" and rhetorical ends that are "achieved." The most comprehensive survey of autobiographical "forms" is Shumaker's chapter on "Shape and Texture," filled with useful, if schematic, hypotheses, and yet chained to the deduction that form must be an achievement of unity, that the means of achievement is the selective principle appropriate to a certain autobiographical "kind," that the autobiographer must find or achieve his form, but that, alas, "autobiography is especially prone to impertinency" and we must be prepared "for the discovery of imperfections" (141) — surely a disconcerting way to look for what actually happens during an autobiographical "wrestling with" form. Shumaker's disciple Mandel forges himself the same critical situation. The critic must first seek an "organizing principle" or "purpose," ask "to what degree does [the work] reveal organic unity based on a defined sense of its own end?" expect "the conscious shaping of a whole life for one informing purpose," demand that the autobiographer as artist "be in control of the way in which he selects and presents" the "ambiguities of his nature" even though he "may not be able" to fathom them, and of course expect some autobiographers to create "dangerously protean" structures and many autobiographies, however impressive, to suffer from a lack of consistency and control (221-4). Such is the restrictiveness of a rhetorical approach to autobiographical form.

Pascal, in a sense the follower of Gusdorf, goes to an opposite pole and makes a prescriptive position out of a "process" view of form and an existentialist view of process. Where there is no voyage of genuine — hence unanticipated — self-discovery, we feel "a partial failure at any rate." The "act of writing [autobiography] is a new act of the man . . . it leaves the man different" (182-3), and presumably where this happens and the autobiographical self reaches the completion of therapeutic process (Wordsworth, Wells) or a new dramatic phase of self-formulation (Sartre, Malcolm X) we are to feel "a partial success at any rate," even though such an end may have emerged out of formal chaos. Basil Willey begins *Spots of Time* unsure in what direction his life has been moving: "It is in the hope of finding out that I am now writing this book."[11] And "reading [*The Buried Day*] through again," C. Day Lewis is "astonished to find that my earlier selves — the schoolboy, the adolescent, the young man — had collaborated in it without my conscious knowledge."[12] Imperatives of exploration have made control in any continuous and deliberate sense impossible — and such often seems the case in autobiography; but to elevate this condition into *the* formal necessity of "true autobiography" is narrowly prescriptive.

Form in an autobiographical work partakes in experimental fluctuation of both control and revelation, and the experimental activity often generates a variety of controlled forms: the tensile forms of inner and outer, man and mask, *Dichtung und Wahrheit*; forms of stylistic and modal counterpoint; metaphoric or parabolic forms — the journey, the penetration, the spiral; rhythmic and expository and therapeutic forms; anti-forms (Malraux, Robert Graves, Mailer) playing against conventional expectations. Some of these are manifest experimentally in the emergent *narrative* patterns of the recovered life. Others appear in the *dramatic* patterns of the evolving act of recovery, the autobiographical situation in which the autobiographer recognizes, interrelates, and attempts to manipulate toward some truth or integrity his relationships with his recoverable past, with his formal or technical options, and with his rhetorical and psychological intentions. Any description of form must take into account this situation in both its narrative momentum and its dramatic evolution, as well as the degree to which one or the other prevails. Or to use Shumaker's terms, every autobiography necessarily moves on "two temporal planes" juxtaposed, narrative past and dramatic present. It is tempting to insist (as some autobiographers do) on the primacy of the present act, hence dramatic form or "process." Dillon Johnston rightly notes: "The autobiography, more than any literary genre, tends to talk about itself: the development of the subject matter is so dependent upon psychological theory and ideas about documentation . . . that a discussion of the formation of autobiography almost always becomes part of the subject matter."[13] But not always; such a devel-

---

11   *Spots of Time* (New York, 1965), p. 10.
12   *The Buried Day* (New York, 1960), p. 240.
13   *The Integral Self in Post-Romantic Autobiography*, Ph.D. dissertation, University of

opment is a formal option; and autobiography is not "process litera-ture" because it does not imitate the creative process enacting itself — it is a recreative act. The occasional primacy of the dramatic present should not be elevated into a formal criterion.

Formal principles in autobiography evolve and fluctuate as auto-biographical intentions interact and shift; a formal problem or option often refocuses the autobiographer's intention or even redefines the nature of his truth. Such is the relation of form to intention. It is not reasonable for the interpretive critic of autobiography to demand or expect unity and consistency of intention. It is certainly not safe to suppose that intention will always be explicit or that intentions are independent of their dramatic locations. No autobiographer writes without reasons for writing or readers to reach, but none has single reasons or readers, and the identification of reasons and readers is itself an experimental feature of the evolving autobiographical situa-tion. Shumaker is far righter in theory than his rage for critical order allows him to be in application: "one has not the right to suggest that some ways of reliving bygone experience are more legitimate than others . . . . At any rate, a study which is meant to be inclusive must accept its materials as they are found" (52) — and this means recog-nizing distinct intentions for what they are and proceeding to identify and interpret their correlations and fluctuating predominances in individual autobiographical works.

Traditional terms will serve, so long as we understand them in their characteristic post-Enlightenment connotations. "Confession" is personal history that seeks to communicate or express the essential nature, the truth, of the self. "Apology" is personal history that seeks to demonstrate or realize the integrity of the self. "Memoir" is per-sonal history that seeks to articulate or repossess the historicity of the self. "Confession" as an intention or impulse places the self relative to nature, reality; "apology" places the self relative to social and/or moral law; "memoir" places the self relative to time, history, cultural pattern and change. Confession is ontological; apology ethical; mem-oir historical or cultural. As these or any comparable definitions suggest, such intentions must overlap; one can hardly appear in total

Virginia, 1969, p. 178. I am generally indebted as well to the dissertations of two other former students: J. M. Firth, *O'Casey and Autobiography*, U. Va., 1965, and an excellent discussion of Moore's *Hail and Farewell* as autobiographical novel in C. P. White *George Moore: From Naturalism to Pure Art*, U. Va., 1970. It is impossible now to particularize my gratitude to the members of English 285. U. Va., Summer, 1969, who helped me formulate these ideas, but I should single out H. H. Sherrill for his study of Wells, B. H. Stone for his analysis of Cleaver and of Mailer's *Armies of the Night*, and F. H. Martz for his discussion of Wright.

independence of the others. In practice, they complement or succeed or conflict with each other. Every autobiography can appropriately and usefully be viewed as in some degree a drama of intention, and its dramatic intentionality is another component of the autobiographical situation for the interpreter to attend to.

What, then, does the interpretive reader find when he seeks the distinctive truth, form, and intention of an autobiography? He is in search of an evolving mixture of pattern and situation — pattern discerned in the life recovered, pattern discovered or articulated in the self or "versions of self" that emerge in that recovery, pattern in the recovery process. The total emergent reciprocity of situation and activity and pattern is what is formative or distinctive, and this he seeks to identify. What follows is a set of interpretive observations made of nearly forty extremely various autobiographical works since and inclusive of those of Rousseau, Franklin, and Gibbon. Their validity remains undemonstrated and controversial; they are offered simply as the kinds of observations I believe one needs to make and test before historical generalization and critical judgment are possible.

We begin with the question of truth, the first relation of which the autobiographical situation is made, the relation between the autobiographer and his personal, historical subject. The relation has various elements. To seek the personal focus of an autobiographical truth is to inquire what kind of "I" is selected, how far the selected "I" is an inductive invention and how far an intentional creation, and whether one single or one multiple "I" persists throughout the work. Moreover, the autobiographer's relation to the pastness or historicity of his selected "I" involves his sense and manipulation of the problem of continuity and discontinuity of identity and perspective. Again, perspective implies access, and the autobiographer's limited and erratic access to the past and present of that ambiguous "I" implies the problem of the form and authority of personal memory. In practice such selections of personal focus are numerous, fluctuating, and often mixed; and the interpreter has no business assuming that certain types and persistences of "I" are more "truly autobiographical" than others. I am not sure there is justification even for Mandel's reasonable postulate that "an autobiographer of great ability will select one aspect of his total personality to stand for the complex whole" (223).

The selection of "I" is made and remade according to such criteria as naturalness, originality, essentiality, continuousness, integrity, and significance. By whatever criteria chosen, the selective "I" plays one or more of a number of structural roles: the "I" that has been hidden or misconstrued; the "I" that has been lost, or gained, regained or sought after in vain; the "I" that has been cultivated, imposed, preserved, developed. The fate of the selective "I" is bound to be of central concern, but the several elements of a multiple "I" may have diverse fates, or a single fate may have various explanations, and the fate or fates may occasion various attitudes: comprehension or bewilderment, celebration or lamentation.

Some autobiographers intend at first to delineate an "I" that is comprehensive, essential, total, while others intend initially only a partial personal truth, chronologically or analytically restricted. Such initial intentions may prove unstable or illusory, and the autobiographer's idea of what is total or essential — of the personal truth that matters — may not persuade or satisfy the reader. Moreover, the "total" autobiographer often discovers motives for restriction or refocusing that he had not anticipated. Rousseau would like "in some way to make my soul transparent to the reader's eye," to let the reader notice all of its movements (169), to recount faithfully the "succession of feelings" that constitute "the history of my soul" (262), and thus let the reader discover the "principle which has produced them." But that history becomes the lamentable record of how the perversities and contradictions of his nature have been exploited by a false and cruel society to prevent his becoming what nature intended him to be. The pervasive longing throughout his true history for the true self he could be only in rare intermittences of idyllic timelessness — with his cousin, with "Mama," with Therese — is, in a sense, the essential, if thwarted, Rousseau. Newman sets out in the *Apologia*[14] to show "what Dr. Newman means," to give "the true key to my whole life," to be "known as a living man," by showing historically how "the concrete being reasons; . . . the whole man moves" (136). Many readers miss "the whole man" in the history of opinions, and are puzzled to find at crucial points — the illness in Sicily, for instance — that it is a divine *mystery* what Newman meant, that the meaning of Dr. Newman may in fact be comprehensible only when it has been sacrificed to the divine meaning — the principle of the Tracts: "we promote truth by a self-sacrifice." The essential or selective self of Ruskin's *Praeterita* is the youthful visionary, and the autobiographer imaginatively recovers identity with that lost self, but falls into confusion when trying to relate to and account for the fallen selves that replaced it after 1850. The selective "I" of Goethe's *Dichtung und Wahrheit*[15] might be equated with the "daemon" that drives him *ohne hast ohne rast* on to some mysterious destiny, or with the

14 *Apologia Pro Vita Sua*, ed. D. J. DeLaura (New York, 1968).
15 The Oxenford trans., pub. as *Autobiography. The Truth and Fiction Relating to My Life*, 2 vols. (New York, 1903).

passion for experience, the capacity to "value highly every thing that contributed to my own cultivation" (II, 18), or with "the organ by which I seized the world," the eye (I, 185), or more properly with the poetic power, the "tendency to turn into an image, into a poem, every thing that delighted or troubled me, or otherwise occupied me" (I, 235), or most likely with that total process of assimilation, that pulsation of self-concentration and self-expansion Goethe calls cultivation.

The selves that undergo crisis in Wordsworth's *Prelude*, Mill's *Autobiography*, and the *Autobiography of Malcolm X*[16] share a duplicity wherein a disintegration or transformation of character somehow leaves a hidden or implicit nature intact; the selective "I" is somehow a transcendence of both. In their brave Rousseauistic candor, setting out to confess shy, unconventional selves, Gide and Spender (in *If It Die* and *World Within World*)[17] both struggle with the secrecy of their moral natures, their backgrounds in a puritanical horror of intimacy. Both find it impossible to describe openly what really matters; both discover what Gide calls "the fear of being led on to say too much" (213); and both rest finally in the acceptance of their own intimate complexities, which prevail over any ultimate articulation of a selective "I." The "spiritual and intellectual auto-biography" of Cleaver, *Soul On Ice*,[18] begins in the sense of lost identity — a common starting point for the autobiographical situation — and moves on experimentally into several new identities — a not uncommon direction for the situation to take. But which is the genuine Cleaver, the one who tells Beverley Axelrod he has lost a sense of who he is, or the one who says this is false — he knows well who he is — he is a vain deceiver and an egoistic prophet of doom? The "autobiography" of Edward Dahlberg, *Because I Was Flesh*,[19] projects as strident a single rhetorical self as the most strident of Cleaver's rhetorical selves. Yet Dahlberg's autobiographical voice asks in Boswellian bewilderment, how many contradictory and unstable selves can a man contain?

The autobiographer provokes a distinct expectation if he initially restricts the "I," analytically or developmentally. The autobiography

---

16   *The Prelude* in the Oxford Standard Authors *Poetical Works of Wordsworth*; Mill's *Autobiography* (New York, 1960); *The Autobiography of Malcolm X* [with Alex Hayley] (New York, 1966).

17   *If It Die* [*Si le grain ne meurt*], pub. 1920, trans. D. Bussy (New York, 1963); Spender, above.

18   *Soul On Ice* (New York, 1968); the descriptive phrase is not Cleaver's.

19   Note 8 above.

that breaks off with some climactic issue from youth or early manhood appears to be a special problem of integrity and continuity. But the restriction may prove less real than the totality. The autobiography whose selective "I" is a suprapersonal significance, a principle of representativeness, sets out from a different kind of restriction, but one equally problematic. "What interests me in any man," says Malraux,[20] "is the human condition; in a great man, the form and essence of his greatness; in a saint, the character of his saintliness. And in all of them, certain characteristics which express not so much an individual personality as a particular relationship with the world." But Malraux has already asked, "what do I care about what matters only to me" (1)? And his answer is momentously personal: "I have never really learned to re-create myself . . . . I do not find myself very interesting" (2). Thus the selection of a personal representativeness may itself be definitive of an idiosyncratic "I." George Kennan's Memoirs[21] cannot segregate the representative history of the modern American diplomat from Kennan's "intellectual autobiography" or, some would add, from his apology. Claude Brown proposes (in Manchild in the Promised Land) to "talk about the first Northern urban generation of Negroes . . . about the experiences of a misplaced generation"[22] and Gosse, Yeats, Henry Adams,[23] and others offer representative personal histories of cultural generations or epochal conflicts, in which the selective "I" is a struggle with historicity for personal freedom and/or unity of being. Mill and Wells[24] profess to give intellectual histories of what one calls an intellectual nature "rather below than above par" and the other calls "a very ordinary brain." But the experimental Wells shifts focus: "Let me alter the pose and the lighting of my experiences so as to bring out in its successive phases the emotional and sensual egoism rather than the intellectual egoism that has hitherto been the focus of attention" (349). And Mill forms his record emphatically on the principle that moral character is of far greater importance than intellectual. When Wordsworth and Goethe trace the growth of a poet's mind, relations between conceptions of poet and of social or political man remain to be worked out. The restrictive idea of a public career for Franklin,

20 Anti-Memoirs, trans. T. Kilmartin (New York, 1968), p. 8.

21 Memoirs (1925-1950) (New York, 1969).

22 Manchild in the Promised Land (New York, n.d.), p. vii.

23 Gosse, Father and Son (Boston, 1965); Adams, The Education of Henry Adams (New York, 1931); Yeats, above.

24 Wells, Experiment in Autobiography (Philadelphia, 1967); Mill, above.

Gibbon, and Podhoretz[25] is a topical focus to be tested, not a sufficient initial signal of selectivity.

A third kind of expectation is initiated by the autobiographer who projects an "I" *more true* somehow than the "versions of self" historically recoverable. Early in *The Words* Sartre says, "I keep creating myself; I am the giver and the gift,"[26] and from the vantage of some new creation looks back — as do Gosse and Dahlberg and Wright — on earlier selves that appear to have been fictions, phantoms, impostures. Yeats says, "if we cannot imagine ourselves as different from what we are and assume that second self, we cannot impose a discipline upon ourselves, though we may accept one from others. . . . Wordsworth is often flat and heavy, partly because his moral sense has no theatrical element, it is an obedience to a discipline which he has not created" (317-18). And presumably — but not in fact — Yeats's *Autobiography* is the history of that disciplined, created self. The autobiographer of *The Prelude* is the true self that has returned to its nature and therein found the power to create a history recounting temporary and unreal lapses into false or fictive selves. But the real autobiographical situation of the poem is as Hartman describes it: "At the beginning of *The Prelude* a poet returns to nature, yet the poem he writes is about the difficulties of that return. He cannot always sustain his quest to link what makes him a poet, the energy of imagination, to the energy of nature."[27] The autobiography of a created "I" must be what Wells describes as any man's struggle for his *persona*: "Our *personas* grow and change and age as we do. And rarely if ever are they the whole even of our conscious mental being. All sorts of complexes are imperfectly incorporated or not incorporated at all, and may run away with us in the most unexpected manner" (9). Thus the deliberate history of the created "I," like that of the restricted "I," is an *experiment* in autobiography. And in the first case the interpretive reader seeks to comprehend the creation, as in the second case the restriction, with reference to an implicit totality with which the restriction or creation is in some kind of tension.

Some autobiographers define the truth of the "I" in terms of such a tension. And it is tempting to single them out normatively as truer to an existential autobiographical situation — tempting, but pre-

25 *Autobiography of Benjamin Franklin* (New York, 1950); *Autobiography of Edward Gibbon* in the new synthetic "edition" of D. A. Saunders (New York, 1961); Podhoretz, *Making It* (New York, 1969).

26 *The Words*, trans. B. Frechtman (New York, 1966), p. 20.

27 G. H. Hartman, *Wordsworth's Poetry 1787-1814* (New Haven, 1964), p. 67.

mature. Goethe's fluctuation between self-expansion and self-concentration is such a formative tension. For Rousseau such a tension persists between the serene and sociable "I" that should have been and the perverse and isolated "I" that nature and society have made. For the autobiographer of cultural conflict the tension may be of the sort T. E. Lawrence describes: "The effort for these years to live in the dress of Arabs, and to imitate their mental foundation, quitted me of my English self . . . . At the same time I could not sincerely take on the Arab skin . . . . I had dropped one form and not taken on the other, and was become like Mohammed's coffin in our [?] legend, with a resultant feeling of intense loneliness . . . . Sometimes these selves would converse in the void; and then madness was very near . . . ."[28] Stephen Spender postulates a tension of perspectival duplicity: "An autobiographer is really writing a story of two lives: his life as it appears to himself, from his own position, when he looks out at the world from behind his eye-sockets; and his life as it appears from outside in the minds of others; a view which tends to become in part his own . . . . However, the great problem of autobiography remains, which is to create the true tension between these inner and outer, subjective and objective, worlds" (viii).

The tension between two lives is often formative in the autobiographical works we call journals. The act of journalizing intensifies the conflict in any autobiographer between life and pattern, movement and stasis, identification and definition, world and self. Journalizing becomes a habit of self-collective withdrawal — for the man of action a time of retrospective stasis (Che in his jungle tree), for the social man a time of solitude (Boswell in the wee hours or confined by the clap), for the artist a moment of undisciplined expression. The habit becomes a problem. Scott gave up journalizing because it made him a solitary egoist. Otto Rank advised Anaïs Nin to "leave your Diary; that is withdrawing from the world," and Henry Miller told her it was her malady, her fear of transformation, her preoccupation with completeness.[29] The tension becomes formative in Gide's journal.[30] For Amiel,[31] too, on occasion, his journal "is a kind of epicurism rather than a discipline" (468); on others, it reestablishes "the integrity of the mind and the equilibrium of the conscience, that is,

28 *Seven Pillars of Wisdom* (Garden City, 1937), pp. 31-2.

29 O. Evans, *Anaïs Nin* (Carbondale, Ill., 1968), p. 7; *Diary of Anaïs Nin 1934-1939* (New York, 1967), pp. 110-12.

30 *Journals of Gide*, trans. and ed. J. O'Brien (New York, n.d.), Vol. I.

31 *The Private Journal of H. F. Amiel*, trans. Brooks and Brooks (New York, 1935).

one's inner health" (566). The journalist's autobiographical tension is a kind of ontologic respiration, an inward and outward of being, itself punctuating and helping to shape the discontinuous life being lived. There may be a reason here why in our times existential autobiographers turn more to the journalistic.

The autobiographer has always had to consider how to manage, and whether to dramatize, the discontinuities inherent in autobiographical recreation. The most basic discontinuities are the intermittences of memory. Autobiographies are always what Morris calls "first of all exercises in recollection — recollection in its simplest conception, as the tactic the mind employs to mitigate the destructive powers of time" (62). But recollection in autobiography is never simple, always the process Berdyaev describes: "Such a cognitive process is not a mere remembering or recapitulation of the past: it is a creative act performed at the present moment."[32] And the first question is whether to dramatize the act. Some do not. Others dramatize memory as a characterizing power, illustrating Malraux's dictum: "One day it will be realized that men are distinguishable as much by the forms their memories take as by their characters. The depths vary, as do the nets they use and the quarry they hunt" (102). It is hardly necessary to cite the complex retrospective mode of Wordsworth's *Prelude*, but equally distinctive are the forms of memory in other autobiographies.

Rousseau is as dependent as Wordsworth (or Proust) on the binoculars of retrospective vision. All that is left him now is memory; that other power his "fearful imagination" has done its worst. Yet the "sweet memories of my best years" are capricious, remind him of painful moments when he sought in vain to recapture remembered innocence, and lead him to chapters wherein sweet memory, like other powers of innocence, is transformed into bitterness and pain. The dominant memory of Nabokov's *Speak, Memory* is reminiscent of Rousseau's. But it is less an ambivalent gift of nature than an aristocratic inheritance, a well-cultivated estate. Nabokov reenters his past. It is his — an intensely personal possession which he jealously reclaims from fictional characters and worlds. Memory's "supreme achievement" is "the masterly use it makes of innate harmonies when gathering to its fold the suspended and wandering tonalities of the past" (70). It creates — it must create — the most densely particularized harmonies, for "I have to make a rapid inventory of the universe. . . . I have to have all space and all time participate in my emotion, in my mortal love, so that the edge of its mortal-

[32] *Dream and Reality: An Essay in Autobiography*, trans. K. Lampert (New York, 1962).

ity is taken off, thus helping me to fight the utter degradation, ridicule, and horror of having developed an infinity of sensation and thought within a finite existence" (297).

Like Ruskin's and Gide's, Yeats's memory is informed by an abiding sense of place: "I only seem to remember things dramatic in themselves or that are somehow associated with unforgettable places" (20) —places with human centers that exemplify proud, traditional, solitary ways of life. But the formative memory of *Reveries* is not just personal. It is fixed in local and family tradition, in legend, and the anecdotal discontinuity of *Reveries* suggests the effect of legendary tales. Identity is having one's story; leaving one's place is losing that story. Creating a new personality is recreating one's legend in association with memorable place. Gide finds in his temporal memory "a person whose eyes cannot properly measure distances and is liable to think things extremely remote which on examination prove to be quite near" (16). Memory fails to provide Sartre with the personal truth that matters:

What I have just written is false. True. Neither true or false, like everything written about madmen, about men. I have reported the facts as accurately as memory permitted me. But to what extent did I believe in my delirium? . . . How could I determine — especially after so many years — the imperceptible and shifting frontier that separates possession from hamming [43-4]?

Dahlberg finds in memory his only reality. Then, as for Rousseau, this only reality becomes a trap and a phantom. The man is prisoner of "the phantasms of his childhood" (49-50). But "did the child who is now the man ever live?" (92) and what remains of that boy who flits like a sapless phantom through my memory? I am more familiar with Theophrastus, Bartram or with Thoreau than I am with him" (122). The remembered past fluctuates wildly between sole reality and nameless phantom, and Dahlberg's commemoration ends strangely. The mother he has confessed to, commemorated, exorcised — the brave, fleshly lady barber portrayed by a fictive omniscience independent of the boy's present consciousness — even she, after all, is beyond memory and understanding. She has been vividly understood, but not by the phantom "I." It is as if the emergence of the "I" had displaced that understanding: "Who was Lizzie Dalberg? I wish to God I knew, but it is my infamy that I do not." Has the fictive narrator's compassionate omniscience redeemed the phantom boy-man from his infamy, or only deepened, articulated it?

Gosse is in an intriguingly similar imaginative paradox *vis-à-vis* his remembered father. Like Nabokov — "The break in my own destiny affords me in retrospect a syncopal kick" (250) — Gosse initiates

Father and Son in a radical discontinuity. He derides the "hallowed proverb" that "the child is father of the man." The child's life is so brief, "its impressions are so illusory and fugitive, that it is as difficult to record its history as it would be to design a morning cloud sailing before the wind. . . . But in memory, my childhood was long, long with interminable hours, hours with the pale cheek pressed against the window pane. . . . I feel now the coldness of the pane, and the feverish heat that was produced, by contrast, in the orbit round the eye" (57). Memory has replaced past reality, yet with an intense and mysterious continuity of sensation, and a power of panoramic visual impression, setting its own terms and limits: "precisely as my life ceases to be solitary, it ceases to be distinct." Memory dictates a distancing vividness wherein child and father attain the same external reality. But, as in Dahlberg, the parent is realized inwardly, as well, with an imaginative compassion denied the ludicrously fictive child. We recall Sartre when Gosse remembers himself as "an adroit little pitcher," and think, too, of the extraordinary distance from which Graves "remembers" the "caricature scenes that now seem to sum up the various stages of my life" (180),[33] moments of absurd visualization by which memory effectively bids "goodbye to all that" in the very act of comic revocation.

Such instances of memory's forms have taken us into considerations of structure and method, problems of retrospective point of view and its essential paradox in autobiography. Effective access to a recollected self or its "versions" begins in a discontinuity of identity or being which permits past selves to be seen as distinct realities. Yet only a continuity of identity or being makes the autobiographical act or purpose meaningful. The paradox of continuity in discontinuity is itself a problem to be experimented with, and it is a problem both of truth and of form. Manipulation of autobiographical point of view is conditioned by the demands of the paradox, but it is also conditioned by rhetorical considerations of intention and emphasis, formal and stylistic considerations of clarity and proportion. And such demands necessarily fluctuate as the autobiographical situation evolves.

Consider two seemingly contradictory manipulations which together illustrate the paradox. Chapter One of Wright's *Black Boy*[34] climaxes a recreation of the experience and awareness of a violent, lonely boy with a visit to the father who had deserted his family for a mistress. The scene closes. The narrator now superimposes Richard's images

33 Graves, *Good-bye to All That* — the passage is only in the revised edn. (Garden City, 1957).

34 *Black Boy* (New York, 1966).

"many times in the years after that" on the boy's sensory immediacy. Finally comes the long interpretive perspective of the man after a lapse of a quarter of a century "during which my mind and consciousness had become so greatly and violently altered" that "I" then looked at the "sharecropper, clad in ragged overalls, holding a muddy hoe in his gnarled, veined hands," with the compassion of a distanced and mature understanding. The separation that had been the father's moral recklessness had become a final condition of the autobiographer's development. The development of the artist, the tragic naturalist whose emergence we trace in the next chapter, is the precondition of the imaginative truth achieved by an intricate conflation of temporal and psychological perspectives. Of such intermingled discontinuities is an autobiographical truth formed.

Or consider the middle chapters of the *Autobiography of Malcolm X*. The autobiographer recalls how he was saved, like Paul on the road to Damascus, by the miraculous intervention of Elijah Muhammed's Muslimism. The historic truth of influence and conversion must be realized. Yet in retrospect the truth comes to include the jealousy and misunderstanding that soon became part of his relation to his leader. This too must be revealed, without compromising the moral power that Malcolm felt and the autobiographer seeks to convey. While editing these chapters, Malcolm was forced to see the truth; and Hayley feared that in his bitterness Malcolm would revise the chapters. Malcolm admitted, "There are a lot of things I could say that passed through my mind at times even then, things I saw and heard, but I threw them out of my mind. I'm going to let it stand the way I've told it. I want the book to be the way it was." The result is truer to the personality of Malcolm revealed in the total reminiscence: his fierce loyalty, his vigorous openness to each new stage of his extraordinary career of changes. The picaresque vitality of the versatile confidence man is reaffirmed in the histrionic exuberance of the autobiographer, recalling the early Harlem days, "scat-singing and popping his fingers, 're-bop-de-bop-blop-bam—'" (391), or recreating with zest the absurdly conked and zootsuited lindy-hopper at Roseland State Ballroom. Historical and psychological truth has been recreated by the careful, even deceptive, manipulation of temporal perspective.

The truth of a particular autobiography demands its own discrimination and conflation of perspectives, and hence its own narrative mode. Even the diurnal unit of the journalist, from Boswell to Che Guevara, is an artifice of multiple perspectives — levels of retrospect, minglings of dramatic and real anticipation, operations of significant selection. Wordsworth and Rousseau, Gosse and Adams and Nabokov, all seem basically to share the mobile panoramic impressionism we associate with Thackeray and Proust, but the distinctive variations are mimetically, as well as formally, crucial. The impressionism of Gosse would be unsuitable for Wright, given *Black Boy's* preoccupation with the potencies and frustrations of words, best represented in a dialogic-scenic mode. Rousseau and Newman are equally committed to a totality of perspective: Rousseau must be seen in every point of view, and Newman must be seen in the dramatic authenticity of each historic moment. The conception of one is pictorial and of the other temporal, however, and so the recreation of the momentous walk to Vincennes demands a different perspectivism than the recreation of the illness in Sicily or the final departure from Oxford. *Dichtung und Wahrheit* necessarily eschews the impressionistic mode. Goethe's idea of a cumulative totality of being, while no more comprehensive than Wordsworth's, amounts to a progressive cultivation and assimilation, not the successive retrospective reassimilation of *The Prelude*. Perhaps the most Thackerayan of major autobiographical narratives is in the panoramic mode of Adams, and for good reason, since the *Education* is a comic epic of maladjustment and discontinuity, whose rational evolutionist relearns repeatedly and in vain that his vision of order in history is an illusive compulsion, that the rule is ludicrous catastrophism.

The inference is clear. The interpretive reader of an autobiography had best interpret its method before fixing it with a general label. And the same is true of structure. The nature of an extended autobiographical act makes it self-defeating for the interpreter to expect some predictable integrity or unity. Form is too experimental, too "accidental," and at the same time too inherent in perspectives still to be recovered or imposed by memory. Conflicts or fluctuations of perspective and intention may themselves become formative, and the personal history that emerges may reveal variant or conflicting assumptions about meaningful orders in life. Furthermore, form is really a multiplicity of formative options in the simplest autobiography: options of selection and exclusion, interpretive refocus or rearrangement, conflations of historical and expository arrangement, developmental rhythms in narrative and situational rhythms in the autobiographer's sense of movement toward his end.

To begin with, autobiographers set out with divergent views of the appropriateness of form. Gauguin insists his *journal intime* is "not a book," and Cocteau confesses in his "journal" that formlessness may itself be an imposition: "Has the book I am writing completed its curve? I who boast, and in its very chapters, of never being preoccupied with it . . . . Can I still speak to you, and keep this journal, which is not really one, in the form of a journal, based on what happens to me? That would be falsifying its mechanism."[35] Gide is constantly preoccupied with form in *If It Die*, troubled by the spatial form memory imposes. He intermittently resists and surrenders to and justifies it, yet insists that "this is not a literary composition; I am just writing down my recollections as they come to me" (44). Boswell's passion for form leads to such finely formed continuities in the *London Journal*[36] as "the Louisa saga." He recognizes in himself a "love of form for its own sake" (128), and his repeated frustrations in trying to live by a form simply lead to marvelous rationalizations of formal variations. The journal was "to contain a consistent picture of a young fellow eagerly pushing through life," but salutary humbling divagations remind him "the hero of a romance or novel must not go uniformly along in bliss. . . . Aeneas met with many disasters in his voyage to Italy, and must not Boswell have his rubs?" (206). The *London Journal* may thus have "more form" than the "approaches to the past made at distinct times in differing modes"[37] that Yeats finally titled *Autobiography*. The formal passion of Gibbon operates to form his autobiography, yet he evidently found form so problematic that he left six finely formed, differently focused, and overlapping fragments. Henry Adams's "idol Gibbon" is reincarnate in the autobiographer of the *Education*, who says, "From cradle to grave this problem of running order through chaos, direction through space, discipline through freedom, unity through multiplicity, has always been, and must always be, the task of education" (12). The rich coherences, the elegant if whimsical patterning and focusing, of Adams's world attest to the control of the philosophical historian, in relentless search of "the working of law in history" (363), determined that "everything must be made to move together" (378), while the "hero" learns by successive false starts that Mont Blanc like other spectacles of being is "a chaos of anarchic and purposeless forces" (289). The result is a curious mock-form, a study in the ludicrous but beautiful balancing of illusion, a protagonist who combines the solemn naivete of Rasselas (378) with the fugitive historicity of Arnold's scholar gypsy, and an autobiographer who, like Chateaubriand and Mark Twain, seems to speak from beyond the grave.

35 *Journals of Jean Cocteau*, trans. W. Fowlie (Bloomington, Ind., 1964), p. 218.

36 *London Journal 1762-1763*, ed. F. A. Pottle (New York, n.d.).

37 Ian Fletcher, "Rhythm and Pattern in *Autobiographies*," in *An Honoured Guest*, ed. Donoghue and Mulryne (New York, 1966), p. 165; contrast J. Ronsley, *Yeats's Autobiography: Life as Symbolic Pattern* (Cambridge, Mass., 1968), pp. 4-5 *et passim*.

But Adams's views of form were at least options of a single "moment" in his history. In other cases the autobiographer's temporal position and his situation changed radically. The Rousseau recreating 1741 in the late 1760's "two years of patient silence" after finishing 1740 has a very different perspective not just on what must follow, but on what has already been written. Franklin at St. Asaph's in 1771 is not the same as Franklin at Passy in 1784 or at home in 1788 — and such shifts, however "accidental," must be formative. Mill's final chapter is punctuated by "In resuming my pen some years after closing the preceding narrative" (170). A silent majority of auto-biographers must have found themselves in the midway metamor-phosis best described by Edwin Muir: "I finished the first part of this book thirteen years ago. . . . The generation to which I belong has survived an age, and the part of our life which is still immobilized there is like a sentence broken off before it could be completed; the future in which it would have written its last word was snatched away and a raw new present abruptly substituted; and that present is reluc-tant now to formulate its own sentence" (194). Form in autobio-graphy is too contingent on shifting situations ever to be interpreted as if it might be a static integrity.

It is contingent as well on shifting principles of selectivity, any one of which may be revised or replaced as each new stage of self-recrea-tion forces a reappraisal of what is relevant. A static interpretation of selectivity would cite the "spots of time" passage in *Prelude XII* and suppose that events throughout have been selected accordingly. Yet the passage with its two long associative "memorials" occurs in the framing of the crucial moment of restoration; the moment becomes continuous with the autobiographical present and thus re-veals a final vision of restorative events. Events in earlier books illustrate earlier visions of events: those testifying to the ministry of beauty and fear, to the reality of vocation or consecration, those that exemplify the imagination's characteristic powers and aspirations, and man's nobility and pathos. Different principles operate at different stages. The shape of the recovered event is the shape of recovery at that point, the shape of the event as then recovered. As *Black Boy* traces the shaping of a literary artist, we see the growth of a vision of human events, and that vision as a selective principle necessarily evolves. At the beginning, Yeats views events as legendary, timeless, antithetical to the action of "inorganic logical straightness." Later, as he "must not only describe events but those patterns into which they fall, when I am the looker-on" (221), certain places and eras of personal development seem in retrospect to identify themselves by a certain form or quality of event: "I see Paris in the Eighteen-nine-ties as a number of events separated from one another, and without cause or consequence, without lot or part in the logical structure of my life" (227). Ruskin in *Praeterita* appears repeatedly confused about what events caused the decay of his visionary power, and how.[38] Wells locates the predominant causes of his own development first in his own will, then in chance or destiny, and finally in history.

To trace such shifts or redefinitions of narrative selection and formation is to identify one essential component of autobiographical form. Some such refocusings are themselves illustrative of a particular history or personality. Others reveal themselves as inherent in life process. Nabokov recognizes that selectivity necessarily changes as memory's focus moves from childhood to adolescence, for the details constituting childhood's "harmonious world" possess "a naturally plastic form in one's memory, which can be set down with hardly any effort; it is only starting with the recollections of one's adolescence that Mnemosyne begins to get choosy and crabbed" (24-5), generating new problems and possibilities of conscious selection. Gibbon regularly discriminates between the characteristic and universal, as his formal sophistication leads him through a succession of selective problems. Early, "since philosophy has exploded all innate ideas and natural propensities" (66) he must include all possible environmental causes and conditions. Later, he is skeptical of the "explosion" (137) and may, therefore, have included irrelevancies. The "delicate subject of my early love" reveals a new selective principle: "the discovery of a sixth sense, the first consciousness of manhood, is a very interesting moment of our lives, but it less properly belongs to the memoirs of an individual than to the natural history of the species" (108) — the same criterion by which Spender postpones recollections of early childhood, Graves mocks them, and Wordsworth and Yeats, seeking the sources of a natural or ancestral identity, stress them. Finally, Gibbon remembers his travels as amusing, but "the narrative of my life must not degenerate into a book of travels" (143), a generic scrupulousness unsuitable in autobiographers with notions of the spatiality or locality of personal identity — e.g., Yeats, Gide, Nabokov, Rousseau, for whom each new relocation is a personally momentous event, or Goethe, Spender, or Adams, for whom it is a significant self-expansion or self-complication.

For all his will to explain himself, Gibbon was not troubled by problems many post-Enlightenment autobiographers have faced. How, asks Muir, can the autobiographer exclude the experience of one-third

---

38 For these interpretive conclusions about Ruskin and Wells I am indebted to Johnston, *Integral Self* (note 13 above), pp. 40-44, 157-66.

of his life, his sleeping experience, his dreams? Imaginary or visionary experiences of all kinds may well seem crucial to self-explanation. Furthermore, the aim of self-explanation may force the autobiographer progressively into the dilemma of reconciling the need for personal historical focus with the claims of philosophical exposition. Adams and Wells, for instance, resolve their struggles for autobiographical form with final expositions of philosophies of world history and government.

The question of the end in autobiographical form is a complex one. Narrative recreation and autobiographical situation somehow terminate at once in a resolution of both narrative pattern and the search for such pattern. Any "end" belongs to both. Goethe's *Dichtung* and Nabokov's *Speak, Memory* both delight in the ever-expanding recapture of past worlds. For Goethe, as Pascal observes, the form is "an irregularly moving expansion," an "ever-widening arc," with no spiral of return, because for Goethe the self is a steady assimilative progression. But there is a counter-rhythm — or rather counter-stasis — in Goethe's lifelong tendency to use his imagination to put his mind at rest, to see how it *stands* relative to the moving world, to use poetry to fix that which is confused or unstable in himself (as he had done with *Werther*). His love of theater, of ritual, of festive ceremony and disguise and sacrament, is the love of one who finds "comfort" in "a regular recurrence of external things" (II, 159). Nabokov too sees the process of repossessing a past world as an achievement of stasis through form — hence, "a colored spiral in a small ball of glass, this is how I see my own life" (275). But the stasis can only seem what Robert Frost called "a momentary stay against confusion." An autobiographical form can seem closed if, like Adams, the autobiographer adopts the final fiction of seeing his whole life as past, or, like Newman and Mill, of seeing all significant movement completed. Or the form may "close" with the cessation of all narrative movement in a climax of the autobiographical act. Sartre's lifelong flight from unreal selves and spurious idealisms comes to rest in a final declaration of self-will in the autobiographer. Podhoretz narrates his decision to try a personal book about the problem of "success," itself a declared bid for success, and announces, "I just have," throwing all past narrative abruptly into the resolution of a dramatic present. The four parts of *Soul On Ice*, a progression of distinct modes like Yeats's *Autobiography*, move from the autobiographical loss of an old self to the mythical affirmation of a new, from colloquial reminiscence and self-portrait, through cultural prophecy, through the intimate personality of the letters to Beverley Axelrod, to mythopoeic vision of a new sexual Jerusalem. *The Prelude*, too, ends in mythopoeia, but the vision is reached by way of an ambiguous journey backwards and forwards, into "fallings away" natural and artificial, and final redemption of a possibly waning power without whose sustaining force the journey could not have been taken. The movement of Spender's *World Within World* is comparably complex: a historico-cultural journey through a decade of crisis; a Conradian movement toward the dark center of an imperative personal complexity; a quest for the "wheels within wheels," the repossessed childhood that at last affirms and encompasses the integrity of the adult. No one has understood better than Spender the complexities of autobiographical form and its relation to the confessional intention.

So we turn at last to the question of intention, the shifting ground of the autobiographer's form, the condition of the truth he struggles for, itself subject to dramatic and narrative redefinition as the personal center fluctuates and formal options are seized or rejected. Having recognized four "kinds" of autobiography — diary or journal, confession, reminiscence, and personal history, Berdyaev declares that *Dream and Reality* will be none of these: "I decided to make this study of myself not only because I feel the need of expressing and communicating myself (a reason for which I cannot possibly claim the attention of the reader), but also because this may help to raise and resolve certain problems concerning man and his destiny and contribute to the understanding of our age. I also feel the necessity of explaining the apparent inconsistencies and contradictions which have been ascribed to my philosophical outlook. . . . I should like memory to overcome oblivion in regard to all that is of value in it" (x-xi). Thus, having disowned all antecedents, Berdyaev embraces all three traditional autobiographical intentions: to communicate one's self (confession); to show the integrity of one's career (apology); to repossess one's past (memoir)! Ostensibly at an opposite pole is the Gibbonian autobiographer, who professes that "my own amusement is my motive, and will be my reward" (27). But such professions probably confirm Sartre's view that "our deeper intentions are plans and evasions which are inseparably linked" (120).

The list is long of autobiographers who commence, like Rousseau, by insisting that what they seek to do is not quite what the reader expects: "It is, I suppose, a hybrid form."[39] Also long is the list of those who periodically discriminate in their motives, reassert control over the reader's generic expectations, and in so doing refine or redefine their intentions: "this is not history but education"; rather, this is the "long mistake" of a "search for education," "the shifting search

---

39 V. Sheean, *Personal History* (Boston, 1969), p. xvii.

for the education he never found," rather "adventures in search of education" (Adams, 172, 185, 162). Each new formal resolution calls for a new justification, hence revelation, of intention; "but I do not judge," repeats the confessor; "I simply relate" — and his protestations accumulate with the force of a devious judicial act. Something inherent in autobiographical process calls for the continuous refocusing of expectation and intention, as each autobiographer discovers his own fluctuating mixture of confession, apology, and memoir.

Rousseau insists on "confession" as his intention, repeatedly disclaims apology, yet Pascal rightly argues that the work is apology. "Confession" is the primary motive of Rousseau's history that gives integrity to his entire social life. The work is the confessor's characteristic act of friendship, an apology for the confessor, intended to achieve at last the society his life has consistently failed to achieve. The interplay of confession and apology is definitive; so precarious and intermittent is his repossession of a historic world that "memoir" is almost irrelevant. Gide resembles Rousseau in his determination to reveal the "secret" of his life as an "act of penance," but there is little apologetic impulse, and there is, intermittently, much of the commemorative passion of the memoirist in distinctive interaction with the confessional intention. Podhoretz resembles Rousseau, too, in confessing his public life around the "dirty little secret" of the desire for success; but memoiristic apology is strong. Like Rousseau, Goethe finds a confessional integrity in a prevalent tendency of his life: "All, therefore, that has been confessed by me, consists of fragments of a great confession; and this little book is an attempt which I have ventured on to render it complete" (I, 235). But this is confession to himself (or his daemon) of his creative relations with the natural and historic world, confession that achieves its end through memoir, the repossession of a rich and expansive experience. Spender's *World Within World* is a mixture of Rousseau and Goethe. But the apologetic intention evolves toward a confessional act of climactic political meaning. The book is as much concerned as Rousseau's with the precariousness of friendship, but the kind of relationship it chiefly defines is one we associate with memoir — personal integrity in a world of history, and what is confessed is a defiant personal balance of individuality and community.

Paradoxically, Newman the "apologist" writes in a situation closer to Rousseau's than the situations of Goethe, Spender, and Gide the "confessors." His initial intention seems closer too: he will replace the phantom deceiver in men's imagination with his truth. But just as his assumptions about personality and history differ, so his confessional-apologetic intention must evolve differently too. What is confessed is the integrity or entelechy of that movement of his "living intelligence" — the "economy" — by which divine providence has revealed the "idea" of his unique personal history. The truth confessed is the immanent idea progressively revealed, quite beyond his foreknowledge or understanding — such is "history" for Newman, and in this is the apology for his life.

Malcolm X's apology is a curious analogue. Malcolm prophesies his own death, and predicts that "the white man, in his press, is going to identify me with 'hate.' He will make use of me dead, as he has made use of me alive, as a convenient symbol of 'hatred'" (381). Malcolm has intended throughout to offer his life as a mirror — and in this exemplary motive he differs from Newman. But the more personal intention has shown itself throughout in the resilient, open, loving man, the antithesis of hate, who has found and now recreates human value and vitality in each new world or underworld he entered. The result is vivid "memoir" with apologetic force, which, of course, he tries to deny: "I want to say before I go on that I have never previously told anyone my sordid past in detail. I haven't done it now to sound as though I might be proud of how bad, how evil, I was. But people are always speculating — why am I as I am? To understand that of any person, his whole life, from birth, must be reviewed. All of our experiences fuse into our personality" (150). The Rousseauistic confessional intention persists, and with it a memoiristic richness of reminiscence, in spite of the apologetic intention of bearing witness to the power and goodness of Allah and the exemplary intention of telling the white man about himself and awakening the black man from his follies.

The evolving intentionality of any autobiography is complicated by an exemplary motive. Podhoretz's whimsical instructions to young writers are dramatically bound up with his apologetic memoir, just as Franklin's maxims and anecdotes mingle with other intentions: to initiate a dynastic chronicle for his posterity, a memoir for his own sense of achieved position, a personal history that will invitingly illustrate the fortunes of his young country. Adams proposes to "fit young men, in universities or elsewhere, to be men of the world" (x); he asserts that "knowledge of human nature is the beginning and end of political education" (180), but he has discovered human nature to be "sheer chaos" (153). He insists the book is education (though he never found education), not history, and not temperament (243). But it is evidently a vividly temperamental last adventure in search of education, and it surely moves through and culminates in a vision of modern history. In his exemplary life, Mill identifies three intentions at the outset, confesses an ulterior propagandistic intention in a letter to his wife, and perhaps reveals others as the original intentions are complicated in interplay. He will record an "unusual and remarkable education"; he will show the successive phases of a mind always pressing forward, achieving intellectual selfhood. "But a motive which weighs more with me than either of these, is a desire to make acknowledgment of the debts which my intellectual and moral development owes to other persons" (1) — most emphatically the person of James Mill, who exemplifies a method and a principle of intellectual individuality, and the person of Harriet Mill, who embodies the fusion of intellectual individuality and imaginative power to which Mill aspires in vain, except insofar as he manifests it in his recreation of other persons. Thus the commemorative-memoiristic motive threatens to overwhelm the apologetic-exemplary one, and in this evolving drama of intention the book acquires its meaning.

To put the static classification of autobiography by "intention" to a final test, consider the present ambiguous status of the "kind" called memoir. If memoir is the personal record of historic events and persons, every autobiography contains some memoir. If memoir is the autobiographical search for the historicity of the self, memoir is scarcely avoidable. But to say that some autobiographies are too much memoir to be "true autobiography" is something else. Orwell's *Homage to Catalonia* and Mailer's *Armies of the Night* are retrospective personal accounts of events that are unique and cataclysmic experiences in historic lives, significant parts of their writers' lives. Each "centers its chief attention on the life of the author as it was lived" (Mandel, 222). It will not do to insist that this "chief attention" must slight the representativeness of the author as witness. It will not do to object that "autobiography proper" gives the wholeness of a life; many autobiographers do not do so, and anyway, an autobiographer may choose to reveal or collect the "wholeness" of his life around one central or cataclysmic event or influence or relationship. Nor can we say that one who is the observer of, rather than a major participant in, his personal history writes memoir rather than autobiography. Adams's autobiography is the history of an (unwilling) observer, and Lawrence of Arabia, whose *Seven Pillars of Wisdom* is allegedly not "true autobiography," could not write a personal history of a significant segment of his life except as a confessional or apologetic participant. Had Orwell written a "true autobiography," it would undoubtedly have been less "autobiographical" than a "memoir" by Spender or Newman or Mailer. What Malraux calls *Anti-Memoirs* is more "memoir" than "autobiography" for autobiographical reasons, as we have seen. George Kennan entitles *Memoirs* a book which he then describes as "primarily . . . an intellectual autobiography" (63) and manifestly intends as apology.

Memoir is not a kind of autobiography, but, like confession and apology, a kind of autobiographical intention. Autobiographers share certain intentions in varying degrees and in numerous distinctive patterns of interaction. Rather than deducing fixed expectations from distinctions of intentional "kind," we should try to see how — why — with what effect distinct intentions evolve and interplay in individual autobiographies. In the same way we should observe and interpret dynamic distinctions of form and evolutions and conflicts of personal focus, as the individual autobiographer wrestles with options of truth and integrity in the recovery of his personal history. The correlation of our observations and interpretations would seem to be the most promising way to the recognition of meaning and value. When such recognitions of individual autobiographies have accumulated and undergone testing and sorting, then and only then will it be possible to make real and meaningful descriptive generalizations about the historical development of modern autobiography. And when, at last, such a "new literary history" of autobiography has been undertaken, then critical judgment can be other than the facile prevention of appreciative understanding it often is at present.

13

Dreaming with Adam: Notes on Imaginary History

George Garrett

I

TWO FACTS, one well-known and often recorded, the other less known and seldom, if ever, related to the first: the first that in her old age Queen Elizabeth ordered all the mirrors, in public rooms where she might pass, to be covered with curtains; the second that she ordered great mirrors, enough to surface walls, ceiling, floor, for her inmost bathing chambers. These things took place at approximately the same time. The biographers of the Queen, and they are excellent, have made a good deal of the covering of the mirrors, also dutifully allowing that fully bewigged and made-up and royally dressed, seen at a respectful distance, she seemed beautiful, even youthful to many observers.

In a work of fiction, where imagination is given more freedom, the two things can properly be joined together. Here is the imagined Walter Ralegh, on the last day before his execution, within the context of an imaginary letter to his young son, Carew.

"In the myth Narcissum is depicted as a man. And rightly so. Only a man (or a brainless beautiful woman) can fall in love with his own appearance. For it is a stranger to him. The woman at her looking glass sees what she sees and knows it. And therefore, I do think, women justly demand the slight subterfuge of flattery from us.

"The old Queen ordered the mirrors in all her palaces removed or covered up in her last years. And this has been taken by some as a sign of vanity and self deceit. They do not know (or do not remember) that her inmost chambers of bathing where she was alone with herself, as naked as God made her, were made of mirrors — walls, floors and ceiling. To see herself. And not in delusion or vanity or self-love. But naked from all sides, as no one sees himself, so that she would know and never forget the plain truth of herself.

"Meaning she knew her appearance as well as any who make a study of themselves. Yet she took that aging body, that withering face, and painted and daubed and costumed and disguised it until, at a decent distance, she was the picture of a proper Queen. Not out of a vanity or self-delusion. Nor out of the wish to deceive others who might know better. But out of the compelling necessity to be what she must be to rule and never to permit the expectations and the pride of her subjects or this kingdom to be diminished or disappointed.

"She was willing, then, to sacrifice even her own integrity of person in the name of her office and for the good of the Kingdom.

"I think it was too much to ask her to look upon herself in the disguises of public mirrors and to beam approval and signify thereby a total self-delusion."

II

Confession is one kind of beginning, apology another of close kin, and neither is advisable except as the last resort of a well-meaning scoundrel. Better to plead guilty and be silent, or to stand mute, than to present at the outset one's last reserves, the extenuating and mitigating circumstances. Yet that dubious strategem is now demanded; for nothing is or can be offered here that by any merciful bending and twisting of definitions can be rightly called critical theory of the uses of history in fiction and of the uneasy, continual kinship between the two. Instead of formulation, founded upon authority or growing out of deep experience, all that can be offered is fragmentary, tentative. More of a "mix" than a blending and without benefit of alchemy or magic.

Which may be just as well, if (once again) necessity can be hopefully named virtue. For there is already an ample weight of authority on all sides; theories of the meaning of history and the telling of it abound, and, to a lesser degree, there are plenty of fully formulated, well-presented, documented and demonstrated notions of the uses, limits, and implications of historical fiction. At best I can only share some parts of an experience, leftovers, the chips and blocks and shards from an unpoliced workshop after the conclusion of a piece of work, done but not yet public. Some are particular and some are general. All are random, lacking even the polish of aphorism which can, at least, disguise mutual doubts and, by sleight of hand, divert attention from awkard innocence.

To be particular. I am writing here in terms of an "historical" novel, my own, recently completed and now scheduled for publication in the fall of 1970. Its title is *Death of the Fox*, and it is subtitled

"An Imaginary Version of the Last Days of Sir Walter Ralegh." It was a long time in the making, begun first in the early 1950's as an attempt at writing a full biography.

Begun then, interrupted by all sorts of circumstances, changing with outward circumstances and with the trial and error of the making and revising, and changing also over that time as I changed my views and feelings, and as experience changed me. Begun, interrupted, but never for long, and constantly changing shape and form, constantly subjected to the process of trial and error, continually and closely questioned. The final writing, myself committed by then by contract and obligation, began in 1964 and continued until the fall of 1969, interrupted sporadically in this second stage only by mundane conditions, not by other work.

Thus, for better or worse, it has been a long time finding its form and coming to be.

My observations and notions are of two kinds: the general, coming from a gradually increasing awareness of the theory and practice of other writers, past and present, in working with past time, and including some reaction to present trends and views; and particular events, technical as it were, created out of the doing and working, the problems, questions, and possibilities which came less out of theoretical or preconceived concerns (though, of course, those are never wholly absent from any literary work if only manifest in the author's interests, impulses, and hidden assumptions) than from what might be called engineering or construction details.

At best, then, I can present here, in advance of and in the absence of the book which must speak for itself and speak differently, some accounting of the gradual formation of an incomplete theory, hand in glove with the particular elements of practice, neither entirely dependent upon the other and neither free of the continuing interchange and influence of the other.

The living writer works within, around, against his literary context and consensus. Even twenty years ago the "historical novel," for American writers, was declining in both prestige and popularity. Those handmaidens of the arts (and especially the commerce of the arts in the marketplace) are more often masters than servants. And prestige and popularity, while not identical twins, are very closely related. There are and will be important exceptions, but present evidence is clear enough. For a time, roughly up through World War II, there was some brief flowering of the form, deceptive in that historical fiction, going in time beyond the hauntings and memories of this nation (what the "new" historians call oral history), leaping an ocean of space backward, has never really been a significant territory for

American writers except, perhaps, in the form of the satirical demonstration of its insignificance (*A Connecticut Yankee in King Arthur's Court*) or in, for example, the bland and popular pieties which, like the poor, are still here: from *Ben Hur* to *The Robe.* For a time the "sword and bosom" school (*Forever Amber*, etc.) flourished adequately in the mass marketplace. And it might have seemed likely that a corresponding prestigious "serious" fiction would develop to take advange of this as, for instance, *Portnoy's Complaint* and *Couples* are advantageous responses to the popularity of pornography. But this did not happen, a fact which might be attributed, though only in small part, to the negative or indifferent (in fact the same) critical consensus of opinion. Witness, for example, the wide-ranging and imaginative work of the late David Stacton, who seemed able to write very well about ancient and utterly alien cultures. Most of his books are still unpublished in the United States despite a considerable recognition in Britain and, in translation, on the continent. The critical distaste for fictional "costume stories" is supported at the highest, most influential level by T. S. Eliot's views of *Murder in the Cathedral,* both in his essays on verse drama and, later, his introduction to the screenplay adaptation of that play. Essentially (and over-simplified) his consistent critical burden is that the directly historical avoids what he seems to have conceived of as the chief duty of the contemporary artist, to bring together, insofar as the dissociated sensibility of the modern artist will allow, the elements of poetry here and now, the past ever a part of the present, but never overwhelming it. At a lower level the vulgar success, followed in more recent years by an almost inevitable failure, of the popular arts — in drama the historical plays of Maxwell Anderson, in film the successes and excesses of a long line of film-makers, from DeMille through George Stevens — did not do much to increase intellectual esteem for the wedding of fiction and history in American letters.

One must stress this national singularity because it is peculiar to our literature and, in fact, goes against the grain of much highly regarded foreign writing. The plays of Camus have enjoyed some interest here, not commensurate with the enthusiasm for his other works, but nevertheless a fact. Par Lagerkvist, in both drama and fiction, is steadily, if modestly admired. And in novel, play, and film the British writers continue the cultivation of the historical muse, and they profit. But the American writer has been steadily more restricted. He remains free to use his own history, provided it is "relevant" to current issues and problems. William Styron's *The Confessions of Nat Turner* is a superb example of the cult of "relevance," of timeliness if not perfect timing. And the American writer may, in form of a *tour de force* within the persistent comic tradition, engage himself in satire and celebrative artifice. Example: John Barth's *The Sot-Weed Factor*. But, in general, historical fiction is of minimal importance today. The best evidence is manifest in the bright rows of paperbacks in bookstores, drugstores, etc. Over the past twenty years the paperback has come to dominate both aspects of the commerce of literature — prestige and popularity. It is the most accurate test of both. There are fewer works of historical fiction to be bought in paper than the small but unvanquished rows of westerns and nurse stories.

At the same time, our time, other slight changes have limited the possibilities of historical fiction. The most widely recognized writers, those who began their careers after World War II, still imagined as young but all now firmly middle-aged, have moved more and more into the field of "non-fiction." One of the first was Shelby Foote — also one of the most articulate theoreticians of the relationship of fiction and history — who fifteen years ago deferred his fiction for the sake of his three-volume history, *The Civil War*. More recently the essays and opinions of Norman Mailer have gained him more stature than the sum of his novels; and, with an ad man's bravado and disregard for inconvenient facts, Truman Capote announced the creation of a "new form," the "non-fiction novel," with his hugely successful *In Cold Blood*.

Perhaps some of the apparent decline, if not the "death" of the novel may be attributed to the novelists themselves, abandoning the sinking ship as early possible. More plausibly, however, one can suggest that the *distinctions*, relatively recent after all, between fiction and non-fiction have blurred beyond much value. This condition is reinforced by the deliberate use of the rhetoric of fiction in contemporary works of non-fiction, the work of Walter Lord, for example, or, more explicitly, Tom Wolfe. And journalism, once the last outpost of "objectivity," has surrendered to the imaginative arrangement of (and suppression of) facts, now dignified as "advocacy journalism."

It could be said that all history, of the moment and of the past, is part of a rhetoric close to that of fiction. Certainly the "revisionist" historians have exposed the imaginative limitations and assumptions of many earlier historians; and they make no great effort to disguise their own. Yet these, too, are limited by their intense concern for the relevant issues. Not all history is irrelevant to the radical activist, but much of it becomes condemned as a game for self-indulgent antiquarians.

Ironically, one result of this stance of shrugging indifference has been a remarkable surge of historical study, and consequently the changing and rearranging of old "ideas," by the historians and by literary scholars. Superb studies have emerged in almost all periods, based more upon a refined definition of the ways and means of modern historical scholarship than upon any desire to "create changes" or to seek relevance to contemporary affairs; resulting, paradoxically, in changes of view more radical than anything yet achieved by the revisionist historians. Paradox within paradox, these historical scholars, bound and perhaps inhibited by a methodology which is insistently inductive, and ravenous for facts, often demanding a weight of evidence far beyond the needs of lawyers or scientists to "prove" a point, have uprooted countless monuments of apparent misconception.

Studies of and in that loose time span we call the Renaissance have increased at an almost inflationary rate, the difference from the economy being that this growth shows no signs of slowing down. In particular all aspects of life and culture, large and small, of the English under the Tudors and the Stuarts have been and are being meticulously reexamined. In specific, there have been, beginning with William Wallace's *Sir Walter Raleigh* and including 1969's addition, *The Shepherd of the Ocean* by J. H. Adamson and H. F. Follard, a whole sequence of biographical studies of Ralegh. These have corrected any number of errors and misapprehensions, brought some facts, previously buried, to light, brought together related information, and, finally, in a speculative way, offered significant reinterpretation of motive and purpose.

Scarcely begun, my biography was out of the question, unnecessary. The impulse to try to come to know the man and the times was undiminished, however. And through his poems, the *History* and the other prose works, I kept close to the original fascination with the man as "subject," not questioning that interest, but accepting it as given. Instead I questioned, sometimes abstractly and sometimes in faulty attempts to begin and finish, what my general guidelines should be. Came back again and again to (among others) lines in the introduction to Agnes M. C. Latham's edition of *The Poems of Sir Walter Ralegh*, especially one — "He might have walked out of an Elizabethan play, a figment of the renaissance-imagination, compact of inordinate vices and virtues and destined to strange ends."

From all these things, then, certain preliminary rules and guidelines took shape.

I would, first of all, ignore the alternative of "relevance" or satire. Others, writers of fiction, were doing both things well enough. The search for direct parallels and practical relevance to our times seemed at worst, which was almost always despite fine writing, high style

DeMille, "camp," itself worthy of satire. Even the finest works I knew of seemed distorted by this inhibition. As for satire, Bob Newhart, the comedian, had done that well enough in a five-minute sketch. The firm assurance in either myself or the values of my own time necessary to satirize another time was lacking.

There was yet another possibility, to treat the subject and story in the "poetic" manner, as, for example, Edith Sitwell had handled Queen Elizabeth in *Fanfare For Elizabeth*, a manner less narrative than evocative, composed of condensed, rich, full-toned images carrying the tune and echoing in the mind long after, as her apt title implied. More successful, in my opinion, at once richer and deeper was Marguerite Yourcenar's *Hadrian's Memoirs*, an almost flawless work; and, for that reason, less influential than exemplary. I would keep those works in mind, models of excellence, if not for imitation. Would, by the same rule and for quite different reasons, think of Anthony Burgess' brilliant and exasperating virtuoso piece on the young Shakespeare — *Nothing Like the Sun*. Which succeeds beyond all expectation though it violates most of the premises I have so far stated. And I would come to know, not systematically but well enough, a variety of past and present fictions of the times, one very great pleasure being the four Tudor novels of R. H. Benson.

But to be interesting enough to work on over a length of time, and, as it happens, to be true to my feelings for the man and the times, my work would have to be different from any I had known and enjoyed. I felt that the strategy of "relevance" was an unnecessary inhibition. Obviously a man writing now could not escape his own time and place. There seemed no virtue or pleasure in asserting the obvious. Biographically there were few things to add to Ralegh's established chronicle. Inevitably a few small factual details and some interesting relationships turned up, things which in an academic work could be footnoted and added to the available evidence. On the other hand there are blank spaces and mysteries in Ralegh's life. Here the writer of fiction could move easily where the biographer and historian must go on tiptoes. The conventional direction of the novelist is to fill in these blank spaces with imagined detail, to stand boldly, attributing one motive or another for the seemingly inexplicable action, siding, then, with one historian or another by turning his careful surmise into a definite stance.

I rejected this possibility for a number of reasons, but in large part because the blank spaces and the dark corners seemed so much a part of the man and his character. Whatever the reasons for them, I would accept them as inherent mysteries, would find another way of using them in fiction.

Perhaps the clearest example is Ralegh's early career as a soldier, several years spent in the brutal religious wars in France when he was a very young man indeed, referred to briskly and memorably in a few instances in his *History of the World* (thus still part of the equipage of his sensibility almost a lifetime later), but otherwise very vague. His military actions in Ireland later are, as they were at the time, well-enough known and have given the biographers considerable material for characterization. Acts of courage, ruthless cunning, and the bloody day's slaughter at Smerwick have been well scrutinized; and these are important. But Ralegh was in his late twenties then and a combat veteran by nearly ten years. Moreover he had already been to the bright center of things, the Court, and thus far, failed in that more complex and more treacherous battlefield of smiles, frowns and false promises.

It was not difficult, nor would be for anyone living in our own time, to imagine a return to combat after ten years and a taste, no more, of a kind of life he could not have well imagined before he had experienced it. Those years in France when a boy became a hardened veteran soldier, remain blank of fact and speculation in my portrait, but are instead conjured up in images, in sudden remembered flashes, imitating his own way in the *History*.

And this, then, was a general rule: though allowing myself the freedom of all imaginary work, I would keep to the decorum of fact except in very rare cases where it seemed to me that the evidence was sufficient to be more definite than speculative. Fitting and proper in *this case*, because it seemed the essential mystery of the man, in his time and ever after, has been essential to his character. And that mystery is larger than the man, is the quality Miss Latham hyphenated as the renaissance-imagination.

The *ideas* of the period have been explored and treated by some great scholars. I know which current explorations of ideas I prefer and admire. But this would not be a book of "ideas," lest it should, like some of the lesser works of scholarship and criticism, become purely and simply a defense of one viewpoint or an attack on another. Ideas, the history of ideas, would be building blocks, not excluded, but not dominating the work.

Critics of contemporary writing often overlook the very large element of choice involved in the writer's language, tone, syntax — all the elements, functional or decorative, we name style. Other writers, especially the poets, do not ignore this in reacting to the work of others; indeed, it is the primary (and often the final) consideration. Auden is directly articulate about this in his essay "Squares and Oblongs," and in several of the prefaces to collections in the Yale

Younger Poets Series. But our critics, even those dealing almost exclusively with language, do not often allow for the writer's responsibility in choosing the language for the work or, in many cases, *a* language for all his work, which then becomes, in the terms of rock music, his "sound." We hear a good deal of the cliché "finding his own voice." Which implies, together with the sense of discovery, an *accidental* process. But any writer, a man attuned to the texture and sensuous affective qualities of words, has at his disposal (and within the physical limitations of his own ear and the predilections of his psychology) a wide range of possibilities (and thus choices) for style as a whole and in the multiple parts which compose it. American writers, blessed and cursed with a singularly shifting, changing language, at once cumulative and acquisitive, and, unlike many of their contemporaries working in other languages, permitted free and easy use of the flexible spoken language (itself, then, being taken into the catholic written language) have more choices to face in proportion to the freedom they possess. When an American writer "finds his own voice" for his own time and place it is no small accomplishment. No wonder, then, that one of the problems bedevilling the American writer who would deal with history, or for that matter anything foreign to his immediate "experience," is language. What style, what sort of dialogue to use? Eliot has written of this dilemma eloquently enough, posing the questions but offering no answers, in any number of critical pieces. In general there are a number of possibilities. Possible, but probably discarded, is the pop novel and Hollywood tradition, most useful in satire or farce: Janet Leigh in "The Vikings" (written by that impeccable stylist, Calder Willingham), "That Viking is the man I love"; Anouk Aimée as the Queen in "Sodom and Gomorrah" — "Greetings, Hebrews and Sodomites!" A more acceptable and conventional solution is the use of a heightened, slightly old-fashioned, neutral sort of language, hopefully not too stilted, and unobtrusive enough to be "transparent." Beyond this, by a step or two, is the creation of a "new" style, by definition personal, therefore eccentric, one which will serve to conjure up the ghosts and ruins for the writer and, rhetorically, permit the reader to participate in this incantation. No doubt the supreme, and unique, example is *Finnegans Wake*, undertaking the dream of all history; but besides being a once-and-for-all-time work, it also works from the present. The dream is the *now* of the novel. Djuna Barnes's *Ryder* is a superb example, but so eccentric as to be almost unreadable. John Berryman's *Homage to Mistress Bradstreet*, allowing for the differences between verse and prose, seems extremely successful despite some great excesses. Where he succeeds most admirably he kept in mind his own chosen motto for the work,

Keats's statement that the delight and surprise of poetry should come from "a fine excess."

My own choice was at least in the direction of these latter, with the private stipulation that the language must be readable, at least within the context of the work, accessible to an imaginary reader. I read and re-read a great many Elizabethan and Jacobean writers. Not systematically, which might have been easier and more efficient, but, I felt, would have arbitrarily inhibited the playful process of assimilation. Thumbed through glossaries and compilations of folk wisdom, etc., occasionally jotting down notes, but these notes to be discarded in the writing. The rule developed: to use what remained in consciousness at the time of writing. More lingered there than I might have expected, but for the most part it served a functional purpose in early drafts, a sense of being physically in *touch* with the language, rhythms, the styles of the times. Later on I could (and did) excise most of the eccentricities. They were expendable. The aim was, like Hemingway's iceberg image in another context, that having been present once in the making, these elements would now be implied, haunting the styles which remained. Since actions of imagination were the chief burden of the story, it was not possible to settle for a neutral tone. The imagination is cloudy, not transparent.

One thing that most aestheticians can agree upon (beyond which they all part company and go separate ways) is that a work of art begins as a sensuous affective experience communicating expressive form. It is one thing to seek to create a sensuous affective experience in words, dealing with known and familiar things. It is quite another to imagine and recreate the surfaces of a world and a time, and a man, that world ever more different the more one "knows" about it, so alien in fact, so removed that it is difficult to believe at all.

Perhaps that's what Keats meant comparing the imagination to Adam's dream. From the one point of view we are able to imagine, Adam's, it is an act of faith.

So it was, though I could not know it until I was done, that a *theme* developed. It grew almost directly out of original choices and predilections. To approach the renaissance-imagination required a commitment of one's own imagination. The proper theme of the work, then, is the human imagination, the possibility, limits and variety of imaginative experience.

To begin to move towards this I had to unlearn much, even as I sought to learn more; to unlearn, if only for dazed heady moments like holding one's breath a long time, some of our simplest assumptions.

A most rudimentary example is our deeply imagined, therefore almost ingrained, chronology of technology. Whether we rejoice in technological accomplishment or, more often, are dismayed and dumbfounded by the awful dangers of it, we accept with only minor exceptions the progressive theory. What we see and feel, what is *our* sensuous affective experience, is constant refinement and "improvement," development of techniques. We therefore work backwards, stripping away the things we know well, to reach the past where they were neither known nor imagined. The result is, even for some of the ablest minds, acceptance of a sense of development, progress and improvement, in technological matters at least. Even the most nostalgic of us are committed to this view.

Tudor and Stuart England, where suddenly so many new things came to be, would seem a likely place to demonstrate the validity of our own myth. And, indeed, it would take an enormous volume merely to list the *things* newly introduced into England during that time.

There is a kind of ritual observance of all historical novelists I know of, regardless of their differing premises. They feel an urgent need to be exact, as precise as they are able to be, about the things of the time, feeling that by means of these they may manage to summon up the ghosts who used them. It is here, in and among things, that novelists can be more pedantic than the most solemn cartoon image of the scholar. With differences, though, scholars and novelists share the same myth or metaphor of technology. I have read brilliant books by scholars whose dedication and intelligence is dazzling, on all aspects of Elizabethan life — architecture, arts and sciences, housekeeping, horsemanship, crafts, labor and social conditions, sailing and navigation, etc. And sooner or later each and every one of these scholars has demonstrated the modern technological myth, what might be called "the technological fallacy."

Take, for example, an area where much extraordinary scholarship has been done — the voyaging and, in particular, the ships, the sailing and seamanship of the times. Our best scholars have long since recognized the marvelous sailing ability of the Elizabethans. Their achievements border on the miraculous when one, working backwards, considers how little they knew, how "primitive" the things they worked with. But. . . . It could be argued persuasively, I think, and with substantial evidence, that the Elizabethan galleon was ideally suited to its purposes. Its sailing and handling defects were offset by virtues and strengths not present in later "improved" sailing vessels. Many of the dangers and troubles of sailing ships a hundred years later and more were simply not present to plague the Elizabethan sailor. The whole concept of sailing changed radically in the century after the death of Elizabeth. Judged by the new concept and purposes, the older methods do not measure up. Seen from another time, when there are more sailors than ever but sailing is a recreation, it can be (though it has not been) convincingly argued that Elizabethan ships and sailors were "better" than most of what came after them. The same thing, here vaguely and there clearly, appears to be true in many things. One great difficulty in any argument is that so very little has survived the times. The wars of the seventeenth century, great fires, and the cheerful discarding of old for new, have left us with a few great houses and a miscellany of things, random odds and ends, for the cases of museums.

In a larger sense this leads towards an abstraction, the idea or metaphor of change. Americans of all persuasions, it would seem, are agreed that we live in "changing times." The conservatives would slow down the changes; the liberals would embrace them; the radicals would hasten the process by *making* changes. Yet there are two positions which cast shadows of doubt upon the truth of the changing. Some thinkers (Aldous Huxley, for example) have pointed out the undeniable fact that in large part all of the apparent changes we have witnessed in fifty years are simply the working out, the inevitable development coming from the *real* changes, which were more theoretical than practical and took place at the turn of the last century and in the first years of this one. For example, after the Wright brothers flew their powered kite it was only a matter of time and engineering before a man could walk on the moon. It may well be said that we, the living, though well-deceived by appearances, have seen very little change, have, in fact, devoted ourselves to exploitation of changes long since made. And, deceived in a larger more metaphysical sense, we call ourselves either victims or celebrants of change. By the same token, it can be well argued that the period of the Tudors witnessed more radical changes than any in our time. And it can be demonstrated that, even as they lamented the aging of the world and the abrasions of mutability, the Elizabethans seem to have welcomed and embraced the new, the changing. The reign of Elizabeth can be detailed as a period of marvels, with outward and visible things changing constantly and, often, overnight. (Symbolically, Ralegh once introduced into England a new style of dress and tailoring in one night after entertaining a distinguished Frenchman and his entourage who affected it.) The Queen herself led the way, apparently delighting in all manner of change. Yet no one, except certain of the puritans, themselves quite new to the scene and soon enough to effect the greatest changes England had ever known, seemed greatly concerned about changes. There was nostalgia, to be sure, conventional longing by a

few for the days of the longbow and the simple life; but for all the
newness, from the introduction of the fork to the implications of
Ramist logic, the prevailing mood is one which takes these changes
for granted . . . like the weather. Dig a little deeper and it soon
becomes apparent that the reign of Elizabeth was deeply conservative,
that one of her great aims was to recover the qualities initiated, then
dissipated by her grandfather, Henry VII. It seems that she was lodged
in the past, studiously seeking to avoid the folly of seeking to master
the future which was the undoing of Henry VIII, likewise turning
away from Mary's attempt to *restore* the lost past, learning her negative lessons from the observed disasters of the reigns of Edward and
Mary. Freed from concern about the future by circumstance and by
choice, schooling herself in the past and aiming to recover rather
than to restore, she found herself oddly free to live (dangerously) in
a continual present. And so, ironically, possessed a longer future and
a longer past than any other monarch before her. Yet while England
burned with change, turn and counterturn for half a century, it was,
we can see now, a time of relative sameness and stability. And with her
death that inner quiet, persistent at the heart of outward clamor, died
too. To be followed, as surely, it seems, as the working out of an
equation, by England's deluge. Which, if true, means finally that
whether she wished it so or not, her refusal to commit herself to the
future made that future inevitable.

This can only be dimly imagined and with difficulty. It *could* have
been imagined easily enough by any number of Elizabethan historians, Ralegh among them for certain and Shakespeare as well, for
they delighted in the working out of intricate mysterious patterns in
time and called that pattern Providence. And because the signs of
Providence were most accessible not to reason alone, but to the reasonable imagination, neither Ralegh nor Shakespeare nor any other
historian of that time seems to have been much troubled by the
unimagined distinction between fact and fiction.

III

Which, by devious ways, leads me to an ending not far from where I
began. Without benefit of much theory, or, perhaps more accurately,
with the benefit of many examples of theory and practice to choose
from and among, my working theory of the use of history in fiction
came from the work. The end is not to *understand* a piece of history
and to make it live again. (Who could presume to follow after
Tolstoy?) I should be condemned under the social and Marxist terms

of Geörgy Lukács, in his profound arrangement of the subject in *The Historical Novel*. Others, my betters and in truth my masters as scholars of the time and place, would (and will no doubt when the time comes) prefer that the distinctions should not be ignored, believing that the distinctions between history and fiction can be liberating to both, can lead the novel, or whatever it is to be called, into new, original, and delightful forms and can free the historian to ignore it if he chooses. Writers of fiction and "non-fiction" will wish the same thing for a different reason, seeing the fusion of methods as confusion. Those who seek radical change, new or reactionary, who find so much of history irrelevant, will find this method lacking in relevance too.

I have no answer to any of these. Except this one, that in the working out in fact of a long-imagined fiction, I came to cling to the notion that the proper subject and theme of historical fiction is what it is — the human imagination in action, itself dramatized as it struggles with surfaces, builds structures with facts, deals out and plays a hand of ideas, and most of all, by conceiving of the imagination of others, wrestles with the angel (Wallace Stevens' "necessary angel") of the imagination.

Therefore to write imaginary history is to celebrate the human imagination. Not one's own, for the subject precludes the possibility of doing what R. P. Blackmur called to *heroize* the sensibility. The subject is not art and the artist. Flaubert did that best in *Salammbo*, and who needs to imitate his triumph? The subject is the larger imagination, the possibility of imagining lives and spirits of other human beings, living or dead, without assaulting their essential and, anyway, ineffable mystery, to dream again in recapitulation the dream of Adam, knowing, as he did not until he awoke, that it is true; for Adam dreamed in innocence. We can only imagine that condition.

And what is the value, if any? Not of a book to be published later and to stand or fall on its own accounting. Not to the writer, who in the writing rather than the publishing, gains all that matters or can be gained. Rather, what use and value from this only vaguely formulated theory of the use of the past in fiction? To which I can answer only this much. We have no poverty of thinkers. If sages are few, honest intellectuals are plentiful, and their voices are heard. And there are plenty, a growing number, of course, equal or superior in intellectual power, who in reaction or revolution would cast aside the mind and follow feeling, sensation, impulse where they may lead. Too often both are abstractionists, peg-legged dancers, one-eyed princes (knaves?) in the kingdom of the blind. The human imagination, an energy in motion and never abstract, permits the wedding and intercourse of thought and feeling, each responsive to, respectful of the other. It may well be that the present (though it is the past by the time two words are on a page or, for that matter, one sequence of images flashes across the movie screen) is the most fitting place to awaken the imagination with some hope of such a felicitous union. To live well in the present demands as much imagination as can be mustered. But to live in the present fully one preserves the possibility of exploring the past. One may choose to deny that one's present world is in any part fictitious. The past, however, is chiefly fiction and must be imagined before it can exist. But the past is forever in the present, even when it is forgotten, and the attempt to imagine it, whether as writer or reader, requires a sacrifice, an expense of vanity (like the old Queen alone in her mirrored room), offering in reward for that a recollection, vague beyond imagining, shared by the living and the dead, of something beautiful, and forever joyously new.